The Android Developer's Cookbook
Building Applications with the Android SDK

Developer's Library Series

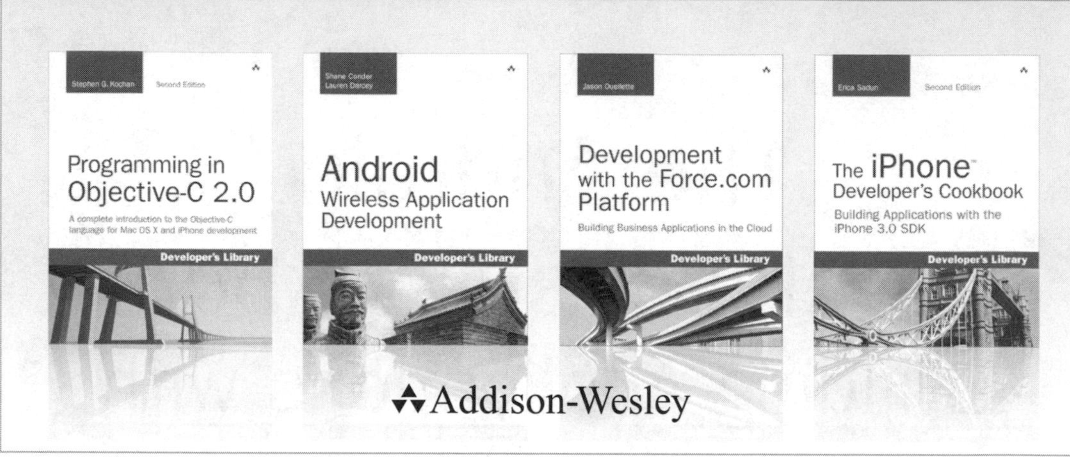

Visit **developers-library.com** for a complete list of available products

---

The **Developer's Library Series** from Addison-Wesley provides practicing programmers with unique, high-quality references and tutorials on the latest programming languages and technologies they use in their daily work. All books in the Developer's Library are written by expert technology practitioners who are exceptionally skilled at organizing and presenting information in a way that's useful for other programmers.

Developer's Library books cover a wide range of topics, from open-source programming languages and databases, Linux programming, Microsoft, and Java, to Web development, social networking platforms, Mac/iPhone programming, and Android programming.

Addison-Wesley Cisco Press EXAM/CRAM IBM Press. QUE 

SAMS | Safari Books Online

The Android Developer's Cookbook
Building Applications with the Android SDK

James Steele
Nelson To

Addison-Wesley

Upper Saddle River, NJ • Boston • Indianapolis • San Francisco
New York • Toronto • Montreal • London • Munich • Paris • Madrid
Cape Town • Sydney • Tokyo • Singapore • Mexico City

The publisher offers excellent discounts on this book when ordered in quantity for bulk purchases or special sales, which may include electronic versions and/or custom covers and content particular to your business, training goals, marketing focus, and branding interests. For more information, please contact:

U.S. Corporate and Government Sales
(800) 382-3419
corpsales@pearsontechgroup.com

For sales outside the United States, please contact:

International Sales
international@pearson.com

Visit us on the Web: informit.com/aw

Library of Congress Cataloging-in-Publication Data

Steele, James, 1971-
The Android developer's cookbook : building applications with the Android SDK / James Steele, Nelson To.
p. cm.
Includes bibliographical references and index.
ISBN-13: 978-0-321-74123-3 (pbk. : alk. paper)
ISBN-10: 0-321-74123-4 (pbk. : alk. paper)
1. Application software—Development. 2. Android (Electronic resource) 3. Mobile computing. 4. Smartphones—Programming. 5. Operating systems (Computers) I. To, Nelson, 1976- II. Title.
QA76.76.A65S743 2011
004.1675—dc22

2010033254

Text printed in the United States on recycled paper at RR Donnelley, Crawfordsville, Indiana.

First Printing: October 2010

ISBN-10: 0-321-74123-4
ISBN-13: 978-0-321-74123-3

Editor-in-Chief
Mark Taub

Acquisitions Editor
Trina McDonald

Development Editor
Michael Thurston

Managing Editor
Sandra Schroeder

Project Editor
Mandie Frank

Copy Editor
Deadline Driven Publishing

Indexer
Erika Millen

Proofreader
Jovana Shirley

Technical Editors
Romin Irani
Douglas Jones

Publishing Coordinator
Olivia Basegio

Designer
Gary Adair

Page Layout
Mark Shirar

❖

To Wei with love.

Jim

To my dear mom.

Nelson

❖

Contents at a Glance

Table of Contents

Preface

Android is the fastest growing mobile operating system (OS). With over 30 smartphones introduced in the last year and over 10,000 applications (apps) being added every month, the Android ecosystem is growing as well. There is enough diversity in device features and wireless carriers to appeal to just about anyone.

Netbooks have always been a natural platform to adopt Android, but the inertia behind Android has fed the growth further into televisions and even automobiles. Many of the world's largest corporations—from banks to fast food chains to airlines—ensure a presence in Android and offer compatible services. Android developers have many opportunities, and relevant apps reach more people than ever before, increasing the satisfaction of creating a relevant app.

Why an Android Cookbook?

The Android OS is simple to learn, and Google provides many libraries to make it easy to implement rich and complex applications. The only aspect lacking, as mentioned by many in the Android developer community, is clear and well-explained documentation. The fact that Android is open source means anyone can dive in and reverse engineer some documentation. Many developer bulletin boards have excellent examples deduced using exactly this method. Still, a book that has a consistent treatment across all areas of the OS is useful.

In addition, a clear working example is worth a thousand words of documentation. Developers faced with a problem usually prefer to do a form of extreme programming; that is, they find examples of working code that does something close to the solution and modify or extend it to meet their needs. The examples also serve as a way to see the coding style and help to shape other parts of the developer's code.

This Android Cookbook serves to fill a need by providing many various self-contained recipes. As each recipe is introduced, the main concepts of the Android OS are also explained.

Who Should Read This Book?

Users who are writing their own Android applications will get the most out of this cookbook. Basic familiarity with Java and the Eclipse development environment is assumed, but not required for the majority of the book. Java is a modular language and most (if not all) of the example recipes can be incorporated with minimal change to the reader's own Android project. The motivation for each topic lends itself well for use as an Android course supplement.

Utilizing Recipes

In general, the code recipes in this cookbook are self-contained and include all the information necessary to run a working application on an Android device. Chapters 1 and 2 give an introduction to the overall use of Android, but feel free to jump around and start using whatever is necessary.

This book is written first as a reference, providing knowledge mostly by example with greatest benefits through implementation of the recipes of interest. The main technique introduced in each recipe is specified in the section heading. However, additional techniques are included in each recipe as needed to support the main recipe.

After reading this book, a developer should

- Be able to write an Android Application from scratch.
- Be able to write code that works across multiple versions of Android.
- Be able to utilize the various Application Programming Interfaces (APIs) provided in Android.
- Have a large reference of code snippets to quickly assimilate into applications.
- Appreciate the various ways to do the same task in Android and the benefits of each.
- Understand the unique aspects of Android programming techniques.

Book Structure

Chapter 1, "Overview of Android," provides an introduction to all aspects of Android outside of the code itself. It is the only chapter that doesn't include recipes, but provides useful background material. Chapter 2, "Application Basics: Activities and Intents," provides an overview of the four Android components and explanation of how an Android project is organized. It also focuses on the activity as a main application building block. Chapter 3, "Threads, Services, Receivers, and Alerts," introduces background tasks such as threads, services, and receivers, as well as notification methods for these background tasks using alerts. Chapter 4, "User Interface Layout," covers the user interface screen layout and views, and Chapter 5, "User Interface Events," covers the user initiated events such as touch events and gestures.

Chapter 6, "Multimedia Techniques," covers multimedia manipulation and record and playback of audio and video. Chapter 7, "Hardware Interface," introduces the hardware APIs available on Android devices and how to utilize them. Chapter 8, "Networking," discusses interaction outside of the Android device with SMS, web browsing, and social networking. Chapter 9, "Data Storage Methods," covers various data storage techniques available in Android including SQLite. Chapter 10, "Location-Based Services," focuses on accessing the location through various methods such as GPS and utilizing services such as the Google Maps API. Chapter 11, "Advanced Android Development," provides some advanced techniques in Android including customizing views, using native code for faster processing, and utilizing the Android Backup Manager. Finally, Chapter 12, "Debugging," provides the testing and debugging framework useful throughout the development cycle.

Additional References

There are many online references for Android. A few essential ones are

- Android Source Code: http://source.android.com/
- Android Developer Pages: http://developer.android.com/
- Android Developer Forums: http://www.svcAndroid.com/
- Open Source Directory: http://osdir.com/
- Stack Overflow Discussion Threads: http://stackoverflow.com/
- Talk Android Developer Forums: http://www.talkandroid.com/android-forums/

About the Authors

James Steele was doing post-doctoral work in physics at MIT when he decided to join a startup in Silicon Valley. Fifteen years later and he continues to innovate, bringing research projects to production in both the consumer and mobile market. He actively presents and participates in various Silicon Valley new technology groups.

Nelson To has more than ten applications of his own in the Android Market. He also has worked on enterprise Android applications for Think Computer, Inc. (PayPhone), AOL (AIM), Stanford University (Education App), and Logitech (Google TV). He also assists in organizing the Silicon Valley Android Meetup Community and teaches Android classes both in the Bay Area and China.

1

Overview of Android

The Android operating system (OS) has come a long way since the announcement of the Open Handset Alliance in late 2007. The idea of an open source OS for embedded systems was not new, but Google aggressively backing it definitely has helped push Android to the forefront in just a few years.

Many wireless carriers in multiple countries across various communication protocols have one or more Android phones available. Other embedded devices, such as tablets, netbooks, televisions, set-top boxes, and even automobiles, have also adopted the Android OS.

This chapter discusses various general aspects of Android useful for a developer. It provides a foundation for the creation of Android applications and a context for the recipes in the rest of this book.

The Evolution of Android

Google, seeing a large growth of Internet use and search in mobile devices, acquired Android, Inc., in 2005 to focus its development on a mobile device platform. Apple introduced the iPhone in 2007 with some ground-breaking ideas including multitouch and an open market for applications. Android was quickly adapted to include these features and to offer definite distinctions, such as more control for developers and multitasking. In addition, Android incorporates enterprise requirements, such as exchange support, remote wipe, and Virtual Private Network (VPN) support, to go after the enterprise market that Research In Motion has developed and held so well with its Blackberry models.

Device diversity and quick adaptation have helped Android grow its user base, but it comes with potential challenges for developers. Applications need to support multiple screen sizes, resolution ratios, keyboards, hardware sensors, OS versions, wireless data rates, and system configurations. Each can lead to different and unpredictable behavior, but testing applications across all environments is an impossible task.

Android has therefore been constructed to ensure as uniform an experience across platforms as possible. By abstracting the hardware differences, Android OS tries to insulate applications from device-specific modifications while providing the flexibility to tune aspects as needed. Future-proofing of applications to the introduction of new hardware platforms and OS updates is also a consideration. This mostly works as long as the developer is well aware of this systematic approach. The generic Application Programming Interfaces (API) that Android offers and how to ensure device and OS compatibility are main threads discussed throughout this book.

Still, as with any embedded platform, extensive testing of applications is required. Google provides assistance to third-party developers in many forms as Android Development Tool (ADT) plugins for Eclipse (also as standalone tools) including real-time logging capabilities, a realistic emulator that runs native ARM code, and in-field error reports from users to developers of Android Market applications.

The Dichotomy of Android

Android has some interesting dichotomies. Knowing about them upfront is useful not only in understanding what Android is, but what it is not.

Android is an embedded OS that relies on the Linux kernel for core system services, but it is not embedded Linux. For example, standard Linux utilities such as X-windows and GNU C libraries are not supported. Writing applications for Android utilizes the Java framework, but it is not Java. Standard Java libraries such as Swing are not supported. Other libraries such as Timer are not preferred; they have been replaced by Android's own libraries, which are optimized for usage in a resource-constrained, embedded environment.

The Android OS is open source, which means developers can view and use any of the system source code, including the radio stack. This source code is one of the first resources for seeing examples of Android code in action, and it helps clarify the usage when documentation is lacking. This also means developers can utilize the system in the same way as any core application and can swap out system components for their own components. However, Android devices do contain some proprietary software that is inaccessible to developers (such as Global Positioning System (GPS) navigation).

A final dichotomy of Android OS is that Google is also backing Chrome OS. Android OS is built for embedded platforms, and Chrome OS is built for cloud-based platforms. However, which is the best choice for embedded devices that live in the cloud? Netbooks, which fill the gap between smart phones and laptop computers, could presumably go either way (and they have). Android has started to utilize the cloud more. Does that mean Chrome OS's days are numbered? Google also backs a web-based market, so Chrome OS enjoys the same developer leverage that Android currently has. This points to a convergence that might have been in the cards all along.

Devices Running Android

There are more than 40 Android phones in the market from more than ten manufacturers. Other hardware also runs Android, such as tablets and televisions. Software can access information on the target device using the `android.os.Build` class, for example:

```
if(android.os.Build.MODEL.equals("Nexus+One")) { ... }
```

Android-supported hardware shares some common features due to the nature of the operating system. The Android OS is organized into the following images:

- Bootloader—Initiates loading of the boot image during startup
- Boot image—Kernel and RAMdisk
- System image—Android operating system platform and apps
- Data image—User data saved across power cycles
- Recovery image—Files used for rebuilding or updating the system
- Radio image—Files of the radio stack

These images are stored on nonvolatile flash memory, so they are protected when the device powers down. The flash memory is used like read-only memory (hence, some call it ROM), but can it be rewritten as necessary (for example, with over-the-air Android operating system updates).

On startup, the microprocessor executes the bootloader to load the kernel and RAMdisk to RAM for quick access. The microprocessor then executes instructions and pages portions of the system and data images into RAM as needed. The radio image resides on the baseband processor, which connects to the radio hardware.

A comparison of some of the early and more recent smart phone models is shown in Table 1.1. It shows that the processing hardware architecture is similar across devices: a microprocessor unit (MPU), synchronous dynamic random access memory (SDRAM or RAM for short), and flash memory (called ROM for short). The screen size is given in pixels, but the dots per inch (dpi) vary depending on the physical screen size. For example, the HTC Magic has a 3.2-inch diagonal screen with 320x480 pixels. This equates to 180 pixels per inch, but is classified as a medium pixel density device by Android (which averages as 160 dpi). All smartphones also offer a CMOS image sensor camera, Bluetooth (BT), and Wi-Fi (802.11), although there are variations.

Table 1.1 **Comparison of Some Representative Android Smartphones. Data from http://en.wikipedia.org/wiki/List_of_Android_devices and http://pdadb.net/.**

Model	MPU	RAM/ ROM	Screen	Other Features
HTC Dream / G1 (October 2008)	528-MHz QCOM MSM7201A	192MB/ 256MB	TFT LCD 320x480 mdpi	GSM/UMTS slide out keyboard, trackball, AGPS BT2.0, 802.11b/g, 3.1-MP camera

Table 1.1 **Continued**

Model	MPU	RAM/ ROM	Screen	Other Features
Samsung Moment (November 2009)	800-MHz ARM1176 JZF-S	288MB/ 512MB	AMOLED 320x480 mdpi	CDMA/1xEV-DO slide out keyboard (backlit), DPAD BT2.0, 802.11b/g, 3.1-MP camera AGPS
Motorola Milestone / Droid (November 2009)	550-MHz TI OMAP3430	256MB/ 512MB	TFT LCD 480x854 hdpi	GSM/UMTS or CDMA/1xEV-DO slide out keyboard, DPAD BT2.1, 802.11b/g, 5-MP camera AGPS
Nexus One / HTC Passion (January 2010)	1-GHz QCOM Snapdragon	512MB/ 512MB	AMOLED 480x800 hdpi	GSM/UMTS Trackball, dual microphones BT2.0, 802.11a/b/g/n, 5-MP camera AGPS, geotagging
HTC Droid Incredible (April 2010)	1-GHz QCOM Snapdragon	512MB/ 512MB	AMOLED 480x800 hdpi	CDMA/1xEV-DO BT2.1, 802.11a/b/g/n, 8-MP camera AGPS, geotagging
HTC EVO 4G (June 2010)	1-GHz QCOM Snapdragon	512MB/ 1GB	TFT LCD 480x800 hdpi	CDMA/1xEV-DO/802.16e-2005 BT2.1, 802.11b/g, 8-MP camera 1.3MP front-facing camera, AGPS

Table 1.1 **Continued**

Model	MPU	RAM/ ROM	Screen	Other Features
Motorola Droid X (July 2010)	1-GHz TI OMAP3630	512MB/ 8GB	TFT LCD 480x854 hdpi	CDMA/1xEV-DO, FM radio BT2.1, 802.11b/g/n, 8-MP camera AGPS, geotagging
Sony-Ericsson Xperia X10a (June 2010)	1-GHz QCOM Snapdragon	256MB/ 1GB	TFT LCD 480x854 hdpi	GSM/UMTS, FM radio BT2.1, 802.11b/g, 8-MP camera AGPS, geotagging
Samsung Galaxy S Pro (August 2010)	1-GHz Samsung Hummingbird	512MB/ 2GB	AMOLED 480x800 hdpi	CDMA/1xEV-DO, 802.16, FM radio slide out keyboard BT3.0, 802.11b/g/n, 5-MP camera 0.3MP front-facing camera, AGPS
Acer Stream / Liquid (September 2010)	1-GHz QCOM Snapdragon	512MB/ 512MB	AMOLED 480x800 hdpi	GSM/UMTS, FM radio BT2.1, 802.11b/g/n, 5-MP camera AGPS, geotagging

Other than improved capacity and performance on newer models, another main differentiator is additional features. Some devices offer 4G, some have FM radio, some have slide-out keyboards, and some have a front-facing camera. Knowing the differentiators helps a developer create great applications. In addition to the built-in hardware, every Android device comes with a secure digital (SD) card slot. An SD card provides additional storage space for multimedia and extra application data. However, until Android 2.2, the apps themselves could be stored only on the internal ROM.

HTC Models

HTC is a Taiwanese company founded in 1997. The first commercially available hardware running Android was the HTC Dream (also known as the G1 with G standing for Google). It was released in October 2008. Since then, HTC has put out over ten phones running Android, including Google's Nexus One.

The Nexus One was one of the first Android devices to use a 1-GHz microprocessor, the Snapdragon platform from Qualcomm. The Snapdragon includes Qualcomm's own core as opposed to an ARM core, and it contains circuitry to decode high-definition video at 720p. Most smartphones that have followed also utilize a 1-GHz microprocessor. Other distinctions of the Nexus One are the use of two microphones to cancel background noise during phone conversations and a backlit trackball that lights up different colors based on the notification.

HTC also released the Droid Incredible in April 2010. As seen in Table 1.1, it is similar to the Nexus One but has a CDMA instead of a GSM radio hardware and a higher pixel density camera. The HTC EVO 4G released in June 2010 produced quite a sensation as the first commercially available phone that supports WiMAX (802.16e-2005).

Motorola Models

Motorola built the first cell phone in the 1980s and has had diverse success in the cell phone market since. More recently, the wireless division was wavering for a direction until it focused efforts on Android. The release of the Motorola Droid for CDMA (also known as the Milestone for the GSM worldwide version) in November 2009 is indeed considered by many as a major milestone for Android. The Droid's impact is apparent in that a significant fraction of Android phones accessing the Android Market are Droids.

In addition, Motorola has put out close to ten additional phone brands running Android. The Motorola Droid X has capabilities similar to the HTC Droid Incredible, including HD video capture.

Samsung Models

Samsung has been a strong force in the mobile market and is starting to come into its own with Android devices. The Samsung Moment was introduced in November 2009, but does not have hardware capability for multitouch. It will not be upgraded beyond Android 2.1. A custom version, including a Mobile TV antenna, is available in select markets for receiving Mobile ATSC signals.

The Samsung Galaxy S is Samsung's answer to the iPhone. It is well known that Samsung processors are used in the iPhone 3G and 3GS. With the Galaxy S, Samsung developed a 1-GHz Hummingbird processor with an ARM Cortex-8 core. It is also one of the first phones to offer Bluetooth 3.0 compatibility.

Tablets

With Apple's introduction of the iPad, Android manufacturers were expected to introduce tablet computers of their own. A tablet computer is loosely defined as having a screen of 4.8 inches or larger and Wi-Fi connectivity. Because many have 3G wireless service, they tend to be more like smartphones with large screens.

Archos was one of the first to market an Android tablet in late 2009. It has a diagonal screen size of 4.8 inches and is called the Archos 5. Archos has since introduced a 7-inch model called the Archos 7. These models come with an actual hard drive for more data storage. Dell has also introduced a 5-inch tablet called the Streak with plans for both a 7-inch and a 10-inch screen size model. Samsung offers the Galaxy Tab with a 7-inch screen. One downside is the inability for many of these tablets to access the Android Market, although that should soon change. A comparison of some tablet computer models is shown in Table 1.2.

Table 1.2 **Comparison of Representative Android Tablet Computers**

Model	MPU	RAM/ disk	Screen	Other Features
Archos 5 (September 2009)	800-MHz TI OMAP 3440	256MB/ 8GB	TFT LCD 4.8 inches 800x480	BT2.0, 802.11b/g/n, FM radio
Archos 7 (June 2010)	600-MHz Rockchip RK2808	128MB/ 8GB	TFT LCD 7 inches 800x480	802.11b/g
Dell Streak (June 2010)	1-GHz QCOM Snapdragon	256MB/ 512MB	TFT LCD 5 inches 800x480	GSM/UMTS, BT2.1, 802.11b/g, 5-MP camera, 0.3-MP front-facing camera AGPS, geotagging
Samsung Galaxy Tablet GT-P1000 (September 2010)	1-GHz Samsung Hummingbird	512MB/ 16GB	TFT LCD 7 inches 1024x600	GSM/UMTS BT3.0, 802.11b/g/n, 3.1-MP camera

Other Devices

Given Android is a generic embedded platform, it is expected to be utilized in many other industries beyond smartphones and tablet computers. The first Android-based automobile is the Roewe 350, which Shanghai Automotive Industry Corporation manufactures. Android is mainly used for GPS navigation but can also support web browsing.

The first Android-based television, Google TV, is a joint development between Google for software, Sony for televisions, Intel for processors, and Logitech for set-top boxes. It brings the Internet to televisions in a natural way, but it also provides access to the Android Market from the television.

Hardware Differences on Android Devices

The hardware available on each Android device varies, as seen in Table 1.1. In general, most of the differences are transparent to the developer and not covered further here. However, a few hardware differences are important to understand to assist in writing device-independent code. Screens, user input methods, and sensors are discussed here.

Screens

Two technologies used for displays are liquid crystal displays (LCD) and light-emitting diodes (LED). The two specific choices in Android phones are thin-film transistor (TFT) LCDs and active-matrix organic LED displays (AMOLED). A benefit of TFT displays is a longer lifetime. A benefit of AMOLED displays is no need for backlighting and therefore deeper blacks and lower power.

Overall, Android devices are categorized into small, normal, and large screens and low-, medium-, and high-pixel density. Note that the actual pixel density might vary but will be chosen as one of these. A summary of currently available device screens is shown in Table 1.3. Note that Table 1.1 provides the screen density classification for each device listed.

Table 1.3 **Summary of Device Screens Supported by Android**

Screen Type	Low-Density (~120ppi), ldpi	Medium-Density (~160ppi), mdpi	High-Density (~240ppi), hdpi
Small screen	**QVGA** (240x320), 2.6-inch to 3.0-inch diagonal		
Normal screen	**WQVGA** (240x400), 3.2-inch to 3.5-inch diagonal **FWQVGA** (240x432), 3.5-inch to 3.8-inch diagonal	**HVGA** (320x480), 3.0-inch to 3.5-inch diagonal	**WVGA** (480x800), 3.3-inch to 4.0-inch diagonal **FWVGA** (480x854), 3.5-inch to 4.0-inch diagonal
Large screen		**WVGA** (480x800), 4.8-inch to 5.5-inch diagonal **FWVGA** (480x854), 5.0-inch to 5.8-inch diagonal	

User Input Methods

Touchscreens enable users to interact with the visual display. There are three types of touchscreen technology:

- Resistive—Two resistive material layers sit on top of a glass screen. When a finger, stylus, or any object applies pressure, the two layers touch together and the location of the touch can be determined. Resistive touchscreens are cost-effective, but only 75 percent of the light shows through, and until recently, multitouch was not possible.
- Capacitive—A charged material layer is overlaid on a glass screen. When a finger or any conductive object touches the layer, some charge is drawn off, changing the capacitance, which is measured to determine the location of the touch. Capacitive touchscreens allow as much as 90 percent of the light through, although accuracy can be less than resistive.
- Surface Acoustic Wave—This uses a more advanced method that sends and receives ultrasonic waves. When a finger or any object touches the screen, the waves are absorbed. The waves are measured to determine the location of the touch. It is the most durable solution, but more suitable for large-scale screens such as automatic bank tellers.

All Android devices use either resistive or capacitive touchscreen technology, and with a few early exceptions, all support multitouch.

In addition, each Android device needs an alternative method to access the screen. This is through one of the following methods:

- D-pad (directional pad)—An up-down-right-left type of joystick
- Trackball—A rolling ball acting as a pointing device that is similar to a mouse
- Trackpad—A special rectangular surface acting as a pointing device

Sensors

Smartphones are becoming sensor hubs in a way, opening a rich experience for users. Other than the microphone that every phone has, the first additional sensor introduced on phones was the camera. Different phone cameras have varying capabilities, and this is an important factor for people in selecting a device. The same type of diversity is now seen with the additional sensors.

Most smartphones have at least three basic sensors: a three-axis accelerometer to measure gravity, a three-axis magnetometer to measure the ambient magnetic field, and a temperature sensor to measure the ambient temperature. For example, the HTC Dream (G1) contains the following sensors (which can be displayed using `getSensorList()` as described further in Chapter 7, "Hardware Interface"):

```
AK8976A 3-axis Accelerometer
AK8976A 3-axis Magnetic field sensor
AK8976A Orientation sensor
AK8976A Temperature sensor
```

The AK8976A is a single package from Asahi Kasei Microsystems (AKM) that combines a piezoresistive accelerometer, Hall-effect magnetometer, and temperature sensor. All provide 8-bit precision data. The orientation sensor is a virtual sensor that uses the accelerometer and magnetometer to determine the orientation.

For comparison, the Motorola Droid contains the following sensors:

```
LIS331DLH 3-axis Accelerometer
AK8973 3-axis Magnetic field sensor
AK8973 Temperature sensor
SFH7743 Proximity sensor
Orientation sensor type
LM3530 Light sensor
```

The LIS331DLH is a 12-bit capacitive accelerometer from ST Microelectronics. It provides much more accurate data and can sample up to 1kHz. The AK8973 is an AKM package with an 8-bit Hall-effect magnetometer and temperature sensor.

In addition, the Droid contains two more sensors. The SFH7743 is an Opto Semiconductor's short-range proximity detector that turns the screen off when an object (such as the ear) is within about 40mm distance. The LM3530 is an LED driver with a programmable light sensor from National Semiconductor that detects ambient light and adjusts the screen backlight and LED flash appropriately.

One other example of sensors available on an Android device is the HTC EVO 4G, which has the following sensors:

```
BMA150 3-axis Accelerometer
AK8973 3-axis Magnetic field sensor
AK8973 Orientation sensor
CM3602 Proximity sensor
CM3602 Light sensor
```

The BMA150 is a Bosch Sensortec 10-bit accelerometer which can sample up to 1.5kHz. The CM3602 is a Capella Microsystems, Inc., short distance proximity sensor and ambient light sensor combined into one.

Overall, it is important to understand each Android model has different underlying hardware. These differences can lead to varying performance and accuracy of the sensors.

Features of Android

The detailed features of Android and how to take advantage of them provide a main theme throughout this book. On a broader level, some key features of Android are major selling points and differentiators. It is good to be aware of these strong points of Android and utilize them as much as possible.

Multiprocess and App Widgets

The Android OS does not restrict the processor to a single application at a time. The system manages priorities of applications and threads within a single application. This has the benefit that background tasks can be run while a user engages the device in a foreground process. For example, while a user plays a game, a background process can check stock prices and trigger an alert as necessary.

App Widgets are mini applications that can be embedded in other applications (such as the Home screen). They can process events, such as start a music stream or update the outside temperature, while other applications are running.

Multiprocessing has the benefit of a rich user experience. However, care must be taken to avoid power-hungry applications that drain the battery. These multiprocess features are discussed further in Chapter 3, "Threads, Services, Receivers, and Alerts."

Touch, Gestures, and Multitouch

The touchscreen is an intuitive user interface for a hand-held device. If utilized well, it can transcend a need for detailed instructions. After a finger touches the screen, drags and flings are natural ways to interact with graphics. Multitouch provides a way to track more than one finger down at the same time. This is often used to zoom or rotate a view.

Some touch events are available transparently to the developer without the need to implement their detailed behaviors. Custom gestures can be defined as needed. It is important to try to maintain a consistent usage of touch events as compared to other applications. These touch events are discussed further in Chapter 5, "User Interface Events."

Hard and Soft Keyboards

One feature on a pocket device that galvanizes users is whether it should have a physical (also called hard) keyboard or software (also called soft) keyboard. The tactile feedback and definite placement of keys provided by a hard keyboard tends to make typing much faster for some, whereas others prefer the sleek design and convenience offered by a software-only input device. With the large variety of Android devices available, either type can be found. A side effect for developers is the need to support both. One downside of a soft keyboard is a portion of the screen needs to be dedicated to the input. This needs to be considered and tested for any user interface (UI) layout.

Android Development

This book is focused on writing Android code, the main aspect of Android development. However, dedicating a few words to the other aspects of development, including design and distribution, is appropriate.

How to Use the Recipes in This Book

In general, the code recipes in this cookbook are self-contained and include all the information necessary to run a working application on an Android device. As discussed in detail in Chapter 2, "Application Basics: Activities and Intents," there are multiple user-generated files needed to get an application working. When even one is omitted from an example, its absence impedes those unfamiliar with the Android setup. Therefore, every recipe contains the necessary files to get code working. Each file is shown as a code listing with the full filename as the title. This helps to convey where the file lives in an Android project.

At the same time, when too many files are shown, it clouds functionality. Therefore, two coding styles are slightly different than would be expected in a normal application:

- The code has limited comments. The text explains the functionality clearer than in-line comments could, and **bolded code** shows the main lines needed to get the particular technique working. In practice, actual code should have more comments than presented in the recipes.
- Strings are explicit and do not point to a global resource. The method of using a global resource for strings is encouraged and discussed in detail in Chapter 4, "User Interface Layout," with multiple examples. In this book, however, when only a few strings are needed for a recipe, the strings are made explicit rather than including a whole additional file just to define them.

People just starting with Android are served well to use Eclipse for the development environment with the Android plugin. As discussed more in Chapter 2, this ensures proper Android project setup and context, and Eclipse even adds a placeholder icon figure. It also helps with more advanced tasks, such as signing an application for distribution.

The emulator provided with the Android Software Development Kit (SDK) is useful, but nothing beats seeing the application run on a true Android device. It leads to faster development and more realistic testing. All code examples in this book have been tested on an actual device running Android 2.1, and as needed, Android 1.5 or Android 2.2. Some functionality (for example, Bluetooth pairing or sensor changes) is difficult and opaque when using the emulator. Therefore, it is recommended that initial testing be done with an action Android device.

Designing Applications Well

Three elements are needed for an excellent application: a good idea, good coding, and good design. Often, the last element is paid the least attention because most developers work alone and are not graphic designers. Google must realize this because it has created a set of design guidelines: icon design, App Widget design, activity and task design, and menu design. These can be found at http://developer.android.com/guide/practices/ui_guidelines/.

Good design cannot be stressed enough. It sets an application apart, improves user adoption, and builds user appreciation. Some of the most successful apps on the Market are a result of the collaboration between a developer and graphic designer. A significant portion of an app's development time should be dedicated to considering the best design for an app.

Maintaining Forward Compatibility

New Android versions are generally additive and forward compatible at the API level. In fact, a device can be called an Android device only if it passes compatibly tests with the Android APIs. However, if an application makes changes to the underlying system, compatibility is not guaranteed. To ensure forward compatibility of an application when future Android updates are installed on devices, follow these rules suggested by Google:

- Do not use internal or unsupported APIs.
- Do not directly manipulate settings without asking the user. A future release might constrain settings for security reasons. For instance, it used to be possible for an app to turn on GPS or data roaming by itself, but this is no longer allowed.
- Do not go overboard with layouts. This is rare, but complicated layouts (more than 10 deep or 30 total) can cause crashes.
- Do not make bad hardware assumptions. Not all Android devices have all possible supported hardware. Be sure to check for the hardware needed, and if it does not exist, handle the exception.
- Ensure device orientations do not disrupt the application or result in unpredictable behavior. Screen orientation can be locked, as described in Chapter 2.

Note that backward compatibility is not guaranteed with Android. It is best to declare the minimum SDK version as described in Chapter 2, so the device can load the proper compatibility settings. Utilizing other new features on older targets is also discussed at various places throughout the book.

Robustness

In the same vein as compatibility support, applications should be designed and tested for robustness. Following are a few tips to help ensure robustness:

- Use the Android libraries before Java libraries. Android libraries are constructed specifically for embedded devices and cover many of the requirements needed in an application. For the other cases, Java libraries are included. However, for cases where either can be used, the Android library is best.
- Take care of memory allocation. Initialize variables. Try to reuse objects rather than reallocate. This speeds up application execution and avoids excessive use of garbage collection. Memory allocations can be tracked using the Dalvik Debug Monitor Server (DDMS) tool as discussed in Chapter 12, "Debugging."

- Utilize the LogCat tool for debugging and check for warnings or errors as also discussed in Chapter 12.
- Test thoroughly, including different environments and devices if possible.

Software Development Kit

The Android SDK is comprised of the platform, tools, sample code, and documentation needed to develop Android applications. It is built as an add-on to the Java Development Kit and has an integrated plugin for the Eclipse Integrated Development Environment.

Installing and Upgrading

There are many places on the Internet that discuss detailed step-by-step instructions on how to install the Android SDK. For example, all the necessary links can be found on the Google website http://developer.android.com/sdk/. Therefore, the general procedure outlined here serves to emphasize the most common installation steps for reference. These steps should be done on a host computer used as the development environment.

1. Install the Java Development Kit (for example, install JDK 6.0 for use with Android 2.1 or above; JDK 5.0 is the minimum version needed for any earlier version of Android).
2. Install Eclipse Classic (for example, version 3.5.2). In the case of Windows, this just needs to be unzipped in place and is ready to use.
3. Install the Android SDK starter package (for example, version r06). In the case of Windows, this just needs to be unzipped in place and is ready to use.
4. Start Eclipse and select **Help → Install New Software...**, and then type https://dl-ssl.google.com/android/eclipse/ and install the Android DDMS and Android Development Tools.
5. In Eclipse, select **Window → Preferences...** (on a Mac, select **Eclipse → Preferences**) and select Android. Browse to the location where the SDK was unzipped and apply.
6. In Eclipse, select **Window → Android SDK and AVD Manager → Available Packages**, and then choose the necessary APIs to install (for example, Documentation for Android SDK, API 8; SDK Platform Android 2.2, API 8; Google APIs by Google Inc.; and Android API 8).
7. From the same Android SDK and AVD Manager menu, create an Android virtual device to run the emulator or install USB drivers to run applications on a plugged-in phone.
8. In Eclipse, select **Run → Run Configurations...** and create a new run configuration to be used with each Android application (or similar for a Debug Configuration). Android JUnit tests can be configured here, too.

Now, the environment should be configured to easily develop any Android application and run on the emulator or an actual Android device. To upgrade to a new version of the SDK, it is simply a matter of selecting **Help → Software Updates...** in Eclipse and choosing the appropriate version.

Software Features and API Level

The Android OS periodically rolls out new features, enhancements such as improved efficiency, and bug fixes. A main driver in OS improvement is the increased capability of hardware on new devices. In fact, major releases of the OS are generally coordinated with new hardware roll-outs (such as Eclair's release with Droid).

Some legacy Android devices cannot support the new version requirements and are not updated with new OS releases. This leads to a user base with a variety of different possible experiences. The developer is left with the task of checking for device capability or at least warning devices of required features. This can be done through a check of a single number: the API level.

The following summarizes the different OS releases and main features from a developer's perspective:

Cupcake: Android OS 1.5, API level 3, Released April 30, 2009

- Linux kernel 2.6.27.
- Smart virtual (soft) keyboard, support for third-party keyboards.
- AppWidget framework.
- Live Folders.
- Raw audio recording and playback.
- Interactive MIDI playback engine.
- Video recording APIs.
- Stereo Bluetooth support.
- Removed end-user root access (unless tethered to computer and using SDK).
- Speech recognition via RecognizerIntent (cloud service).
- Faster GPS location gathering (using AGPS).

Donut: Android OS 1.6, API Level 4, Released September 15, 2009

- Linux kernel 2.6.29.
- Support for multiple screen sizes.
- Gesture APIs.
- Text-to-speech engine.
- Integrate with the Quick Search Box using the SearchManager.
- Virtual Private Network (VPN) support.

Eclair: Android OS 2.0, API Level 5, Released October 26, 2009
Android OS 2.0.1, API Level 6, Released December 3, 2009
Android OS 2.1, API Level 7, Released January 12, 2010

- Sync adapter APIs to connect to any backend.
- Embed Quick Contact accessible in applications.
- Applications can control the Bluetooth connection to devices.
- HTML5 support.
- Microsoft Exchange support.
- Multitouch is accessible through the MotionEvent class.
- Animated wallpaper support.

FroYo: Android OS 2.2, API Level 8, Released May 20, 2010

- Linux kernel 2.6.32.
- Just-In-Time compilation (JIT) enabled, leading to faster code execution.
- Voice dialing using Bluetooth.
- Car and desk dock themes.
- Better definition of multitouch events.
- Cloud-to-device APIs.
- Applications can request to be installed on the SD memory card.
- Wi-Fi tether support on select devices.
- Thumbnail utility for videos and images.
- Multiple language support on keyboard input.
- Application error reporting for Market apps.

Android is starting to mature in that releases are less frequent. Although possible, the over-the-air updates are logistically tricky and carriers prefer to avoid them. Hardware manufacturers also appreciate a level of stability, which does not mean the first flashed devices in stores need an immediate update. However, when a release is made, the level of additional features for developers remains high and worthwhile to utilize.

Emulator and Android Device Debug

The emulator launches a window on the development computer that looks like an Android phone and runs actual ARM instructions. Note the initial startup is slow, even on high-end computers. Although there are ways to configure the emulator to try to emulate many aspects of a real Android device such as incoming phone calls, limited data rate, and screen orientation change, some features (such as sensors and audio/video) are not the same. The emulator should be considered a useful way to validate basic functionality for devices not available to the user. For example, the tablet screen size can be tried without purchasing a tablet.

Note that a target virtual device must be created before the emulator can properly run. Eclipse provides a nice method to manage Android Virtual Devices (AVD). A handy list of keyboard shortcuts for emulator functions is shown in Table 1.4.

Table 1.4 **Android OS Emulator Controls**

Key	Emulated Function
Escape	Back button
Home	Home button
F2, PageUp	Menu button
Shift-F2, PageDown	Start button
F3	Call/Dial button
F4	Hangup/EndCall button
F5	Search button
F7	Power button
Ctrl-F3, Ctrl-KEYPAD_5	Camera button
Ctrl-F5, KEYPAD_PLUS	Volume up button
Ctrl-F6, KEYPAD_MINUS	Volume down button
KEYPAD_5	DPAD center
KEYPAD_4, KEYPAD_6	DPAD left, DPAD right
KEYPAD_8, KEYPAD_2	DPAD up, DPAD down
F8	Toggle cell network on/off
F9	Toggle code profiling (when **-trace** set)
Alt-ENTER	Toggle fullscreen mode
Ctrl-T	Toggle trackball mode
Ctrl-F11, KEYPAD_7	Rotate screen orientation to previous or next layout
Ctrl-F12, KEYPAD_9	

In general, the first testing is best done with an Android phone. This ensures full functionality and real-time issues that cannot be fully recreated with the emulator. For an Android device to be used as a developer platform, just hook it to the USB using the USB cable that came with the phone and ensure the USB driver is detected (this is automatic with a MAC; the drivers are included with the SDK for Windows; and see Google's web page for Linux).

Some settings on the Android device need to be changed to enable developer usage. From the home screen, select **MENU→Settings→Applications→Unknown sources** and **MENU→Settings→Applications→Development→USB debugging** to enable installation of applications through the USB cable. More details about Android debugging are provided in Chapter 12.

Using the Android Debug Bridge

It is often convenient to use the command line to access the Android device. This is possible when it is connected to a computer using the USB cable. The Android Debug Bridge, which comes with the SDK, can be used to access the Android device. For example, to log into the Android device as if it were a Linux computer, type the following:

```
> adb shell
```

Then, many UNIX commands are usable on the device. Use `exit` to exit the shell. A single command can be appended to this to be executed without needing to enter and exit the shell:

```
> adb shell mkdir /sdcard/app_bkup/
```

To copy files off the device, use `pull` and rename it as needed:

```
> adb pull /system/app/VoiceSearchWithKeyboard.apk VSwithKeyboard.apk
```

To copy a file onto the device, use `push`:

```
> adb push VSwithKeyboard.apk /sdcard/app_bkup/
```

To delete an application, for example `com.dummy.game`, from the device, type the following:

```
> adb uninstall com.dummy.game
```

These commands are the most commonly used, but more are available. Some additional commands are introduced in Chapter 12.

Signing and Publishing

For an application to be accepted on the Android Market, it needs to be signed. To do this, a private key needs to be generated and kept in a secure place. Then, the app needs to be packaged in release mode and signed with the private key. When an application is upgraded, the same key needs to sign it to ensure a transparent update for the user.

Eclipse automatically does all of this. Just right-click on the project to be signed and select **Export... → Export Android Application** to initiate packaging. A password can be used to create a private key, which is saved for future applications and upgrades. Then, continue through the menu to the creation of an APK file. This is a packaged version of the Android project in release mode and signed with the private key. It is ready for upload to the Android Market.

Android Market

After an application is designed, developed, tested, and signed, it is ready to be deployed into the Android Market. To use Google's Android Market, a Google Checkout account needs to be created. It is used not only to pay for the initial developer fee of $25, but is also used for payment back to the developer for any charged apps. Public exposure to a developer's creation is often exciting. Within hours of upload, the application can get hundreds of views, downloads, ratings, and reviews from around the world. A few considerations for publication of an app are provided here for reference.

End-User License Agreement

Any original content distributed in a tangible form is automatically copyrighted in most of the world under the Berne Convention. Still, it is common practice to add a copyright with a date of publication to the content, such as © 2010. The method for adding this symbol to an Android app is discussed in Chapter 4.

This can be taken one step further in an End User License Agreement (EULA), which is a contract between the developer (or company) and the customer (or end user) providing the developer a form of protection for publicly distributed software. Most EULAs contain sections such as "Grant of License," "Copyright," and "No Warranties." It is common practice to add a EULA to an application, especially if it is offered for sale. The method for adding a EULA to an Android app is discussed in Chapter 9, "Data Storage Methods."

Improving App Visibility

Users find applications in three different ways. Catering to these methods helps to increase visibility for an application.

The first way users see an app is by choosing to list the "Just in" apps. Choose a good descriptive name for the application and place it in an appropriate category, such as **Games** or **Communication**. Keep the description simple and to the point to get more views. The **Games** category is over laden with apps, so there are sub-categories. If the app is fun but has no score or goal, consider the **Entertainment** category. Even so, with over 10,000 applications uploaded to the Android Market each month, an uploaded application is pushed off the "Just in" list within a day or two.

The second way users see an app is by keyword search. Determine the essential keywords users might use and include those in either the title or description of the app. Some users might speak a different language, so including appropriate international keywords can help.

The third way users see an app is by choosing the "Top" apps. This is a combination of the highest rating and the most downloads. To get in this category takes time and effort with possible updates to fix bugs. This points to the last consideration for app visibility:

robustness. Ensure the app does not contain major bugs, does not waste excessive battery, and has a foolproof way to exit the application. Nothing turns off a potential customer more than seeing reviews that say, "This app uses all of my battery," or, "I can't uninstall this app."

One side note to mention: Almost all interactions between the developer and users are done through the Android Market. Providing developer contact information or a supporting website is often superfluous, as people browsing the mobile market rarely use it.

Differentiating an App

Sometimes, the developer creates an application only to find a similar variant already in the Android Market. This should be treated as an opportunity rather than a discouragement. Differentiating the app simply through a better design, interface, or execution can quickly win over a user base. Basically, originality is nice, but it is not required. That being said, one must be careful to avoid using copyrighted material.

Charging for an App

Every time a new application or its update is uploaded to the Android Market, the developer must choose whether to provide it for free or charge for it. Following are the main options:

- Provide the app for free. Everyone who can access the Android market can see and install the app.
- Provide a free app, but include advertisements. In some cases, the developer negotiates sponsorship for an app. More often, the developer works with a third-party aggregator. Payouts are provided for clicked ads and less often for impressions (ad views). Figure 1.1 shows an example banner ad from AdMob. Such ads require the application have permission to access the Internet and the location of the device. Consider using coarse location instead of fine location to avoid deterring some potential customers from installing the app.
- Provide the app for a charge. Google handles its charges, but takes 30 percent of the proceeds. Countries that are not set up for charges through Google Checkout cannot see or cannot install an app for charge. For these reasons, some developers turn to third-party app stores for distribution.
- Post a free, limited version, but charge for a full version. This gives users the opportunity to try the app and if they like it, they will have less resistance to purchasing the full version. For some apps, this is a natural model (such as a game with ten free levels), but not all apps can be partitioned this way.
- Sell virtual goods inside the app. This is an important way Facebook apps work, and it is catching on in the mobile world.

Figure 1.1 Example mobile banner ad from AdMob.

Free applications tend to get a lot of views. Even the most obscure and odd applications seem to be downloaded and viewed by at least 1,000 people in the first month the application is on the Market. There are some developers who explicitly say, "This app is absolutely useless," and yet, they get over 10,000 downloads and a four-star rating. Somewhat relevant free applications can get as many as 50,000 downloads, and extremely useful free applications have over 100,000 downloads. For most developers, such exposure is quite impressive.

Mobile advertisement is still in its infancy and usually does not entice enough users to click the ad. For now, monetizing apps is best done by charging on the Market. As long as the app is useful for some people, has a clear description, and has a good selection of positive reviews, users purchase it. If an app is successful, it might make sense to raise the price of the app.

Managing Reviews and Updates

Most successful apps from independent developers come through a process of releasing a version and adapting to the user feedback. Users like to see a developer who is responsive. This leads to more people downloading an app, and as the number of downloads increases, it adds validity to the app.

In general, it seems about 1 in 200 people rate an application, and a small subset of those actually leaves a review. If someone takes the time to type a review, it is usually worth listening to it, especially if the review comments are constructive, such as "Doesn't work on the HTC Hero," or "Nice app, just wish it did so on and so forth."

Updates that respond to user comments are seen in a positive light by new potential customers. In any case, the reason for the update should be clearly highlighted. Most users get 10 to 20 notifications a day of applications that have updates. If they do not see a good reason to upgrade, they might not.

Alternatives to the Android Market

Other independent Android app stores exist. They might not have as convenient access to Android devices as the Google market does, but they provide other benefits for developers such as better app visibility, more places to charge for apps, and taking no portion of the proceeds from an app. Also, some Android manufacturers create customized app stores accessible from their devices. For example, getting app visibility onto Motorola Android phones in the China and Latin American markets can be done through the Motorola app market at http://developer.motorola.com/shop4apps.

2

Application Basics: Activities and Intents

Each Android application is represented by a single Android project. An overview of the project structure, including a brief introduction to the basic building blocks of an application, is provided as useful background information for the recipes in this book. Then the focus of this chapter turns to activities and the intents that launch them.

Android Application Overview

An Android application consists of various functionalities. Some examples are editing a note, playing a music file, ringing an alarm, or opening a phone contact. These functionalities can be classified into four different Android components, shown in Table 2.1, each of which is specified by a Java base class.

Table 2.1 **The Four Possible Components of an Android Application**

Functionality	Java Base Class	Examples
Focused thing a user can do	`Activity`	Edit a note, play a game
Background process	`Service`	Play music, update weather icon
Receive messages	`BroadcastReceiver`	Trigger alarm upon event
Store and retrieve data	`ContentProvider`	Open a phone contact

Every application is made up of one or more of these components. They are instantiated by the Android operating system (OS) as needed. Other applications are allowed to use them, too, within the specified permissions.

As multiple functionalities play out in the OS (some not even related to the intended application, such as an incoming phone call), each component goes through a lifecycle of getting created, focused, defocused, and destroyed. The default behavior can be overridden for a graceful operation, such as saving variables or restoring user interface (UI) elements.

With the exception of `ContentProvider`, each component is activated by an asynchronous message called an `Intent`. The `Intent` can contain a `Bundle` of supporting information describing the component. This provides a method of passing information between components.

The rest of this chapter demonstrates the previous concepts using the most common component: the `Activity`. Because activities almost always specify an interaction with a user, a window is automatically created with each activity. Therefore, a short introduction to the UI is also included. Of the other components, `Service` and `BroadcastReceiver` are covered in Chapter 3, "Threads, Services, Receivers, and Alerts," and `ContentProvider` is covered in Chapter 9, "Data Storage Methods."

Recipe: Creating a Project and an Activity

A straightforward way to create an Android project or any of its components is to use the Eclipse Integrated Development Environment (IDE). This method ensures proper setup of the supporting files. The steps to create a new Android project are

1. In Eclipse, choose **File → New → Android Project**. This displays a New Android Project creation screen.
2. Fill in the Project name, such as **SimpleActivityExample**.
3. Select a Build Target from the choices provided. These choices are based on the Software Development Kit (SDK) versions that are installed on the development computer.
4. Fill in the Application name, such as **Example of Basic Activity.**
5. Fill in the Package name, such as **com.cookbook.simple_activity.**
6. To create the main activity in the same step, be sure **Create Activity** is checked and fill in an Activity name, such as **SimpleActivity.**

All activities extend the abstract class `Activity` or one of its subclasses. The entry point to each activity is the `onCreate()` method. It is almost always overridden to initialize the activity, such as setting up the UI, creating button listeners, initializing parameters, and starting threads.

If the main activity is not created with the project or another activity needs to be added, the steps to create an activity are

1. Create a class to extend `Activity`. (In Eclipse, this can be done by right-clicking on the project, choosing **New → Class**, and then specifying `android.app.Activity` as the super class.)
2. Override the `onCreate()` function. (In Eclipse, this can be done by right-clicking on the class file, choosing **Source → Override/Implement Methods...**, and then checking the `onCreate()` method.)

3. As with most overridden functions, it must invoke the super class method, too; otherwise, an exception may be thrown at run-time. Here, the `super.onCreate()` should be called first to properly initialize the activity, as shown in Listing 2.1.

Listing 2.1 **src/com/cookbook/simple_activity/SimpleActivity.java**

```
package com.cookbook.simple_activity;

import android.app.Activity;
import android.os.Bundle;

public class SimpleActivity extends Activity {

    @Override
    public void onCreate(Bundle savedInstanceState) {
        super.onCreate(savedInstanceState);
        setContentView(R.layout.main);
    }
}
```

4. If a UI is used, specify the layout in an XML file in the **res/layout/** directory. Here it is called **main.xml,** as shown in Listing 2.2.
5. Set the layout of the activity using the `setContentView()` function and passing it the resource ID for the XML layout file. Here, it is `R.layout.main`, as shown in Listing 2.1.

Listing 2.2 **res/layout/main.xml**

```
<?xml version="1.0" encoding="utf-8"?>
<LinearLayout xmlns:android="http://schemas.android.com/apk/res/android"
    android:orientation="vertical"
    android:layout_width="fill_parent"
    android:layout_height="fill_parent"
    >
<TextView
    android:layout_width="fill_parent"
    android:layout_height="wrap_content"
    android:text="@string/hello"
    />
</LinearLayout>
```

6. Declare the properties of the activity in the AndroidManifest XML file. This is covered in more detail in Listing 2.5.

Note that the string resources are defined in the **strings.xml** file in the **res/values/** folder, as shown in Listing 2.3. This provides a central place for all strings in case text needs to be changed or reused.

Listing 2.3 **res/values/strings.xml**

```
<?xml version="1.0" encoding="utf-8"?>
<resources>
    <string name="hello">Hello World, SimpleActivity!</string>
    <string name="app_name">SimpleActivity</string>
</resources>
```

Now a more detailed look at the directory structure of this project and the additional auto-generated content is explored.

Directory Structure of Project and Autogenerated Content

Figure 2.1 shows an example project structure, as seen from the Eclipse Package Explorer.

Figure 2.1 Android project directory structure, as seen in the Eclipse IDE.

With the exception of the Android 2.0 library, the project structure is a mix of user-generated and auto-generated files.

User-generated files include

- **src/** contains the Java packages the developer writes or imports for the application. Each package can have multiple .java files representing different classes.
- **res/layout/** contains the XML files that specify the layout of each screen.
- **res/values/** contains the XML files used as references by other files.
- **res/drawable-hdpi/**, **res/drawable-mdpi/**, and **res/drawable-ldpi/** are directories that contain pictures the application uses. They have high, medium, and low dots-per-inch resolution, respectively.
- **assets/** contains additional nonmedia files the application uses.
- **AndroidManifest.xml** specifies the project to the Android OS.

Autogenerated files include

- **gen/** contains autogenerated code, including the generated class **R.java.**
- **default.properties** contains project settings. Although autogenerated, it should be kept under revision control.

An application's resources include XML files describing the layout, XML files describing values such as strings, labels of UI elements, and additional supporting files such as pictures and sounds. At compile time, references to the resources are gathered into an autogenerated wrapper class called **R.java.** The Android Asset Packaging Tool (aapt) autogenerates this file. Listing 2.4 shows what it looks like for the "Creating a Project and an Activity" recipe.

Listing 2.4 **gen/com/cookbook/simple_activity/R.java**

```
/* AUTO-GENERATED FILE.  DO NOT MODIFY.
 *
 * This class was automatically generated by the
 * aapt tool from the resource data it found.  It
 * should not be modified by hand.
 */

package com.cookbook.simple_activity;

public final class R {
    public static final class attr {
    }
    public static final class drawable {
        public static final int icon=0x7f020000;
    }
    public static final class layout {
        public static final int main=0x7f030000;
```

```
    }
    public static final class string {
        public static final int app_name=0x7f040001;
        public static final int hello=0x7f040000;
    }
}
```

Here, each resource is mapped to a unique integer value. In this way, the **R.java** class provides a way to reference external resources within Java code. For example, to reference the **main.xml** layout file in Java, the `R.layout.main` integer is used. To reference the same within XML files, the `"@layout/main"` string is used.

Referencing resources from within Java or XML files is demonstrated in Table 2.2. Note that to define a new button ID called `home_button`, the plus sign is added to the identifying string: `@+id/home_button`. More complete details on resources are given in Chapter 4, "User Interface Layout," but this suffices to cover the recipes in this chapter.

Table 2.2 **How Different Resources Are Referenced from Within Java and XML Files**

Resource	Reference in Java	Reference in XML
res/layout/main.xml	`R.layout.main`	`@layout/main`
res/drawable-hdpi/icon.png	`R.drawable.icon`	`@drawable/icon`
`@+id/home_button`	`R.id.home_button`	`@id/home_button`
`<string name="hello">`	`R.string.hello`	`@string/hello`

Android Package and Manifest File

The Android project, sometimes also referred to as an Android package, is a collection of Java packages. Different Android packages can have the same Java package names, whereas the Android package name must be unique across all applications installed on the Android device.

For the OS to access them, each application must declare its available components in a single AndroidManifest XML file. In addition, this file contains the required permissions and behavior for the application to run. Listing 2.5 shows what it looks like for the "Creating a Project and an Activity" recipe.

Listing 2.5 **AndroidManifest.xml**

```
<?xml version="1.0" encoding="utf-8"?>
<manifest xmlns:android="http://schemas.android.com/apk/res/android"
          package="com.cookbook.simple_activity"
          android:versionCode="1"
          android:versionName="1.0">
    <application android:icon="@drawable/icon"
```

```
                android:label="@string/app_name">
        <activity android:name=".SimpleActivity"
                 android:label="@string/app_name">
            <intent-filter>
              <action android:name="android.intent.action.MAIN" />
              <category android:name="android.intent.category.LAUNCHER" />
            </intent-filter>
        </activity>
    </application>
    <uses-sdk android:minSdkVersion="3" />
</manifest>
```

The first line is required and standard across all XML files in Android to specify the encoding. The `manifest` element defines the Android package name and version. The `versionCode` is an integer that can be evaluated in programs to determine the upgrade or downgrade relationship. The `versionName` represents a human readable format that can have major and minor revisions declared.

The `application` element defines the icon and label the user sees from the Android device menu. The label is a string and should be short enough to display under the icon on a user's device. Generally the name can be up to two words of ten characters each without being cut off.

The `activity` element defines the main activity that is launched when the application is started and the name shown in the title bar when the activity is active. Here, the Java package name needs to be specified, which is `com.cookbook.simple_activity.SimpleActivity` in this case. Because the Java package name is usually the same as the Android package name, the shorthand notation is often used: `.SimpleActivity`. However, it is best to remember that the Android package and Java package are distinct.

The `intent-filter` element informs the Android system of the capabilities of the component. It can have multiple action, category, or data elements for this purpose. This is seen as it is utilized in different recipes.

The `uses-sdk` element defines the application programming interface (API) level required to run this application. In general, the API level is specified as follows:

```
<uses-sdk android:minSdkVersion="integer"
          android:targetSdkVersion="integer"
          android:maxSdkVersion="integer" />
```

Because the Android OS is constructed to be forward compatible, the `maxSdkVersion` is highly discouraged and not even adhered on devices with Android 2.0.1 or later. Specifying the `targetSdkVersion` is not required, but allows devices of the same SDK version to disable compatibility settings that might speed up operation. The `minSdkVersion` should always be specified to ensure the application does not crash when run on a platform that does not support the required features in the application. Always choose the lowest API level possible when specifying this.

The AndroidManifest can also contain permission settings needed to run the application. More complete details about the options are provided in later chapters, but this suffices to cover the recipes in this chapter.

Renaming Parts of an Application

Sometimes a portion of an Android project needs to be renamed. Maybe a file was copied manually into the project, such as from this book. Maybe the application name has changed during development, and it needs to be reflected in the filesystem tree. Automatic tools help with this and ensure cross-references are automatically updated. For example, in the Eclipse IDE, the different ways to rename portions of an application are

- Rename the Android project, as follows:
    1. Right-click the project and **Refactor** → **Move** to a new directory in the filesystem.
    2. Right-click the project and **Refactor** → **Rename** the project.
- Rename an Android package, as follows:
    1. Right-click the package and **Refactor** → **Rename** the package.
    2. Edit the **AndroidManifest.xml** to ensure the new package name is reflected.
- Rename an Android class (such as the major components `Activity`, `Service`, `BroadcastReceiver`, `ContentProvider`), as follows:
    1. Right-click the **.java** file and **Refactor** → **Rename** the class.
    2. Edit the **AndroidManifest.xml** to ensure the `android:name` has the new component name.

Note that renaming other files, such as XML files, usually requires manually changing the corresponding references in the Java code.

Activity Lifecycle

Each activity in an application goes through its own lifecycle. Once and only once when an activity is created, is the `onCreate()` function executed. If the activity exits, the `onDestroy()` function is executed. In between, various events can lead to the activity being in multiple different states, as illustrated in Figure 2.2. The next recipe provides an example of each of these functions.

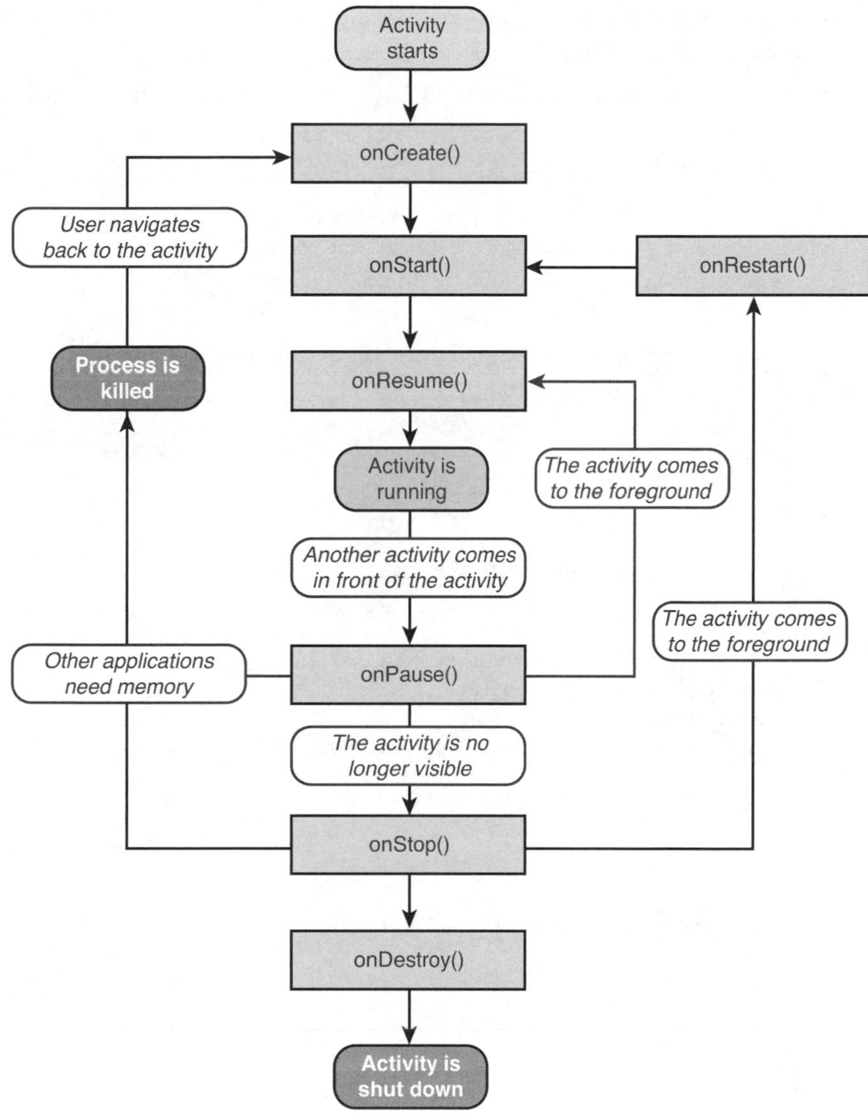

Figure 2.2 Activity Lifecycle from http://developer.android.com/.

Recipe: Utilizing Other Lifecycle Functions

The following recipe provides a simple way to see the activity lifecycle in action. For illustration purposes, each overridden function is explicit and a `Toast` command is added to show on screen when the function is entered (more detail on the Toast widget is provided in Chapter 3). The activity is shown in Listing 2.6. Run it on an Android device and try various cases. In particular, note the following:

- Changing the screen orientation destroys and recreates the activity from scratch.
- Pressing the Home button pauses the activity, but does not destroy it.
- Pressing the Application icon might start a new instance of the activity, even if the old one was not destroyed.
- Letting the screen sleep pauses the activity and the screen awakening resumes it. (This is similar to taking an incoming phone call.)

Listing 2.6 **src/com/cookbook/activity_lifecycle/ActivityLifecycle.java**

```
package com.cookbook.activity_lifecycle;

import android.app.Activity;
import android.os.Bundle;
import android.widget.Toast;

public class ActivityLifecycle extends Activity {

    @Override
    public void onCreate(Bundle savedInstanceState) {
        super.onCreate(savedInstanceState);
        setContentView(R.layout.main);
        Toast.makeText(this, "onCreate", Toast.LENGTH_SHORT).show();
    }

    @Override
    protected void onStart() {
        super.onStart();
        Toast.makeText(this, "onStart", Toast.LENGTH_SHORT).show();
    }

    @Override
    protected void onResume() {
        super.onResume();
        Toast.makeText(this, "onResume", Toast.LENGTH_SHORT).show();
    }

    @Override
    protected void onRestart() {
        super.onRestart();
        Toast.makeText(this, "onRestart", Toast.LENGTH_SHORT).show();
    }
```

```
    @Override
    protected void onPause() {
        Toast.makeText(this, "onPause", Toast.LENGTH_SHORT).show();
        super.onPause();
    }

    @Override
    protected void onStop() {
        Toast.makeText(this, "onStop", Toast.LENGTH_SHORT).show();
        super.onStop();
    }

    @Override
    protected void onDestroy() {
        Toast.makeText(this, "onDestroy", Toast.LENGTH_SHORT).show();
        super.onDestroy();
    }
}
```

As seen here, various common actions by the user can cause the activity to be paused, killed, or even launch multiple versions of the application. Before moving on, it is worth mentioning two additional simple recipes that can control this behavior.

Recipe: Forcing Single Task Mode

As an application is navigated away from and launched again, it can lead to multiple instances of the activity on the device. Eventually the redundant instance of the activity is killed to free up memory, but in the meantime, it can lead to odd situations. To avoid these, the developer can control this behavior for each activity in the AndroidManifest.

To ensure only one instance of the activity runs on the device, specify the following in an `activity` element that has the `MAIN` and `LAUNCHER` intent filters:

```
android:launchMode="singleInstance"
```

This keeps a single instance of each activity in a task at all times. In addition, any child activity is launched as its own task. To constrain even further to only have a single task for all activities of an application, use the following:

```
android:launchMode="singleTask"
```

This allows the activities to share information easily as the same task.

In addition, it might be desirable to retain the task state, regardless of how a user navigates to the activity. For example, if a user leaves the application and relaunches it later, the default behavior often resets the task to its initial state. To ensure the user always returns to the task in its last state, specify the following in the `activity` element of the root activity of a task:

```
android:alwaysRetainTaskState="true"
```

Recipe: Forcing Screen Orientation

Any Android device with an accelerometer can determine which way is down. As the device is tilted from portrait to landscape mode, the default action is to rotate the application view accordingly. However, as seen from the "Other Lifecycle Functions" recipe, the activity is destroyed and restarted on screen orientation changes. When this happens, the current state of the activity might be lost, disrupting the user experience.

One option to handle screen orientation changes gracefully is to save state information before the change and restore information after the change. A simpler method that might be useful is to force the screen orientation to stay constant. For each activity in the AndroidManifest, the `screenOrientation` can be specified. For example, to specify that the activity always stays in portrait mode, the following can be added to the `activity` element:

```
android:screenOrientation="portrait"
```

Similarly, landscape mode can be specified using the following:

```
android:screenOrientation="landscape"
```

However, the previous still causes the activity to be destroyed and restarted when a hard keyboard is slid out. Therefore, a third method is possible: Tell the Android system that the application should handle orientation and keyboard slide-out events. This is done by adding the following attribute to the activity element:

```
android:configChanges="orientation|keyboardHidden"
```

This can be used alone or in combination with the `screenOrientation` attribute to specify the required behavior to the application.

Recipe: Saving and Restoring Activity Information

Whenever an activity is about to be killed, the `onSaveInstanceState()` function is called. Override this to save relevant information that should be retained. When the activity is then recreated, the `onRestoreInstanceState()` is called. Override this function to retrieve the saved information. This allows for a seamless user experience when an application undergoes lifecycle changes. Note that most UI states do not need to be managed because they are, by default, taken care of by the system.

This function is distinct from `onPause()`. For example, if another component is launched in front of the activity, the `onPause()` function is called. Later, if the activity is still paused when the OS needs to reclaim resources, it calls `onSaveInstanceState()` before killing the activity.

An example of saving and restoring the instance state consisting of a string and a float array is shown in Listing 2.7.

Listing 2.7 **Example of onSaveInstanceState() and onRestoreInstanceState()**

```
float[] localFloatArray = {3.14f, 2.718f, 0.577f};
String localUserName = "Euler";

@Override
protected void onSaveInstanceState(Bundle outState) {
        super.onSaveInstanceState(outState);
        //save the relevant information
        outState.putString("name", localUserName);
        outState.putFloatArray("array", localFloatArray);
}

@Override
public void onRestoreInstanceState(Bundle savedInstanceState) {
        super.onRestoreInstanceState(savedInstanceState);
        //restore the relevant information
        localUserName = savedInstanceState.getString("name");
        localFloatArray = savedInstanceState.getFloatArray("array");
}
```

Note that `onCreate()` also contains the `Bundle savedInstanceState`. In the case of an activity reinitializing after previously being shut down, the bundle saved in `onSaveInstanceState()` is also passed to `onCreate()`. In all cases, the saved bundle is passed to the `onRestoreInstanceState()` function, so it is more natural to utilize this to restore states.

Multiple Activities

Even the simplest applications have more than one functionality. Hence, there is often a need to deal with multiple activities. For example, a game can have two activities: a high scores screen and a game screen. A notepad can have three activities: view a list of notes, read a selected note, and edit a selected or new note.

The main activity, as defined in the AndroidManifest XML file, is started when the application is started. This activity can launch another activity, usually after a trigger event. This causes the main activity to pause while the secondary activity is active. When the secondary activity ends, the main activity is brought to the foreground and resumed.

To activate a particular component of the application, an intent naming the component explicitly is used. If instead the requirements of an application can be specified by intent filters, an implicit intent can be used. The system then determines the best component or components to use, even if it is in a separate application or native to the OS. Note that unlike other activities, implicit intents that reside in other applications do not need to be declared in the current application's AndroidManifest file.

Android utilizes implicit intents as often as possible, providing a powerful framework for modular functionality. When a new component is developed that meets the required implicit intent filter, it can be used in place of an Android internal intent. For example, say a new application for displaying phone contacts is loaded on an Android device. When a user selects a contact, the Android system finds all available activities with the proper intent filter for viewing contacts and asks the user to decide which one should be used.

Recipe: Using Buttons and TextView

To fully demonstrate multiple activities, it is useful to use a trigger event. A button press is introduced here for that purpose. The steps to adding a button to a given layout and assigning an action to a button press are

1. Put a button in the designated layout XML file:
```
<Button android:id="@+id/trigger"
   android:layout_width="100dip" android:layout_height="100dip"
   android:text="Press this button" />
```
2. Declare a button that points to the button ID in the layout file:
```
Button startButton = (Button) findViewById(R.id.trigger);
```
3. Specify a listener for when the button is clicked:
```
//setup button listener
startButton.setOnClickListener(new View.OnClickListener() {
    //insert onClick here
});
```
4. Override the `onClick` function for the listener to do the required action:
```
public void onClick(View view) {
    // do something here

}
```

To show the result of an action, it is useful to change the text on the screen. The steps for defining a text field and changing it programmatically are

1. Put a text field in the designated layout XML file with an ID. It can also be initialized to some value (here, it can be initialized to the string named "hello" in the strings.xml file):
```
<TextView android:id="@+id/hello_text"
   android:layout_width="fill_parent"
   android:layout_height="wrap_content"
   android:text="@string/hello"
/>
```

2. Declare a TextView that points to the TextView ID in the layout file:
   `private TextView tv = (TextView) findViewById(R.id.hello_text);`
3. If the text needs to be changed, use the setText function:
   `tv.setText("new text string");`

These two UI techniques are used in the subsequent recipes in this chapter. A more complete demonstration of UI techniques is covered in Chapter 4.

Recipe: Launching Another Activity from an Event

In this recipe, `MenuScreen` is the main activity as shown in Listing 2.8. It launches the `PlayGame` activity. Here the trigger event is implemented as a button click using the `Button` widget.

When a user clicks the button, the `startGame()` function runs; it launches the `PlayGame` activity. When a user clicks the button in the `PlayGame` activity, it calls `finish()` to return control to the calling activity. The steps for launching an activity are

1. Declare an Intent that points to the activity to be launched.
2. Call startActivity on this intent.
3. Declare the additional activity in the AndroidManifest.

Listing 2.8 **src/com/cookbook/launch_activity/MenuScreen.java**

```
package com.cookbook.launch_activity;

import android.app.Activity;
import android.content.Intent;
import android.os.Bundle;
import android.view.View;
import android.widget.Button;

public class MenuScreen extends Activity {

    @Override
    public void onCreate(Bundle savedInstanceState) {
        super.onCreate(savedInstanceState);
        setContentView(R.layout.main);

        //setup button listener
        Button startButton = (Button) findViewById(R.id.play_game);
        startButton.setOnClickListener(new View.OnClickListener() {
            public void onClick(View view) {
                startGame();
            }
        });
```

```
    }

    private void startGame() {
        Intent launchGame = new Intent(this, PlayGame.class);
        startActivity(launchGame);
    }
}
```

Provide Current Context in an Anonymous Inner Class

Note the additional consideration needed for launching an activity with a Button press, as shown in Listing 2.8. The intent needs a context. However, using the `this` shortcut in the `onClick` function is not properly resolved. Different ways to provide current context in an anonymous inner class are

- Use `Context.this` instead of `this`.
- Use `getApplicationContext()` instead of `this`.
- Explicitly use the class name `MenuScreen.this`.

Call a function that is declared at the right context level. This is what is used in Listing 2.8: startGame().

Each of these methods can usually be interchanged. Utilize the one that works best for the clarity of the situation.

The `PlayGame` activity shown in Listing 2.9 is simply a button with a `onClick` listener that calls `finish()` to return control to the main activity. More functionality can be added as needed to this activity, and multiple branches of the code can each lead to their own `finish()` calls.

Listing 2.9 **src/com/cookbook/launch_activity/PlayGame.java**

```
package com.cookbook.launch_activity;

import android.app.Activity;
import android.os.Bundle;
import android.view.View;
import android.widget.Button;

public class PlayGame extends Activity {

    public void onCreate(Bundle savedInstanceState) {
        super.onCreate(savedInstanceState);
        setContentView(R.layout.game);

        //setup button listener
        Button startButton = (Button) findViewById(R.id.end_game);
        startButton.setOnClickListener(new View.OnClickListener() {
```

```
            public void onClick(View view) {
                finish();
            }
        });
    }
}
```

The button must be added to the `main` layout as shown in Listing 2.10, with the ID `play_game` to match what was declared in Listing 2.8. Here, the size of the button is also declared in device-independent pixels (dip), as discussed more in Chapter 4.

Listing 2.10 **res/layout/main.xml**

```
<?xml version="1.0" encoding="utf-8"?>
<LinearLayout xmlns:android="http://schemas.android.com/apk/res/android"
    android:orientation="vertical"
    android:layout_width="fill_parent"
    android:layout_height="fill_parent"
    >
<TextView
    android:layout_width="fill_parent"
    android:layout_height="wrap_content"
    android:text="@string/hello"
    />
 <Button android:id="@+id/play_game"
    android:layout_width="100dip" android:layout_height="100dip"
    android:text="@string/play_game"
    />
</LinearLayout>
```

The `PlayGame` activity references its own button ID `end_game` in the `R.layout.game` layout resource that corresponds to the layout XML file **game.xml**, as shown in Listing 2.11.

Listing 2.11 **res/layout/game.xml**

```
<?xml version="1.0" encoding="utf-8"?>
<LinearLayout xmlns:android="http://schemas.android.com/apk/res/android"
    android:orientation="vertical"
    android:layout_width="fill_parent"
    android:layout_height="fill_parent"
    >
<Button android:id="@+id/end_game"
    android:layout_width="100dip" android:layout_height="100dip"
    android:text="@string/end_game" android:layout_centerInParent="true"
    />
</LinearLayout>
```

Although the text can be written explicitly in each case, it is good coding practice to define variables for each string. In this recipe, the two string values `play_game` and `end_game` need to be declared in the string XML resource file, as shown in Listing 2.12.

Listing 2.12 **res/values/strings.xml**

```
<?xml version="1.0" encoding="utf-8"?>
<resources>
    <string name="hello">This is the Main Menu</string>
    <string name="app_name">LaunchActivity</string>
    <string name="play_game">Play game?</string>
    <string name="end_game">Done?</string>
</resources>
```

Finally, the AndroidManifest XML file needs to register a default action to the new class `PlayGame`, as shown in Listing 2.13.

Listing 2.13 **AndroidManifest.xml**

```
<?xml version="1.0" encoding="utf-8"?>
<manifest xmlns:android="http://schemas.android.com/apk/res/android"
      android:versionCode="1"
      android:versionName="1.0" package="com.cookbook.launch_activity">
    <application android:icon="@drawable/icon"
                 android:label="@string/app_name">
        <activity android:name=".MenuScreen"
                  android:label="@string/app_name">
            <intent-filter>
              <action android:name="android.intent.action.MAIN" />
              <category android:name="android.intent.category.LAUNCHER" />
            </intent-filter>
        </activity>
        <activity android:name=".PlayGame"
                  android:label="@string/app_name">
            <intent-filter>
              <action android:name="android.intent.action.VIEW" />
              <category android:name="android.intent.category.DEFAULT" />
            </intent-filter>
        </activity>
    </application>
    <uses-sdk android:minSdkVersion="3" />
</manifest>
```

Recipe: Launching an Activity for a Result Using Speech to Text

In this recipe, launching an activity for a result is demonstrated. It also demonstrates how to utilize speech to text functionality from Google's `RecognizerIntent` and print the result to the screen. Here, the trigger event is a button press. It launches the `RecognizerIntent` activity, which does speech recognition on sound from the microphone and converts it into text. When finished, the text is passed back to the calling activity.

Upon return, the `onActivityResult()` function is first called with the returned data, and then the `onResume()` function is called to continue the activity as normal. The calling activity can have a problem and not return properly. Therefore, the `resultCode` should always be checked to ensure `RESULT_OK` before continuing to parse the returned data.

Note that in general any launched activity that returns data causes the same `onActivityResult()` function to be called. Therefore, a request code is customarily used to distinguish which activity is returning. When the launched activity finishes, it returns control to the calling activity and calls `onActivityResult()` with the same request code.

The steps for launching an activity for result are

1. Call startActivityForResult() with an intent, defining the launched activity and an identifying requestCode.
2. Override the onActivityResult() function to check on the status of the result, check for the expected requestCode, and parse the returned data.

The steps for using `RecognizerIntent` are

1. Declare an intent with action ACTION_RECOGNIZE_SPEECH.
2. Add any extras to the intent; at least EXTRA_LANGUAGE_MODEL is required. This can be set as either LANGUAGE_MODEL_FREE_FORM or LANGUAGE_MODEL_WEB_SEARCH.
3. The returned data bundle contains a list of strings with possible matches to the original text. Use `data.getStringArrayListExtra` to retrieve this data. This should be cast as an ArrayList for use later.

A `TextView` is used to display the returned text to the screen. The main activity is shown in Listing 2.14.

The additional supporting files needed are the **main.xml** and **strings.xml**, which need to define a button and the TextView to hold the result. This is accomplished using Listing 2.10 and 2.12 in the "Launching Another Activity from an Event" recipe. The Android-Manifest needs to declare only the main activity, which is the same as the basic "Creating an Activity" recipe. The RecognizerIntent activity is native to the Android system and does not need to be declared explicitly to be utilized.

Listing 2.14 **src/com/cookbook/launch_for_result/RecognizerIntent Example.java**

```
package com.cookbook.launch_for_result;

import java.util.ArrayList;

import android.app.Activity;
import android.content.Intent;
import android.os.Bundle;
import android.speech.RecognizerIntent;
import android.view.View;
import android.widget.Button;
import android.widget.TextView;

public class RecognizerIntentExample extends Activity {
    private static final int RECOGNIZER_EXAMPLE = 1001;
    private TextView tv;

    protected void onCreate(Bundle savedInstanceState) {
        super.onCreate(savedInstanceState);
        setContentView(R.layout.main);

        tv = (TextView) findViewById(R.id.text_result);

        //setup button listener
        Button startButton = (Button) findViewById(R.id.trigger);
        startButton.setOnClickListener(new View.OnClickListener() {
            public void onClick(View view) {
                // RecognizerIntent prompts for speech and returns text
                Intent intent =
                    new Intent(RecognizerIntent.ACTION_RECOGNIZE_SPEECH);

                intent.putExtra(RecognizerIntent.EXTRA_LANGUAGE_MODEL,
                        RecognizerIntent.LANGUAGE_MODEL_FREE_FORM);
                intent.putExtra(RecognizerIntent.EXTRA_PROMPT,
                "Say a word or phrase\nand it will show as text");
                startActivityForResult(intent, RECOGNIZER_EXAMPLE);
            }
        });
    }

    @Override
    protected void onActivityResult(int requestCode,
                                int resultCode, Intent data) {
        //use a switch statement for more than one request code check
        if (requestCode==RECOGNIZER_EXAMPLE && resultCode==RESULT_OK) {
```

```
            // returned data is a list of matches to the speech input
            ArrayList<String> result =
            data.getStringArrayListExtra(RecognizerIntent.EXTRA_RESULTS);

            //display on screen
            tv.setText(result.toString());
        }

        super.onActivityResult(requestCode, resultCode, data);
    }
}
```

Recipe: Implementing a List of Choices

A common situation in applications is to provide a user with a list of choices that can be selected by clicking them. This can be easily implemented utilizing `ListActivity`, a subclass of `Activity`, and triggering an event based on what choice was made.

The steps for creating a list of choices are

1. Create a class that extends the ListActivity class instead of the Activity class:
```
public class ActivityExample extends ListActivity {
  //content here
}
```
2. Create a String array of labels for each choice:
```
static final String[] ACTIVITY_CHOICES = new String[] {
        "Action 1",
        "Action 2",
        "Action 3"
};
```
3. Call `setListAdapter()` with the `ArrayAdapter` specifying this list and a layout:
```
setListAdapter(new ArrayAdapter<String>(this,
        android.R.layout.simple_list_item_1, ACTIVITY_CHOICES));
getListView().setChoiceMode(ListView.CHOICE_MODE_SINGLE);
getListView().setTextFilterEnabled(true);
```
4. Launch an OnItemClickListener to determine which choice was selected and act accordingly:
```
getListView().setOnItemClickListener(new OnItemClickListener()
{
   @Override
    public void onItemClick(AdapterView<?> arg0, View arg1,
           int arg2, long arg3) {
       switch(arg2) {//extend switch to as many as needed
       case 0:
           //code for action 1
```

```
                break;
            case 1:
                //code for action 2
                break;
            case 2:
                //code for action 3
                break;
            default: break;
            }
        }
    });
```

This technique is utilized in the next recipe.

Recipe: Using Implicit Intents for Creating an Activity

Implicit intents do not specify an exact component to use. Instead, they specify the functionality required through a filter, and the Android system must determine the best component to utilize. An intent filter can be either an action, data, or a category.

The most commonly used intent filter is an action, and the most common action is `ACTION_VIEW`. This mode requires a uniform resource identifier (URI) to be specified and then displays the data to the user. It does the most reasonable action for the given URI. For example, the implicit intents in case 0, 1, and 2 in the following example have the same syntax but produce different results.

The steps for launching an activity using an implicit intent are

1. Declare the intent with the appropriate filter specified (ACTION_VIEW, ACTION_WEB_SEARCH, and so on).
2. Attach any extra information to the intent required to run the activity.
3. Pass this intent to startActivity().

This is shown for multiple intents in Listing 2.15.

Listing 2.15 **src/com/cookbook/implicit_intents/ListActivityExample.java**

```
package com.cookbook.implicit_intents;

import android.app.ListActivity;
import android.app.SearchManager;
import android.content.Intent;
import android.net.Uri;
import android.os.Bundle;
import android.view.View;
import android.widget.AdapterView;
import android.widget.ArrayAdapter;
```

```
import android.widget.ListView;
import android.widget.AdapterView.OnItemClickListener;

public class ListActivityExample extends ListActivity {
    static final String[] ACTIVITY_CHOICES = new String[] {
        "Open Website Example",
        "Open Contacts",
        "Open Phone Dialer Example",
        "Search Google Example",
        "Start Voice Command"
    };
    final String searchTerms = "superman";

    protected void onCreate(Bundle savedInstanceState) {
        super.onCreate(savedInstanceState);

        setListAdapter(new ArrayAdapter<String>(this,
                android.R.layout.simple_list_item_1, ACTIVITY_CHOICES));
        getListView().setChoiceMode(ListView.CHOICE_MODE_SINGLE);
        getListView().setTextFilterEnabled(true);
        getListView().setOnItemClickListener(new OnItemClickListener()
        {
            @Override
            public void onItemClick(AdapterView<?> arg0, View arg1,
                    int arg2, long arg3) {
                switch(arg2) {
                case 0: //opens web browser and navigates to given website
                    startActivity(new Intent(Intent.ACTION_VIEW,
                            Uri.parse("http://www.android.com/")));
                    break;
                case 1: //opens contacts application to browse contacts
                    startActivity(new Intent(Intent.ACTION_VIEW,
                            Uri.parse("content://contacts/people/")));
                    break;
                case 2: //opens phone dialer and fills in the given number
                    startActivity(new Intent(Intent.ACTION_VIEW,
                            Uri.parse("tel:12125551212")));
                    break;
                case 3: //search Google for the string
                    Intent intent= new Intent(Intent.ACTION_WEB_SEARCH );
                    intent.putExtra(SearchManager.QUERY, searchTerms);
                    startActivity(intent);
                    break;
                case 4: //starts the voice command
                    startActivity(new
                                Intent(Intent.ACTION_VOICE_COMMAND));
```

```
                    break;
                default: break;
                }
            }
        });
    }
}
```

Recipe: Passing Primitive Data Types Between Activities

Sometimes data needs to be passed to a launched activity. Sometimes a launched activity creates data that needs to be passed back to the calling activity. For example, a final score of a game needs to be returned to a high-scores screen. The different ways to pass information between activities are

- Declare the relevant variable in the calling activity (for example, public `int finalScore`) and set it in the launched activity (for example, `CallingActivity.finalScore=score`).
- Attach extras onto Bundles (demonstrated here).
- Use Preferences to store data to be retrieved later (covered in Chapter 5, "User Interface Events").
- Use the SQLite database to store data to be retrieved later (covered in Chapter 9).

A `Bundle` is a mapping from String values to various parcelable types. It can be created by adding extras to an intent. The following example shows data being passed from the main activity to the launched activity, where it is modified and passed back.

The variables (in this case, an `integer` and a `String`) are declared in the `StartScreen` activity. When the intent is created to call the `PlayGame` class, these variables are attached to the intent using the `putExtra` method. When the result is returned from the called activity, the variables can be read using the `getExtras` method. These calls are shown in Listing 2.16.

Listing 2.16 **src/com/cookbook/passing_data_activities/StartScreen.java**

```
package com.cookbook.passing_data_activities;

import android.app.Activity;
import android.content.Intent;
import android.os.Bundle;
import android.view.View;
import android.widget.Button;
import android.widget.TextView;

public class StartScreen extends Activity {
    private static final int PLAY_GAME = 1010;
```

```
    private TextView tv;
    private int meaningOfLife = 42;
    private String userName = "Douglas Adams";

    @Override
    public void onCreate(Bundle savedInstanceState) {
        super.onCreate(savedInstanceState);
        setContentView(R.layout.main);
        tv = (TextView) findViewById(R.id.startscreen_text);

        //display initial values
        tv.setText(userName + ":" + meaningOfLife);

        //setup button listener
        Button startButton = (Button) findViewById(R.id.play_game);
        startButton.setOnClickListener(new View.OnClickListener() {
            public void onClick(View view) {
                startGame();
            }
        });
    }

    @Override
    protected void onActivityResult(int requestCode,
            int resultCode, Intent data) {
        if (requestCode == PLAY_GAME && resultCode == RESULT_OK) {
            meaningOfLife = data.getExtras().getInt("returnInt");
            userName = data.getExtras().getString("userName");
            //show it has changed
            tv.setText(userName + ":" + meaningOfLife);
        }
        super.onActivityResult(requestCode, resultCode, data);
    }

    private void startGame() {
        Intent launchGame = new Intent(this, PlayGame.class);

        //passing information to launched activity
        launchGame.putExtra("meaningOfLife", meaningOfLife);
        launchGame.putExtra("userName", userName);

        startActivityForResult(launchGame, PLAY_GAME);
    }
}
```

The variables passed into the `PlayGame` activity can be read using the `getIntExtra` and `getStringExtra` methods. When the activity finishes and prepares an intent to return, the `putExtra` method can be used to return data back to the calling activity. These calls are shown in Listing 2.17.

Listing 2.17 **src/com/cookbook/passing_data_activities/PlayGame.java**

```
package com.cookbook.passing_data_activities;

import android.app.Activity;
import android.content.Intent;
import android.os.Bundle;
import android.view.View;
import android.widget.Button;
import android.widget.TextView;

public class PlayGame extends Activity {
    private TextView tv2;
    int answer;
    String author;

    public void onCreate(Bundle savedInstanceState) {
        super.onCreate(savedInstanceState);
        setContentView(R.layout.game);

        tv2 = (TextView) findViewById(R.id.game_text);

        //reading information passed to this activity
        //Get the intent that started this activity
        Intent i = getIntent();
        //returns -1 if not initialized by calling activity
        answer = i.getIntExtra("meaningOfLife", -1);
        //returns [] if not initialized by calling activity
        author = i.getStringExtra("userName");

        tv2.setText(author + ":" + answer);

        //change values for an example of return
        answer = answer - 41;
        author = author + " Jr.";

        //setup button listener
        Button startButton = (Button) findViewById(R.id.end_game);
        startButton.setOnClickListener(new View.OnClickListener() {
            public void onClick(View view) {
                //return information to calling activity
```

```
                Intent i = getIntent();
                i.putExtra("returnInt", answer);
                i.putExtra("returnStr", author);
                setResult(RESULT_OK, i);
                finish();
            }
        });
    }
}
```

3

Threads, Services, Receivers, and Alerts

This chapter continues the introduction of the basic building blocks of an application. First, the explicit specification of threads is introduced as a method to separate tasks. Then, services and broadcast receivers are introduced. These can also benefit from threads, as shown in some recipes. The application widget, which utilizes receivers, is then covered. This leads naturally to the discussion of various alerts available to the developer.

Threads

Every application by default runs a single process upon creation that contains all the tasks. To avoid hanging the user interface, time-consuming tasks, such as network downloads or computationally intensive calculations, should reside in a separate background thread. It is up to the developer to implement this properly, but then the Android operating system (OS) prioritizes the threads accordingly.

Most applications can benefit from the use of threads. If such occasions are not detected in the software design phase, they quickly display during testing because the Android system provides an alert to the user when the user interface (UI) hangs, as shown in Figure 3.1.

Recipe: Launching a Secondary Thread

In this recipe, a ring-tone song is played when an onscreen button is pressed. This provides a simple illustration of how threads can be used with a time-consuming operation. In the following, calling the `play_music()` function without specifying a separate thread blocks the application during music playback.

```
Button startButton = (Button) findViewById(R.id.trigger);
startButton.setOnClickListener(new View.OnClickListener() {
    public void onClick(View view){
        // BAD USAGE: function call to time-consuming
        //   function causes main thread to hang
```

```
        play_music();
    }
});
```

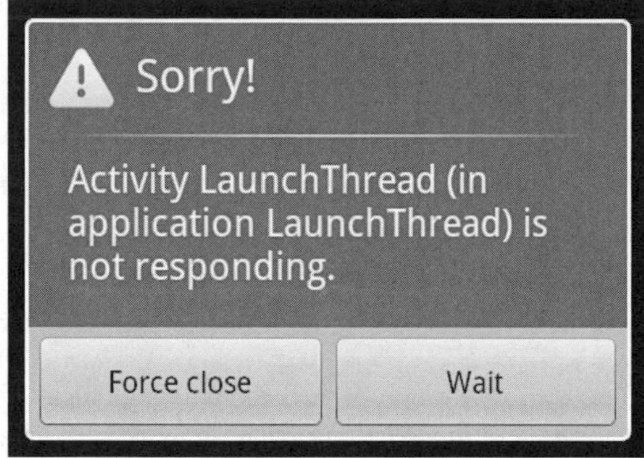

Figure 3.1 An example of the message that displays when a thread hangs.

This means any user request such as navigating back to the home screen or multiple pushes of an onscreen button are not registered until the music is completely finished playing. The unresponsive UI might even cause the Android system to show an error such as the previous one in Figure 3.1.

This is resolved by launching a secondary thread to call the `play_music()` function. The steps to do this are

1. Create a new thread to hold a `Runnable` object:
   ```
   Thread initBkgdThread = new Thread(
       //insert runnable object here
   );
   ```
2. Create a `Runnable` object that overrides the `run()` method to call the time-consuming task:
   ```
   new Runnable() {
     public void run() {
       play_music();
     }
   }
   ```
3. Start the thread, which then runs the task:
   ```
   initBkgdThread.start();
   ```

The setup of the secondary thread to contain the time-consuming task is quick, so the main thread can continue servicing other events.

Before showing the code for the full activity, the supporting files are discussed. Media playback is covered more fully in Chapter 6, "Multimedia Techniques," but for illustration, the song is implemented here as a sequence of notes specified using ring-tone text transfer language (RTTTL). For example, the RTTTL code describing a quarter note of the A(220Hz) just below middle C is shown in Listing 3.1. Putting this in a single-line text file in the **res/raw/** directory registers it as the `R.raw.a4` resource.

Listing 3.1 **RTTTL file res/raw/a4.rtttl, which denotes A just below middle-C.**

```
<a4:d=4,o=5,b=250:a4;
```

Then, a call in the activity to the media player plays this ring-tone note:

```
m_mediaPlayer = MediaPlayer.create(this, R.raw.a4);
                m_mediaPlayer.start();
```

This recipe uses four different notes in four separate RTTTL files: **g4.rtttl, a4.rtttl, b4.rtttl,** and **c5.rtttl.** These are just exact copies of Listing 3.1 with the `a4` changed in the file to reflect the new note in each case, but it can also be expanded to other notes or formats.

One aside is that the `MediaPlayer` launches its own background thread to play the media. So, if this was a single longer file to play, it is possible to avoid the use of an explicit thread as explained in Chapter 6. That fact does not help when multiple files need to be played quickly, as here, but it is important to know that threads are not always necessary.

The trigger for starting the music is a button press. The Button widget needs to be specified in the main layout file (here called **main.xml**) and is identified with the name `trigger`, as shown in Listing 3.2.

Listing 3.2 **res/layout/main.xml**

```
<?xml version="1.0" encoding="utf-8"?>
<LinearLayout xmlns:android="http://schemas.android.com/apk/res/android"
    android:orientation="vertical"
    android:layout_width="fill_parent"
    android:layout_height="fill_parent"
    >
  <Button android:id="@+id/trigger"
    android:layout_width="100dip" android:layout_height="100dip"
    android:text="Press Me"
  />
</LinearLayout>
```

One side-effect of launching a separate thread is that it still continues even if the main activity is paused. This is seen by implementing the background thread and navigating back to the home screen during music play. The music keeps playing until it is completed. If this is not the preferred behavior, the `play_music()` function can check a flag (here called `paused`), which is set during the main activity's `onPause()` function to stop music playback when the main thread is paused.

All the previous items are combined into the full activity `PressAndPlay` in Listing 3.3.

Listing 3.3 **src/com/cookbook/launch_thread/PressAndPlay.java**

```
package com.cookbook.launch_thread;

import android.app.Activity;
import android.media.MediaPlayer;
import android.os.Bundle;
import android.view.View;
import android.widget.Button;

public class PressAndPlay extends Activity {

    @Override
    public void onCreate(Bundle savedInstanceState) {
        super.onCreate(savedInstanceState);
        setContentView(R.layout.main);

        Button startButton = (Button) findViewById(R.id.trigger);
        startButton.setOnClickListener(new View.OnClickListener() {
            public void onClick(View view){

                //standalone play_music() function call causes
                //main thread to hang.  Instead, create
                //separate thread for time-consuming task
                Thread initBkgdThread = new Thread(new Runnable() {
                    public void run() {
                        play_music();
                    }
                });
                initBkgdThread.start();
            }
        });
    }

    int[] notes = {R.raw.c5, R.raw.b4, R.raw.a4, R.raw.g4};
    int NOTE_DURATION = 400; //millisec
    MediaPlayer m_mediaPlayer;
    private void play_music() {
```

```
        for(int ii=0; ii<12; ii++) {
            //check to ensure main activity not paused
            if(!paused) {
                if(m_mediaPlayer != null) {m_mediaPlayer.release();}
                m_mediaPlayer = MediaPlayer.create(this, notes[ii%4]);
                m_mediaPlayer.start();
                try {
                    Thread.sleep(NOTE_DURATION);
                } catch (InterruptedException e) {
                    e.printStackTrace();
                }
            }
        }
    }

    boolean paused = false;
    @Override
    protected void onPause() {
        paused = true;
        super.onPause();
    }
    @Override
    protected void onResume() {
        super.onResume();
        paused = false;
    }
}
```

Note the `Thread.sleep()` method pauses the thread for approximately the amount specified (in milliseconds). This is used to implement the note duration.

Also note the convention used in the lifecycle methods: Additional activity-specific logic is bracketed by the super methods. This is good practice to ensure proper completion of commands. So the internal pause flag is set to true before truly pausing the activity, and the activity is fully resumed before setting the internal pause flag to false.

Recipe: Creating a Runnable Activity

This recipe is an activity that evaluates a computationally intensive function, such as edge detection in an image. Here, a dummy function called `detectEdges()` is run to emulate the actual image-processing algorithm.

If `detectEdges()` is called in `onCreate()` by itself, it hangs the main thread and does not display the UI layout until computation is done. Therefore, a separate thread needs to be created and started for the time-consuming function. Because the main purpose of the activity is this time-consuming operation, it is natural to have the activity itself implement `Runnable`. As shown in Listing 3.4, the background thread is declared in the `onCreate()`

method. When the background thread is started, it calls the activity's `run()` method, which is overridden with the intended functionality.

The button is implemented exactly as in the previous "Launching a Secondary Thread" recipe. Pressing the button shows the UI is still responsive when the background task `detectEdges()` runs.

Listing 3.4 **src/com/cookbook/runnable_activity/EdgeDetection.java**

```
package com.cookbook.runnable_activity;

import android.app.Activity;
import android.os.Bundle;
import android.view.View;
import android.widget.Button;
import android.widget.TextView;

public class EdgeDetection extends Activity implements Runnable {
    int numberOfTimesPressed=0;

    @Override
    public void onCreate(Bundle savedInstanceState) {
        super.onCreate(savedInstanceState);
        setContentView(R.layout.main);
        final TextView tv  = (TextView) findViewById(R.id.text);
        //in-place function call causes main thread to hang:
        /* detectEdges(); */
        //instead, create background thread for time-consuming task
        Thread thread = new Thread(EdgeDetection.this);
        thread.start();

        Button startButton = (Button) findViewById(R.id.trigger);
        startButton.setOnClickListener(new View.OnClickListener() {
            public void onClick(View view){

                tv.setText("Pressed button " + ++numberOfTimesPressed
                        + " times\nAnd computation loop at "
                        + "(" + xi + ", " + yi + ") pixels");
            }
        });
    }

    @Override
    public void run() {
        detectEdges();
    }
```

```
    //Edge Detection
    int xi, yi;
    private double detectEdges() {
        int x_pixels = 4000;
        int y_pixels = 3000;
        double image_transform=0;

        //double loop over pixels for image processing
        //meaningless hyperbolic cosine emulates time-consuming task
        for(xi=0; xi<x_pixels; xi++) {
            for(yi=0; yi<y_pixels; yi++) {
                image_transform = Math.cosh(xi*yi/x_pixels/y_pixels);
            }
        }
        return image_transform;
    }
}
```

Recipe: Setting a Thread's Priority

The Android system handles thread priorities. By default, a new thread `myThread` gets a priority of 5. The developer can suggest a different priority by calling `myThread.setPriority(priority)` before `myThread.start()`. The priority cannot be set higher than `Thread.MAX_PRIORITY` (which is 10) or lower than `Thread.MIN_PRIORITY` (which is 1).

Recipe: Canceling a Thread

Sometimes when a component is finished or killed, the developer wants the threads it spawns to also be killed. For example, take a thread defined in an activity:

```
private volatile Thread myThread;
```

The `myThread.stop()` method is deprecated because it might leave the application in an unpredictable state. Instead, use the following when needed, such as in the `onStop()` method of the parent component:

```
//use to stop the thread myThread
if(myThread != null) {
   Thread dummy = myThread;
   myThread = null;
   dummy.interrupt();
}
```

At the application level, there is another way to do this: Declare all spawned threads as daemon threads using the `setDaemon(true)` method. This ensures threads associated with that application are killed when the application's main thread is killed.

```
//use when initially starting a thread
myThread.setDaemon(true);
myThread.start();
```

Finally, there is always the method of using a `while(stillRunning)` loop in the `run()` method and externally setting `stillRunning=false` to kill the thread. However, this might not provide sufficient control over the timing of when the thread stops.

Recipe: Sharing a Thread Between Two Applications

The previous recipes motivated the use of multiple threads in a single application. The converse case is also sometimes useful: use of multiple applications in a single thread. For example, if two applications need to communicate between each other, they can do so using binders rather than the more complicated inter-process communication (IPC) protocol. The steps are

1. Make sure each application, when packaged for release, is signed with the same key for security reasons.
2. Make sure each application is run with the same user ID. This is done by declaring the same attribute `android:sharedUserId="my.shared.userid"` in the **ActivityManifest.xml** for each application.
3. Declare each relevant activity or component to be run in the same process. This is done by declaring the same attribute `android:process="my.shared.process-name"` in the **ActivityManifest.xml** for each component.

These simple steps ensure the two components are run in the same thread and transparently share the same information. The more complex case where permissions cannot be shared is covered in the "Implementing a Remote Procedure Call" recipe in Chapter 11, "Advanced Android Development."

Messages Between Threads: Handlers

After multiple threads run concurrently, such as a main application thread and a background thread, there needs to be a way to communicate between them. Some examples are

- A main thread serves time-critical information and passes messages to the background time-consuming thread to update.
- A large computation completes and sends a message back to the calling thread with the result.

This can be accomplished with handlers, which are objects for sending messages between threads. Each handler is bound to a single thread, delivering messages to it and executing commands from it.

Recipe: Scheduling a Runnable Task from the Main Thread

This recipe implements a clock timer, which is often needed in applications. For example, it can be used in a game to keep track of how long a player takes to complete a level. This provides a simple way to handle user interaction while a background thread continues to run.

The timer is run in a background thread so it does not block the UI thread, but it needs to update the UI whenever the time changes. As shown in Listing 3.5, the `TextView text` starts with a welcome message and the button text with `trigger` ID starts with the value "Press Me."

Listing 3.5 **res/layout/main.xml**

```
<?xml version="1.0" encoding="utf-8"?>
<LinearLayout xmlns:android="http://schemas.android.com/apk/res/android"
    android:orientation="vertical"
    android:layout_width="fill_parent"
    android:layout_height="fill_parent"
    >
<TextView android:id="@+id/text"
    android:layout_width="fill_parent"
    android:layout_height="wrap_content"
    android:text="@string/hello"
    />
<Button android:id="@+id/trigger"
    android:layout_width="100dip" android:layout_height="100dip"
    android:text="Press Me"
    />
</LinearLayout>
```

These text resources in the layout XML file are associated with `TextView` variables in the `BackgroundTimer` Java activity using the following initializers:

```
mTimeLabel = (TextView) findViewById(R.id.text);
mButtonLabel = (TextView) findViewById(R.id.trigger);
```

After identified in Java, the text can be modified during run-time. When the application starts, the `mUpdateTimeTask` starts a counting timer and overwrites the text `mTimeLabel` with the new time in minutes and seconds. When the button is pressed, its `onClick()` method overwrites the text `mButtonLabel` with the number of times the button was pressed.

The handler `mHandler` is created and used to queue the runnable object `mUpdateTimeTask`. It is first called in the `onCreate()` method and then the recursive call in the task itself continues to update the time every 200ms. This is more often than needed to ensure a smooth time change each second without excessive overhead in task calls. The complete activity is shown in Listing 3.6.

Listing 3.6 **src/com/cookbook/background_timer/BackgroundTimer.java**

```
package com.cookbook.background_timer;

import android.app.Activity;
import android.os.Bundle;
import android.os.Handler;
import android.os.SystemClock;
import android.view.View;
import android.widget.Button;
import android.widget.TextView;

public class BackgroundTimer extends Activity {
    //keep track of button presses, a main thread task
    private int buttonPress=0;
    TextView mButtonLabel;

    //counter of time since app started, a background task
    private long mStartTime = 0L;
    private TextView mTimeLabel;

    //Handler to handle the message to the timer task
    private Handler mHandler = new Handler();

    @Override
    public void onCreate(Bundle savedInstanceState) {
        super.onCreate(savedInstanceState);
        setContentView(R.layout.main);

        if (mStartTime == 0L) {
            mStartTime = SystemClock.uptimeMillis();
            mHandler.removeCallbacks(mUpdateTimeTask);
            mHandler.postDelayed(mUpdateTimeTask, 100);
        }

        mTimeLabel = (TextView) findViewById(R.id.text);
        mButtonLabel = (TextView) findViewById(R.id.trigger);

        Button startButton = (Button) findViewById(R.id.trigger);
        startButton.setOnClickListener(new View.OnClickListener() {
            public void onClick(View view){
                mButtonLabel.setText("Pressed " + ++buttonPress
                                                + " times");
            }
        });
    }
```

```
    private Runnable mUpdateTimeTask = new Runnable() {
        public void run() {
            final long start = mStartTime;
            long millis = SystemClock.uptimeMillis() - start;
            int seconds = (int) (millis / 1000);
            int minutes = seconds / 60;
            seconds     = seconds % 60;

            mTimeLabel.setText("" + minutes + ":"
                              + String.format("%02d",seconds));
            mHandler.postDelayed(this, 200);
        }
    };

    @Override
    protected void onPause() {
        mHandler.removeCallbacks(mUpdateTimeTask);
        super.onPause();
    }

    @Override
    protected void onResume() {
        super.onResume();
        mHandler.postDelayed(mUpdateTimeTask, 100);
    }
}
```

Recipe: Using a Countdown Timer

The previous recipe is an example of handlers and a functional timer. Another timer is provided with the built-in class `CountDownTimer`. This encapsulates the creation of a background thread and the handler queuing into a convenient class call.

The countdown timer takes two arguments: the number of milliseconds until the countdown is done and how often in milliseconds to process `onTick()` callbacks. The `onTick()` method is used to update the countdown text. Note that otherwise the recipe is identical to the previous recipe. The full activity is shown in Listing 3.7.

Listing 3.7 **src/com/cookbook/countdown/CountDownTimerExample.java**

```
package com.cookbook.countdown;

import android.app.Activity;
import android.os.Bundle;
import android.os.CountDownTimer;
import android.view.View;
import android.widget.Button;
import android.widget.TextView;
```

```
public class CountDownTimerExample extends Activity {
    //keep track of button presses, a main thread task
    private int buttonPress=0;
    TextView mButtonLabel;

    //count down timer, a background task
    private TextView mTimeLabel;

    @Override
    public void onCreate(Bundle savedInstanceState) {
        super.onCreate(savedInstanceState);
        setContentView(R.layout.main);

        mTimeLabel = (TextView) findViewById(R.id.text);
        mButtonLabel = (TextView) findViewById(R.id.trigger);

        new CountDownTimer(30000, 1000) {
            public void onTick(long millisUntilFinished) {
                mTimeLabel.setText("seconds remaining: "
                        + millisUntilFinished / 1000);
                }
            public void onFinish() {
                mTimeLabel.setText("done!");
                }
        }.start();

        Button startButton = (Button) findViewById(R.id.trigger);
        startButton.setOnClickListener(new View.OnClickListener() {
            public void onClick(View view){
              mButtonLabel.setText("Pressed " + ++buttonPress + " times");
            }
        });
    }
}
```

Recipe: Handling a Time-Consuming Initialization

This recipe addresses a common case of needing to run a time-consuming initialization when an application starts. Initially, the layout is set to show a specific "Loading..." splash screen specified in the **loading.xml** file. In this example, it is a simple text message as shown in Listing 3.8, but it could be a company logo or introductory animation.

Listing 3.8 **res/layout/loading.xml**

```
<?xml version="1.0" encoding="utf-8"?>
<LinearLayout
  xmlns:android="http://schemas.android.com/apk/res/android"
  android:layout_width="wrap_content"
  android:layout_height="wrap_content">
  <TextView android:id="@+id/loading"
    android:layout_width="fill_parent"
    android:layout_height="wrap_content"
    android:text="Loading..."
    />
</LinearLayout>
```

While this layout is being displayed, the function `initializeArrays()`, which takes time to complete, is launched in a background thread to avoid hanging the UI. The initialization uses static variables to ensure a screen change or another instance of the activity does not require a recalculation of the data.

When the initialization is done, a message is sent to the handler `mHandler`. Since the act of sending a message is all the information needed, just an empty message is sent as `mHandler.sendEmptyMessage(0)`.

Upon receiving the message, the UI thread runs the `handleMessage()` method. It is overridden to continue on with the activity after the starting initialization, here setting up the main screen specified in the **main.xml** layout file. The full activity is shown in Listing 3.9.

Listing 3.9 **src/com/cookbook/handle_message/HandleMessage.java**

```
package com.cookbook.handle_message;

import android.app.Activity;
import android.os.Bundle;
import android.os.Handler;
import android.os.Message;

public class HandleMessage extends Activity implements Runnable {

    @Override
    public void onCreate(Bundle savedInstanceState) {
        super.onCreate(savedInstanceState);
        setContentView(R.layout.loading);

        Thread thread = new Thread(this);
        thread.start();
    }
```

```
    private Handler mHandler = new Handler() {
        public void handleMessage(Message msg) {
            setContentView(R.layout.main);
        }
    };

    public void run(){
        initializeArrays();
        mHandler.sendEmptyMessage(0);
    }

    final static int NUM_SAMPS = 1000;
    static double[][] correlation;
    void initializeArrays() {
        if(correlation!=null) return;

        correlation = new double[NUM_SAMPS][NUM_SAMPS];
        //calculation
        for(int k=0; k<NUM_SAMPS; k++) {
            for(int m=0; m<NUM_SAMPS; m++) {
                correlation[k][m] = Math.cos(2*Math.PI*(k+m)/1000);
            }
        }
    }
}
```

Services

A *service* is an Android component that runs in the background without any user interaction. It can be started and stopped by any component. While it is running, any component can bind to it. A service can also stop itself. Some illustrative scenarios are

- An activity provides the user a way to select a set of music files, which then starts a service to play back the files. During playback, a new activity starts and binds to the existing service to allow the user to change songs or stop playback.
- An activity starts a service to upload a set of pictures to a website. A new activity starts and binds to the existing service to determine which file is currently being uploaded and displays the picture to the screen.
- A broadcast receiver receives a message that a picture was taken and launches a service to upload the new picture to a website. The broadcast receiver then goes inactive and is eventually killed to reclaim memory, but the service continues until the picture is uploaded. Then, the service stops itself.

The general lifecycle of a service is illustrated in Figure 3.2.

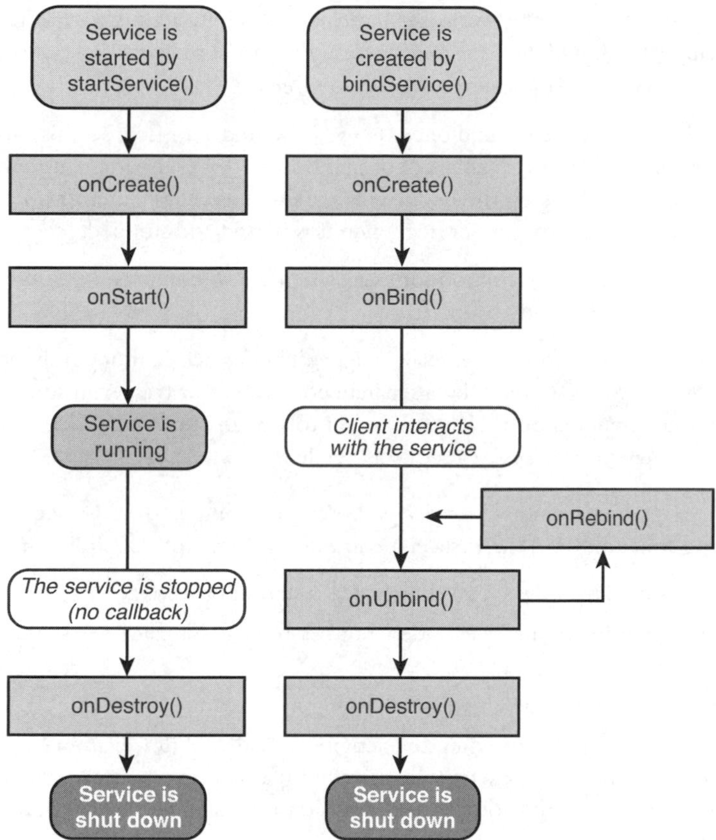

Figure 3.2 Service Lifecycle from http://developer.android.com/.

An aside on the third scenario: Any background task within a component will be killed when the component is killed. Therefore, tasks that are meaningful to continue even after the component stops should be done by launching a service. This ensures the operating system is aware active work is still being done by the process.

All services extend the abstract class `Service` or one of its subclasses. Similar to an Activity, the entry point to each service is the `onCreate()` method. There is no concept of pausing a service, but it can be stopped, which calls the `onDestroy()` method.

Recipe: Creating a Self-Contained Service

The steps to create a self-contained service associated with a single component are

1. Create a class to extend `Service`. (In Eclipse, this can be done by right-clicking the project, choosing **New → Class** and specifying `android.app.Service` as the super class.)

2. Declare the service in the **AndroidManifest.xml** file by adding a variation of the following (this should be done automatically with the previous Eclipse step):
   `<service android:name=".myService"></service>`
3. Override the `onCreate()` and `onDestroy()` methods. (In Eclipse, this can be done by right-clicking on the class file, choosing **Source → Override/Implement Methods...**, and checking the `onCreate()` and `onDestroy()` methods.) These contain the functionality of the service when it is started and stopped.
4. Override the `onBind()` method for cases when a new component binds to this service after it has already been created.
5. Activate the service from an external trigger. The service cannot run by itself, but instead needs to be activated by a separate component or trigger in some way. For example, a component can create an intent to start or stop the service using `startService()` or `stopService()` as needed.

To illustrate the previous, a simple service is shown in Listing 3.10 to use the `play_music()` function from the first recipe in this chapter. Note the following:

- A `Toast` is used to show when the service is started or stopped.
- The `onBind()` method is overridden, but not used. (This can be extended as needed.)
- A thread still needs to be created for playing music to not block the UI.
- The service does not stop when the activity is destroyed (for example, by changing the screen orientation) or when the activity is paused (for example, when pressing the home button). This shows the service, although launched by the activity, runs as its own entity.

Listing 3.10 **src/com/cookbook/simple_service/SimpleService.java**

```
package com.cookbook.simple_service;

import android.app.Service;
import android.content.Intent;
import android.media.MediaPlayer;
import android.os.IBinder;
import android.widget.Toast;

public class SimpleService extends Service {
    @Override
    public IBinder onBind(Intent arg0) {
          return null;
    }

    boolean paused = false;
```

```
    @Override
    public void onCreate() {
          super.onCreate();
          Toast.makeText(this,"Service created ...",
                         Toast.LENGTH_LONG).show();
          paused = false;
          Thread initBkgdThread = new Thread(new Runnable() {
              public void run() {
                  play_music();
              }
          });
          initBkgdThread.start();
    }

    @Override
    public void onDestroy() {
          super.onDestroy();
          Toast.makeText(this, "Service destroyed ...",
                         Toast.LENGTH_LONG).show();
          paused = true;
    }

    int[] notes = {R.raw.c5, R.raw.b4, R.raw.a4, R.raw.g4};
    int NOTE_DURATION = 400; //millisec
    MediaPlayer m_mediaPlayer;
    private void play_music() {
        for(int ii=0; ii<12; ii++) {
            //check to ensure main activity not paused
            if(!paused) {
                if(m_mediaPlayer != null) {m_mediaPlayer.release();}
                m_mediaPlayer = MediaPlayer.create(this, notes[ii%4]);
                m_mediaPlayer.start();
                try {
                    Thread.sleep(NOTE_DURATION);
                } catch (InterruptedException e) {
                    e.printStackTrace();
                }
            }
        }
    }
}
```

The **AndroidManifest.xml** now has both the activity and service declared, as shown in Listing 3.11.

Listing 3.11 **AndroidManifest.xml**

```
<?xml version="1.0" encoding="utf-8"?>
<manifest xmlns:android="http://schemas.android.com/apk/res/android"
          package="com.cookbook.simple_service"
          android:versionCode="1"
          android:versionName="1.0">
    <application android:icon="@drawable/icon"
                 android:label="@string/app_name">
        <activity android:name=".SimpleActivity"
                  android:label="@string/app_name">
            <intent-filter>
              <action android:name="android.intent.action.MAIN" />
              <category android:name="android.intent.category.LAUNCHER" />
            </intent-filter>
        </activity>
        <service android:name=".SimpleService"></service>
    </application>
    <uses-sdk android:minSdkVersion="3" />
</manifest>
```

The example activity that sets up the UI to trigger the start and stop of this service is shown in Listing 3.12, and the associated layout file is shown in Listing 3.13 for the two buttons.

Listing 3.12 **src/com/cookbook/simple_service/SimpleActivity.java**

```
package com.cookbook.simple_service;

import android.app.Activity;
import android.content.Intent;
import android.os.Bundle;
import android.view.View;
import android.widget.Button;

public class SimpleActivity extends Activity {
    @Override
    protected void onCreate(Bundle savedInstanceState) {
        super.onCreate(savedInstanceState);
        setContentView(R.layout.main);

        Button startButton = (Button) findViewById(R.id.Button01);
        startButton.setOnClickListener(new View.OnClickListener() {
            public void onClick(View view){
                startService(new Intent(SimpleActivity.this,
                                        SimpleService.class));
            }
        });

        Button stopButton = (Button)findViewById(R.id.Button02);
```

```
        stopButton.setOnClickListener(new View.OnClickListener() {
            public void onClick(View v){
                stopService(new Intent(SimpleActivity.this,
                                       SimpleService.class));
            }
        });
    }
}
```

Listing 3.13 **res/layout/main.xml**

```
<?xml version="1.0" encoding="utf-8"?>
<LinearLayout xmlns:android="http://schemas.android.com/apk/res/android"
    android:orientation="vertical"
    android:layout_width="fill_parent"
    android:layout_height="fill_parent">
  <TextView
    android:layout_width="fill_parent"
    android:layout_height="wrap_content"
    android:text="@string/hello"
    />
  <Button android:text="Do it" android:id="@+id/Button01"
    android:layout_width="wrap_content"
    android:layout_height="wrap_content"></Button>
  <Button android:text="Stop it" android:id="@+id/Button02"
    android:layout_width="wrap_content"
    android:layout_height="wrap_content"></Button>
</LinearLayout>
```

Adding a Broadcast Receiver

A broadcast receiver listens for relevant broadcast messages to trigger an event. Some examples of broadcasted events already sent from the OS are

- The camera button was pressed.
- The battery is low.
- A new application was installed.

A user-generated component can also send a broadcast, such as:

- A calculation was finished.
- A particular thread has started.

All broadcast receivers extend the abstract class `BroadcastReceiver` or one of its subclasses. The lifecycle of a broadcast receiver is simple. A single method, `onReceive()`, is called when a message arrives for the receiver. After this method is finished, the `BroadcastReceiver` instance goes inactive.

A broadcast receiver normally initiates a separate component or sends a notification to the user in its `onReceive()` method, as discussed later in this chapter. If a broadcast receiver needs to do something more time-consuming, it should start a service instead of spawn a thread because an inactive broadcast receiver might be killed by the system.

Recipe: Starting a Service When the Camera Button Is Pressed

This recipe shows how to start a service based on a broadcasted event, such as when the camera button is pressed. The broadcast receiver is needed to listen for the specified event(s) and subsequently launch the service. The broadcast receiver itself is started in another component. (Here, it is implemented as a standalone activity, `SimpleActivity`.)

The activity shown in Listing 3.14 sets up a broadcast receiver and sets up an intent with the filter for the camera button. The filter for package-added messages is also added for illustration purposes. Then, the broadcast receiver is started and this intent filter is passed to it using the `registerReceiver()` method.

Listing 3.14 **src/com/cookbook/simple_receiver/SimpleActivity.java**

```
package com.cookbook.simple_receiver;

import android.app.Activity;
import android.content.Intent;
import android.content.IntentFilter;
import android.os.Bundle;

public class SimpleActivity extends Activity {
    SimpleBroadcastReceiver intentReceiver =
        new SimpleBroadcastReceiver();

    /** Called when the activity is first created. */
    @Override
    public void onCreate(Bundle savedInstanceState) {
        super.onCreate(savedInstanceState);
        setContentView(R.layout.main);

        IntentFilter intentFilter =
            new IntentFilter(Intent.ACTION_CAMERA_BUTTON);
        intentFilter.addAction(Intent.ACTION_PACKAGE_ADDED);
        registerReceiver(intentReceiver, intentFilter);
    }

    @Override
    protected void onDestroy() {
        unregisterReceiver(intentReceiver);
```

```
        super.onDestroy();
    }
}
```

Note the receiver is unregistered if the activity is ever destroyed. This is unnecessary, but useful. The `BroadcastReceiver` component is shown in Listing 3.15. The single lifecycle method `onReceive()` is overridden to check for any broadcasted event. If it matches the specified event (here, it is the `ACTION_CAMERA_BUTTON` event), a service is started in the original context.

Listing 3.15 **src/com/cookbook/simple_receiver/SimpleBroadcastReceiver .java**

```
package com.cookbook.simple_receiver;

import android.content.BroadcastReceiver;
import android.content.Context;
import android.content.Intent;

public class SimpleBroadcastReceiver extends BroadcastReceiver {
    @Override
    public void onReceive(Context rcvContext, Intent rcvIntent) {
        String action = rcvIntent.getAction();
        if (action.equals(Intent.ACTION_CAMERA_BUTTON)) {
            rcvContext.startService(new Intent(rcvContext,
                    SimpleService2.class));
        }
    }
}
```

The service that is started in the `SimpleBroadcastReceiver` of Listing 3.15 is shown in Listing 3.16. The service simply shows whether it was started or stopped using `Toast`.

Listing 3.16 **src/com/cookbook/simple_receiver/SimpleService2.java**

```
package com.cookbook.simple_receiver;

import android.app.Service;
import android.content.Intent;
import android.os.IBinder;
import android.widget.Toast;

public class SimpleService2 extends Service {
    @Override
    public IBinder onBind(Intent arg0) {
        return null;
    }
```

```
    @Override
    public void onCreate() {
        super.onCreate();
        Toast.makeText(this,"Service created ...",
                Toast.LENGTH_LONG).show();
    }

    @Override
    public void onDestroy() {
        super.onDestroy();
        Toast.makeText(this, "Service destroyed ...",
                Toast.LENGTH_LONG).show();
    }
}
```

App Widgets

App Widgets are small icon-like views into an application. They implement a subclass of the broadcast receiver for use in updating this view. Called widgets for short, they can be embedded into other applications, such as the home screen, by *long clicking* (in other words, pressing and holding) an empty area of the touchscreen. This displays a menu where a widget can be selected to install at that location. They can be removed by a long click on the widget and dragging to the trash can. In all, they require the following:

- A view describing the appearance of the widget. This is defined in an XML layout resource file and contains text, background, and other layout parameters.
- An App Widget provider that receives broadcast events and interfaces to the widget to update it.
- Detailed information about the App Widget, such as the size and update frequency. Note that the home screen is divided into 4x4 cells and so a widget is often a multiple of a single cell size (which is 80x100dp in Portrait mode and 106x74dp in Landscape mode).
- Optionally, an App Widget configuration activity can be defined to properly set any parameters of the Widget. This activity is launched upon creation of the Widget.

Recipe: Creating an App Widget

This recipe creates a simple App Widget that displays some text on the home screen. The text is configured to update every second, but note that by default, the Android system forces the minimum update time to be 30 minutes. This helps avoid poorly written widgets from draining the battery. Listing 3.17 implements an `AppWidgetProvider`, which is a subclass of `BroadcastReceiver`. The main method to override is the `onUpdate()` function, which gets called when the system determines it is time to update the widgets.

Listing 3.17 **src/com/cookbook/widget_example/SimpleWidgetProvider.java**

```
package com.cookbook.simple_widget;

import android.appwidget.AppWidgetManager;
import android.appwidget.AppWidgetProvider;
import android.content.Context;
import android.widget.RemoteViews;

public class SimpleWidgetProvider extends AppWidgetProvider {
    final static int APPWIDGET = 1001;
    @Override
    public void onUpdate(Context context,
            AppWidgetManager appWidgetManager, int[] appWidgetIds) {
        super.onUpdate(context, appWidgetManager, appWidgetIds);
        // Loop through all widgets to display an update
        final int N = appWidgetIds.length;
        for (int i=0; i<N; i++) {
            int appWidgetId = appWidgetIds[i];
            String titlePrefix = "Time since the widget was started:";
            updateAppWidget(context, appWidgetManager, appWidgetId,
                            titlePrefix);
        }
    }

    static void updateAppWidget(Context context, AppWidgetManager
            appWidgetManager, int appWidgetId, String titlePrefix) {
        Long millis = System.currentTimeMillis();
        int seconds = (int) (millis / 1000);
        int minutes = seconds / 60;
        seconds     = seconds % 60;

        CharSequence text = titlePrefix;
        text += " " + minutes + ":" + String.format("%02d",seconds));

        // Construct the RemoteViews object.
        RemoteViews views = new RemoteViews(context.getPackageName(),
                R.layout.widget_layout);
        views.setTextViewText(R.id.widget_example_text, text);

        // Tell the widget manager
        appWidgetManager.updateAppWidget(appWidgetId, views);
    }
}
```

The XML file describing the detailed information on the widget is shown in Listing 3.18. It shows the size the widget takes on the home screen and how often it should be updated in milliseconds. (The system minimum is 30 minutes.)

Listing 3.18 **src/res/xml/widget_info.xml**

```
<?xml version="1.0" encoding="utf-8"?>
<appwidget-provider xmlns:android="http://schemas.android.com/apk/res/android"
    android:minWidth="146dp"
    android:minHeight="72dp"
    android:updatePeriodMillis="1000"
    android:initialLayout="@layout/widget_layout">
</appwidget-provider>
```

The view describing the appearance of the widget is laid out in an XML file, as shown in Listing 3.19.

Listing 3.19 **src/res/layout/widget_layout.xml**

```
<?xml version="1.0" encoding="utf-8"?>
<TextView xmlns:android="http://schemas.android.com/apk/res/android"
    android:id="@+id/widget_example_text"
    android:layout_width="wrap_content"
    android:layout_height="wrap_content"
    android:textColor="#ff000000"
    android:background="#ffffffff"
/>
```

Alerts

Alerts provide a quick message to the user outside of the application's main UI. It can be in an overlay window such as a Toast or AlertDialog box. It can also be in the notification bar at the top of the screen. The Toast alert provides a printed message to the screen with a single line of code. There is no need to work with the layout files. For this reason, it is also a handy debug tool, equivalent to the `printf` statement in C programs.

Recipe: Using Toast to Show a Brief Message on the Screen

The Toast method has been introduced in the previous chapter in a compact form:

```
Toast.makeText(this, "text", Toast.LENGTH_SHORT).show();
```

It can also be written as a multiline command:

```
Toast tst = Toast.makeText(this, "text", Toast.LENGTH_SHORT);
        tst.show();
```

This form is useful when the text needs to be shown multiple times, as the instance in the first line can be reused.

Two other uses for the multiline `Toast` command are to reposition the text location or to add an image. To reposition the text location, or to center the Toast in the screen display, use `setGravity` before calling the `show()` method:

```
tst.setGravity(Gravity.CENTER, tst.getXOffset() / 2,
                               tst.getYOffset() / 2);
```

To add an image to a Toast, use the following:

```
Toast tst = Toast.makeText(this, "text", Toast.LENGTH_LONG);
ImageView view = new ImageView(this);
view.setImageResource(R.drawable.my_figure);
tst.setView(view);
tst.show();
```

Recipe: Using an Alert Dialog Box

Providing a user with an alert and up to three buttons of possible actions can be done with the AlertDialog class. Some examples are

- "Your final score was 80/100: Try this level again, advance to next level, or go back to the main menu."
- "The image file is corrupt, choose another or cancel action."

This recipe takes the first example and shows how to provide an action on each choice depending on which button is clicked. The example code is shown in Listing 3.20.

The `AlertDialog` is initialized using the `create()` method; the text is specified using the `setMessage()` method; the three possible button text and corresponding actions are specified using the `setButton()` method; and finally, the dialog box is displayed to the screen using the `show()` method. Note the logic in each of the `onClick()` callback functions is just an example to show how to specify button actions.

Listing 3.20 **Example of AlertDialog**

```
AlertDialog dialog = new AlertDialog.Builder(this).create();

dialog.setMessage("Your final score: " + mScore + "/" + PERFECT_SCORE);
dialog.setButton(DialogInterface.BUTTON_POSITIVE, "Try this level again",
       new DialogInterface.OnClickListener() {
            public void onClick(DialogInterface dialog, int which) {
                mScore = 0;
                start_level();
            }
        });
dialog.setButton(DialogInterface.BUTTON_NEGATIVE, "Advance to next level",
       new DialogInterface.OnClickListener() {
```

```
            public void onClick(DialogInterface dialog, int which) {
                mLevel++;
                start_level();
            }
        });
dialog.setButton(DialogInterface.BUTTON_NEUTRAL, "Back to the main menu",
        new DialogInterface.OnClickListener() {
            public void onClick(DialogInterface dialog, int which) {
                mLevel = 0;
                finish();
            }
        });
dialog.show();
```

This produces the pop-up dialog box shown in Figure 3.3. Note that the buttons are displayed in the order `BUTTON_POSITIVE`, `BUTTON_NEUTRAL`, and `BUTTON_NEGATIVE`. If a dialog box with two options or one option is needed, do not specify all three button choices.

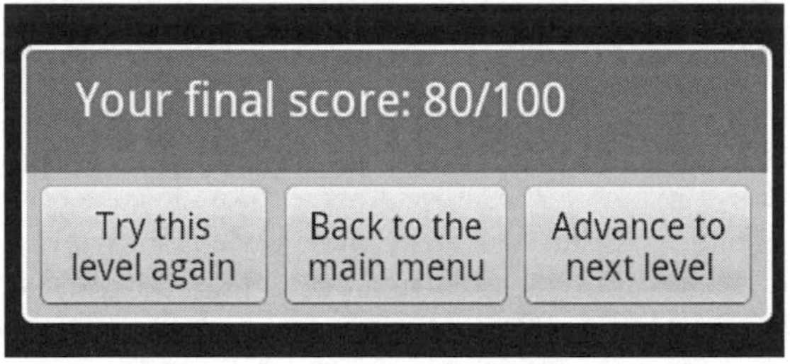

Figure 3.3 Example of an alert dialog box.

Recipe: Showing Notification in Status Bar

The status bar across the top of the device screen shows pending notifications for the user to read at a convenient time. In general, because an activity mostly interacts with the user, services are more likely to utilize this feature. As a rule, notifications should be concise and minimal for the best user experience.

The steps for creating a status bar notification are

1. Declare a notification and specify how it displays on the status bar:

```
String ns = Context.NOTIFICATION_SERVICE;
mNManager = (NotificationManager) getSystemService(ns);
final Notification msg = new Notification(R.drawable.icon,
        "New event of importance",
        System.currentTimeMillis());
```

2. Define how it looks when the status bar is expanded for details and the action taken when clicked (this future action is defined by a `PendingIntent` class):

```
Context context = getApplicationContext();
CharSequence contentTitle = "ShowNotification Example";
CharSequence contentText = "Browse Android Cookbook Site";
Intent msgIntent = new Intent(Intent.ACTION_VIEW,
                       Uri.parse("http://www.pearson.com"));
PendingIntent intent =
            PendingIntent.getActivity(ShowNotification.this,
                    0, msgIntent,
                    Intent.FLAG_ACTIVITY_NEW_TASK);
```

3. Add any further configurable information, such as whether to blink an LED, play a sound, or automatically cancel the notification after it is selected. The latter two are shown here:

```
msg.defaults |= Notification.DEFAULT_SOUND;
msg.flags |= Notification.FLAG_AUTO_CANCEL;
```

4. Set the info for the notification event to the system:

```
msg.setLatestEventInfo(context,
                       contentTitle, contentText, intent);
```

5. On the event of interest, trigger notification with a unique identifier:

```
mNManager.notify(NOTIFY_ID, msg);
```

6. Upon completion, clear notification as needed with the same identifier.

If any information gets changed, the notification should be updated rather than sending another notification. This can be done by updating the relevant information in step 2, and then again calling `setLatestEventInfo`. An example activity to show a notification is shown in Listing 3.21.

Listing 3.21 **src/com/cookbook/show_notification/ShowNotification.java**

```
package com.cookbook.show_notification;

import android.app.Activity;
import android.app.Notification;
import android.app.NotificationManager;
import android.app.PendingIntent;
import android.content.Context;
import android.content.Intent;
import android.net.Uri;
import android.os.Bundle;
import android.view.View;
import android.view.View.OnClickListener;
import android.widget.Button;
```

```
public class ShowNotification extends Activity {

    private NotificationManager mNManager;
    private static final int NOTIFY_ID=1100;

    /** Called when the activity is first created. */
    @Override
    public void onCreate(Bundle savedInstanceState) {
        super.onCreate(savedInstanceState);
        setContentView(R.layout.main);

        String ns = Context.NOTIFICATION_SERVICE;
        mNManager = (NotificationManager) getSystemService(ns);
        final Notification msg = new Notification(R.drawable.icon,
                "New event of importance",
                System.currentTimeMillis());

        Button start = (Button)findViewById(R.id.start);
        Button cancel = (Button)findViewById(R.id.cancel);

        start.setOnClickListener(new OnClickListener() {
            public void onClick(View v) {
                Context context = getApplicationContext();
                CharSequence contentTitle = "ShowNotification Example";
                CharSequence contentText = "Browse Android Cookbook Site";
                Intent msgIntent = new Intent(Intent.ACTION_VIEW,
                        Uri.parse("http://www.pearson.com"));
                PendingIntent intent =
                    PendingIntent.getActivity(ShowNotification.this,
                            0, msgIntent,
                            Intent.FLAG_ACTIVITY_NEW_TASK);

                msg.defaults |= Notification.DEFAULT_SOUND;
                msg.flags |= Notification.FLAG_AUTO_CANCEL;

                msg.setLatestEventInfo(context,
                        contentTitle, contentText, intent);
                mNManager.notify(NOTIFY_ID, msg);
            }
        });

        cancel.setOnClickListener(new OnClickListener() {
            public void onClick(View v) {
                mNManager.cancel(NOTIFY_ID);
            }
        });
    }
}
```

4

User Interface Layout

The Android user interface (UI) consists of screen views, screen touch events, and key presses. The framework for specifying the UI is constructed to support the various different Android devices. This chapter focuses on the utilization of this framework for the initial graphical layout and its changes. Chapter 5, "User Interface Events," handles key presses and gestures.

Resource Directories and General Attributes

The UI display utilizes developer-generated resource files, some of which are discussed in Chapter 2, "Application Basics: Activities and Intents," in the context of the directory structure of an Android project. For completeness, the entire set of resource directories is summarized here:

- res/anim/—Frame-by-frame animation or tweened animation objects.
- res/drawable/—Image resources. Note these images can be modified and optimized during compilation.
- res/layout/—eXtensible Markup Language (XML) files specifying screen layouts.
- res/values/—XML files with resource descriptors. As with other resource directories, filenames are arbitrary, but common ones, as utilized in this book, are **arrays.xml, colors.xml, dimens.xml, strings.xml,** and **styles.xml**.
- res/xml/—Other arbitrary XML files not covered previously.
- res/raw/—Other arbitrary resources not covered previously, including images that should not be modified or optimized.

Each UI object has three definable attributes that customize the look and feel of the UI: the dimension of the object, text in the object, and the color of the object. The possible values for these three general UI attributes are summarized in Table 4.1. Note that for dimension, it is best to use **dp** or **sp** for device-independent compliance.

Table 4.1 **Possible Values for the Three General UI Attributes**

Attribute	Possible Values
Dimension	Any number followed by one of the following dimensions: **px**—Actual pixels on the screen **dp** (or **dip**)—Device-independent pixels relative to a 160dpi screen **sp**—Device-independent pixels scaled by user's font size preference **in**—Inches based on physical screen size **mm**—Millimeters based on physical screen size **pt**—1/72 of an inch based on physical screen size
String	Any string, as long as apostrophes/quotes are escaped: **Don\'t worry** Any properly quoted string: **"Don't worry"** Any formatted string, for example: **Population: %1$d** Can include HTML tags, such as **<b>**, **<i>**, or **<u>** Can include special characters, such as © given by **©**
Color	Possible values are a 12-bit color **#rgb**, 16-bit color with alpha opacity **#argb**, 24-bit color **#rrggbb**, or 32-bit color with alpha opacity **#aarrggbb**. It is also possible to utilize the predefined colors in the Color class within Java files, such as **Color.CYAN**.

To unify the look and feel of the application, a global resource file can be used for each of these attributes. This is also useful in that it is easy to redefine the attributes later, as they are all collected in three files:

- Measurements and dimensions of items are declared in the XML resource file **res/values/dimens.xml.** For example:
  - XML declaration—`<dimen name="large">48sp</dimen>`
  - XML reference—`@dimen/large`
  - Java reference—`getResources().getDimension(R.dimen.large)`
- Label and text of items are declared in the XML resource file **res/values/strings.xml**. For example:
  - XML declaration—`<string name="start_pt">I\'m here</string>`
  - XML reference—`@string/start_pt`
  - Java reference—`getBaseContext().getString(R.string.start_pt)`
- The colors of items are declared in the XML resource file **res/values/colors.xml**. For example:
  - `XML declaration—<color name="red">#f00</color>`
  - `XML reference—@color/red`
  - `Java reference—getResources().getColor(R.color.red)`

Recipe: Specifying Alternate Resources

The resources described in the previous section provide a generic configuration that Android can use by default. The developer has the ability to specify different values for specific configurations distinguished by various qualifiers.

To support multiple languages, the strings can be translated and used in different language **values** directories. For example, American English, British English, French, simplified Chinese (used in mainland China), traditional Chinese (used in Taiwan), and German strings are added using:

```
res/values-en-rUS/strings.xml
res/values-en-rGB/strings.xml
res/values-fr/strings.xml
res/values-zh-rCN/strings.xml
res/values-zh-rTW/strings.xml
res/values-de/strings.xml
```

Not all strings need to be redefined in these files. Any missing strings from the selected language file fall back to the default **res/values/strings.xml** file, which should contain a complete set of all strings used in the application. If any drawables contain text and require a language-specific form, a similar directory structure should also apply to them (such as **res/drawables-zh-hdpi/**).

To support multiple screen pixel densities, the drawables and raw resources (as needed) can be scaled and used in different dots per inch (dpi) value directories. For example, an image file can belong to each of the following directories:

```
res/drawable-ldpi/
res/drawable-mdpi/
res/drawable-hdpi/
res/drawable-nodpi/
```

The low-, medium-, and high-density screens are defined as 120dpi, 160dpi, and 240dpi. Not all dpi choices need to be populated. At run-time, Android determines the closest available drawables and scales them appropriately. The `nodpi` choice can be used with bitmap images to prevent them from being scaled. In case both a language and dpi choice are specified, the directory can contain both qualifiers: **drawable-en-rUS-mdpi/**.

The various types of screens available for Android devices are discussed in Chapter 1, "Overview of Android." It is often useful to define separate XML layouts for the different screen types. The most often used qualifiers are

- Portrait and landscape screen orientations: **-port** and **-land**
- Regular (QVGA, HVGA, and VGA) and wide aspect ratios (WQVGA, FWVGA, and WVGA): **-notlong** and **-long**
- Small (up to 3.0-inch diagonal), normal (up to 4.5-inch diagonal), and large (above 4.5-inch diagonal) screen sizes: **-small**, **-normal**, and **-large**

If screen orientation or aspect ratio are not defined, the Android system auto-scales the UI for the screen (although not always elegantly). However, if layouts for different screens are defined, a special element should be added to the Android Manifest XML file at the application element level to ensure proper support:

```
<supports-screens
  android:largeScreens="true"
  android:normalScreens="true"
  android:smallScreens="true"
  android:resizable="true"
  android:anyDensity="true" />
```

Note that if `android:minSdkVersion` or `android:targetSdkVersion` is "3" (Android 1.5), then by default only `android:normalScreens` (the screen for the G1) is set to "true." Therefore, it is useful to explicitly declare the `supports-screens` element for the application so more recent phones have a properly scaled UI.

Views and ViewGroups

The basic building block of a graphical layout is a view. Each view is described by a `View` Object, which is responsible for drawing a rectangular area and handling events in that area. The `View` is a base class for objects that interact with the user; they are called widgets. Examples of widgets are buttons and check boxes.

A `ViewGroup` Object is a type of `View` that acts as a container to hold multiple `Views` (or other `ViewGroups`). For example, a `ViewGroup` can hold a vertical or horizontal placement of views and widgets, as shown in Figure 4.1. The `ViewGroup` is a base class for screen layouts.

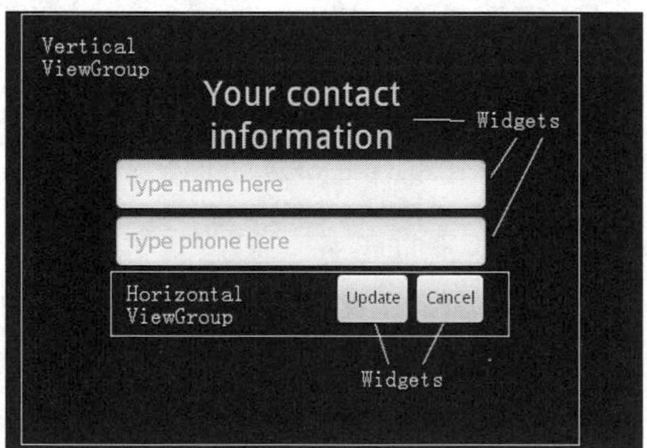

Figure 4.1 View example that contains `ViewsGroups` and widgets.

The layout defines the user interface elements, their positions, and their actions. It can be specified from either XML or Java. Most often, an initial base layout is declared in XML and any run-time changes are handled in Java. This combines the ease of developing the overall position of View and ViewGroup Objects using XML and the flexibility to change any component within the application using Java.

Another benefit of separating the XML layout from the Java activity is that the same Android application can produce a different behavior depending on the screen orientation, type of device (such as phone versus tablet), and locale (such as English versus Chinese). These customizations can be abstracted into various XML resource files without cluttering the underlying activity.

Recipe: Building Layouts in the Eclipse Editor

A quick way to get started with layouts is to use the handy graphical layout editor in Eclipse. Take a new activity and open its layout resource XML file. Here, it is the **main.xml** file. Then, click the Layout tab. This shows how the layout would look graphically. Click the black screen and remove everything to start from scratch. Then, follow these steps:

1. Click and drag a layout from the Layouts Selector to the screen area. For example, choose `TableLayout`, which holds multiple `Views` or `ViewGroups` down a column.
2. Click and drag any other layouts to nest them inside the first one. For example, choose `TableRow`, which hold multiples `Views` or `ViewGroups` along a row. Add three of these for this example.
3. Right-click each `TableRow` in the Outline view and add view elements from the Views Selector. For example, add a `Button` and `CheckBox` to the first `TableRow`, two `TextViews` to the second, and a `TimePicker` to the third.
4. Add a `Spinner` and `VideoView` view below the `TableRow` elements.

This looks like Figure 4.2, and the landscape and portrait view can be toggled to see the difference in the layout. Clicking the **main.xml** tab shows XML code like that shown in Listing 4.1. This provides a simple method to build UIs with the Android look and feel.

Listing 4.1 **main.xml**

```
<?xml version="1.0" encoding="utf-8"?>
<TableLayout android:id="@+id/TableLayout01"
    android:layout_width="fill_parent"
    android:layout_height="fill_parent"
    xmlns:android="http://schemas.android.com/apk/res/android">
    <TableRow android:id="@+id/TableRow01"
        android:layout_width="wrap_content"
        android:layout_height="wrap_content">
        <Button android:text="@+id/Button01"
            android:id="@+id/Button01"
```

```
            android:layout_width="wrap_content"
            android:layout_height="wrap_content" />
        <CheckBox android:text="@+id/CheckBox01"
            android:id="@+id/CheckBox01"
            android:layout_width="wrap_content"
            android:layout_height="wrap_content" />
    </TableRow>
    <TableRow android:id="@+id/TableRow02"
        android:layout_width="wrap_content"
        android:layout_height="wrap_content">
        <TextView android:text="@+id/TextView01"
            android:id="@+id/TextView01"
            android:layout_width="wrap_content"
            android:layout_height="wrap_content" />
        <TextView android:text="@+id/TextView02"
            android:id="@+id/TextView02"
            android:layout_width="wrap_content"
            android:layout_height="wrap_content" />
    </TableRow>
    <TableRow android:id="@+id/TableRow03"
        android:layout_width="wrap_content"
        android:layout_height="wrap_content">
        <TimePicker android:id="@+id/TimePicker01"
            android:layout_width="wrap_content"
            android:layout_height="wrap_content" />
    </TableRow>
    <Spinner android:id="@+id/Spinner01"
        android:layout_width="wrap_content"
        android:layout_height="wrap_content" />
    <VideoView android:id="@+id/VideoView01"
        android:layout_width="wrap_content"
        android:layout_height="wrap_content" />
</TableLayout>
```

Another way to view the layout is using the Hierarchy Viewer. Running an application in the emulator, the **hierarchyviewer** can be run from the command line. It resides in the **tools/** directory of the Software Development Kit (SDK) installation. For security reasons, this works only with the emulator as the device because running the **hierarchyviewer** on an actual device might reveal secure settings. Click the window of interest and select **Load View Hierarchy.** This produces a relational view of the different layouts. For this recipe, the result is as shown in Figure 4.3.

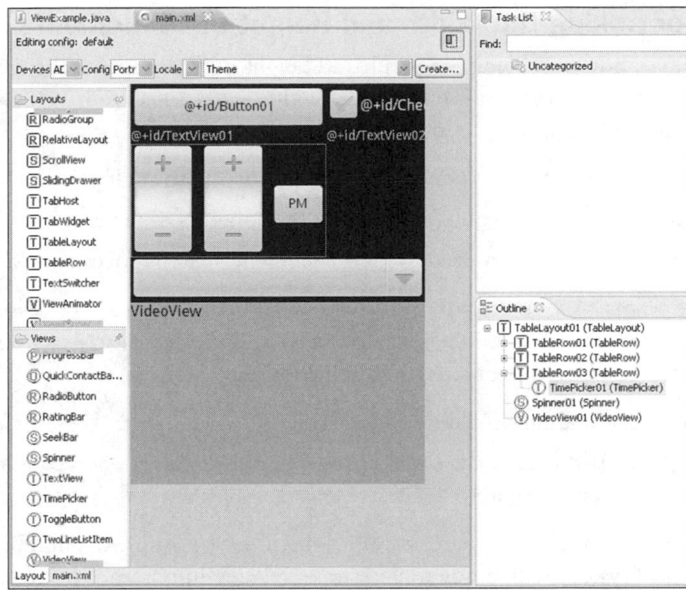

Figure 4.2 Android layout builder example, as seen in Eclipse.

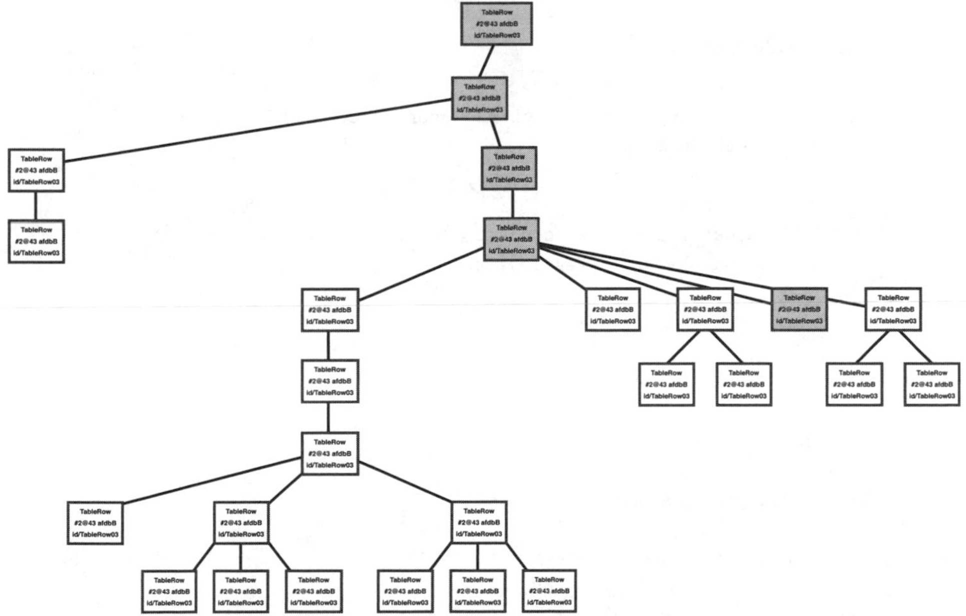

Figure 4.3 Android hierarchy viewer on the example in Listing 4.1.

Recipe: Controlling the Width and Height of UI Elements

This recipe shows how specifying the width and height of UI elements changes the overall layout. Each View object must specify a total width `android:layout_width` and total height `android:layout_height` in one of three ways:

- exact dimension—Provides control, but does not scale to multiple screen types well.
- `wrap_content`—Just big enough to enclose the contents of the element plus padding.
- `fill_parent`—Size maximized to fill the element's parent, including padding.

Padding is the blank space surrounding an element, and defaults to zero if it is not specified. It is part of the size of an UI element and must be specified as an exact dimension, but can be specified using one of two types of attributes:

- `padding`—Sets padding equal on all four sides of an element.
- `paddingLeft`, `paddingRight`, `paddingTop`, `paddingBottom`—Sets padding on each side of an element separately.

Another attribute is `android:layout_weight`, which can be assigned a number. It provides the Android system with a way to determine relative importance between different elements of a layout.

Listing 4.2 shows the main layout file as a linear layout with four buttons. This aligns them horizontally on the screen, as shown in Figure 4.4.

Listing 4.2 **res/layout/main.xml**

```
<?xml version="1.0" encoding="utf-8"?>
<LinearLayout xmlns:android="http://schemas.android.com/apk/res/android"
 android:layout_width="fill_parent"
 android:layout_height="fill_parent">
       <Button android:text="add"
        android:layout_width="wrap_content"
        android:layout_height="wrap_content"
        />
        <Button android:text="subtract"
        android:layout_width="wrap_content"
        android:layout_height="wrap_content"
        />
        <Button android:text="multiply"
        android:layout_width="wrap_content"
        android:layout_height="wrap_content"
        />
        <Button android:text="divide"
        android:layout_width="wrap_content"
        android:layout_height="wrap_content"
        />
</LinearLayout>
```

Figure 4.4 LinearLayout with four buttons aligned horizontally, as shown in Listing 4.2.

If the height of the "add" button is changed to `fill_parent`, the button fills the vertical space of its parent while keeping the words aligned. If the width of any button is changed to `fill_parent`, then all subsequent buttons in the horizontal layout are washed out. These are shown in Figure 4.5.

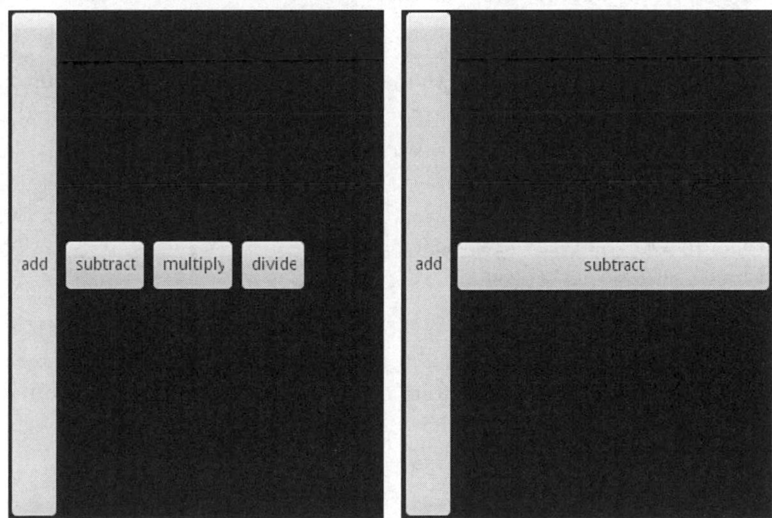

Figure 4.5 The fill_parent in height keeps the horizontal alignment, but a fill_parent in width washes out the remaining buttons.

Another thing to point out in Figure 4.4 is that the "multiply" and "divide" buttons have a portion of the last letter cut off. This can be fixed by appending a space to the text, such as "multiply" and "divide". However, a more general method to resolve this utilizes the layout. Take a look at the various button formats in Figure 4.6.

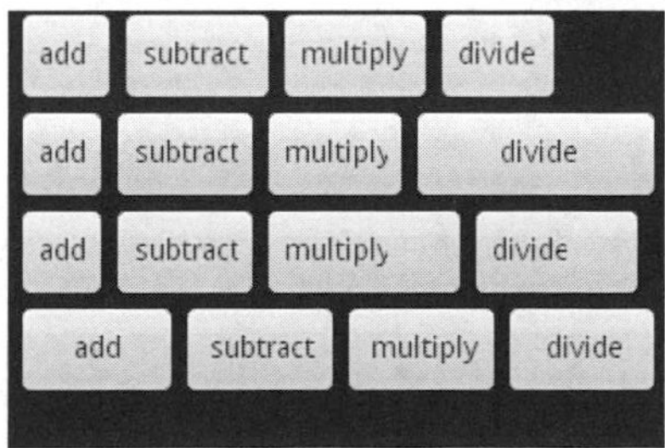

Figure 4.6 Various methods to tweak the layout of four buttons.

The four rows of buttons in Figure 4.6 are as follows:

- The first row is the same as Listing 4.2, but with spaces appended to the end of each word.
- In the second row, the layout width is changed to `fill_parent` for the last button, providing the space needed for the button, but it cannot be used for the earlier buttons on the line as evidenced by the right part of Figure 4.5:

```
<Button android:text="divide"
  android:layout_width="fill_parent"
  android:layout_height="wrap_content"
/>
```

- In the third row, padding is added to the multiply button to make the button bigger, but it does not add this space to the word itself because it was declared as `wrap_content`:

```
<Button android:text="multiply"
  android:layout_width="wrap_content"
  android:layout_height="wrap_content"
  android:paddingRight="20sp"
/>
```

- In the fourth row, all buttons use `fill_parent`, but also add `layout_weight` and assign it the same value for all buttons. This gives the most satisfying layout:

```
<Button android:text="add"
  android:layout_width="fill_parent"
  android:layout_height="wrap_content"
  android:layout_weight="1"
/>
<Button android:text="subtract"
  android:layout_width="fill_parent"
  android:layout_height="wrap_content"
  android:layout_weight="1"
/>
<Button android:text="multiply"
  android:layout_width="fill_parent"
  android:layout_height="wrap_content"
  android:layout_weight="1"
/>
<Button android:text="divide"
  android:layout_width="fill_parent"
  android:layout_height="wrap_content"
  android:layout_weight="1"
/>
```

Recipe: Setting Relative Layout and Layout ID

Sometimes it is more convenient to set the layout relative to a starting object or parent object rather than absolute rules. Also, if the UI starts nesting `LinearLayouts`, it might be simpler to use relative layouts. This can be done using a `RelativeLayout` view, as shown in Listing 4.3. The layout is shown in Figure 4.7.

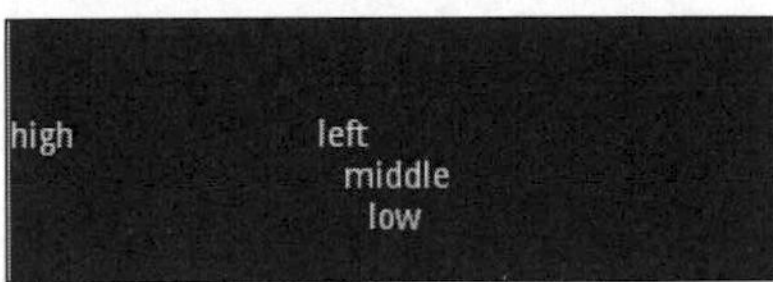

Figure 4.7 Four text views from the `RelativeLayout` example.

Listing 4.3 **`RelativeLayout` example**

```
<?xml version="1.0" encoding="utf-8"?>
<RelativeLayout xmlns:android="http://schemas.android.com/apk/res/android"
    android:layout_width="fill_parent"
    android:layout_height="fill_parent">
    <TextView android:id="@+id/mid" android:text="middle"
         android:layout_width="wrap_content"
         android:layout_height="wrap_content"
         android:layout_centerInParent="true"/>
    <TextView android:id="@+id/high" android:text="high"
        android:layout_width="wrap_content"
        android:layout_height="wrap_content"
        android:layout_above="@id/mid"/>
    <TextView android:id="@+id/low" android:text="low"
        android:layout_width="wrap_content"
        android:layout_height="wrap_content"
        android:layout_centerHorizontal="true"
        android:layout_below="@id/mid"/>
    <TextView android:id="@+id/left" android:text="left"
        android:layout_width="wrap_content"
        android:layout_height="wrap_content"
        android:layout_alignBottom="@id/high"
        android:layout_toLeftOf="@id/low"/>
</RelativeLayout>
```

The explanation of these attributes and a list of the different available rules for relative layout are collected in Table 4.2. Because every layout can have portions declared in XML files and other portions in Java code, both methods of referring to layouts are shown. The first three rows of the table show attributes that need to point to a view ID, and the last two rows show attributes that are boolean.

Table 4.2 **Possible Rules for Children in a Relative Layout**

Relative Layout Rule	XML Attribute (All Start with the **`android:`** Tag)	Java Constant

Align this view's edge relative to anchor view's edge	`layout_above`
	`layout_below`
	`layout_toRightOf`
	`layout_toLeftOf`
		`ABOVE`
		`BELOW`
		`RIGHT_OF`
		`LEFT_OF`

Align this view's edge with anchor view's edge	`layout_alignTop`
	`layout_alignBottom`
	`layout_alignRight`
	`layout_alignLeft`
		`ALIGN_TOP`
		`ALIGN_BOTTOM`
		`ALIGN_RIGHT`
		`ALIGN_LEFT`

Align this view's text baseline with anchor view's text baseline	`layout_alignBaseline`	`ALIGN_BASELINE`

Align this view's edge with parent view's edge	`layout_alignParentTop`
	`layout_alignParentBottom`
	`layout_alignParentRight`
	`layout_alignParentLeft`
		`ALIGN_PARENT_TOP`
		`ALIGN_PARENT_BOTTOM`
		`ALIGN_PARENT_RIGHT`
		`ALIGN_PARENT_LEFT`

Center this view within parent	`layout_centerInParent`
	`layout_centerHorizontal`
	`layout_centerVertical`
		`CENTER_IN_PARENT`
		`CENTER_HORIZONTAL`
		`CENTER_VERTICAL`

Recipe: Declaring a Layout Programmatically

The XML layout framework in Android is the preferred method for enabling general device changes and simple development. However, sometimes it is useful to change some layout aspects programmatically—using Java, for example. In fact, the entire layout can be declared using Java. For illustration, a portion of the previous recipe's layout is shown implemented as Java code in Listing 4.4. It should be stressed that not only is coding layout in Java cumbersome, but it is also discouraged because it does not take advantage of the modular approach to resource directories where a layout can be changed simply without modification of Java code, as discussed in the "Specifying Alternate Resources" recipe.

Listing 4.4 **src/com/cookbook/programmaticlayout/ProgrammaticLayout.java**

```
package com.cookbook.programmatic_layout;

import android.app.Activity;
import android.os.Bundle;
import android.view.ViewGroup;
import android.view.ViewGroup.LayoutParams;
import android.widget.RelativeLayout;
import android.widget.TextView;

public class ProgrammaticLayout extends Activity {
    private int TEXTVIEW1_ID = 100011;
    @Override
    public void onCreate(Bundle savedInstanceState) {
        super.onCreate(savedInstanceState);

        //Here is an alternative to: setContentView(R.layout.main);
        final RelativeLayout relLayout = new RelativeLayout( this );
        relLayout.setLayoutParams( new RelativeLayout.LayoutParams(
                                       LayoutParams.FILL_PARENT,
                                       LayoutParams.FILL_PARENT ) );
        TextView textView1 = new TextView( this );
        textView1.setText("middle");
        textView1.setTag(TEXTVIEW1_ID);

        RelativeLayout.LayoutParams text1layout = new
            RelativeLayout.LayoutParams(   LayoutParams.WRAP_CONTENT,
                                           LayoutParams.WRAP_CONTENT );
        text1layout.addRule( RelativeLayout.CENTER_IN_PARENT );
        relLayout.addView(textView1, text1layout);
        TextView textView2 = new TextView( this );
        textView2.setText("high");

        RelativeLayout.LayoutParams text2Layout = new
            RelativeLayout.LayoutParams(   LayoutParams.WRAP_CONTENT,
                                           LayoutParams.WRAP_CONTENT );
        text2Layout.addRule(RelativeLayout.ABOVE, TEXTVIEW1_ID );
        relLayout.addView( textView2, text2Layout );

        setContentView( relLayout );
    }
}
```

Recipe: Updating a Layout from a Separate Thread

As discussed in Chapter 3, "Threads, Services, Receivers, and Alerts," when a time-consuming activity is being run, care must be taken to ensure the UI thread stays responsive. This is done by creating a separate thread for the time-consuming task and letting the UI thread continue at high priority. If the separate thread subsequently needs to update the UI, a handler can be used to post updates to the UI thread.

This recipe uses a button to trigger a time-consuming computation in two parts and updates to the screen when each part is done. The layout, represented by the XML in Listing 4.5, consists of status text called `computation_status` and a trigger button called `action`. It utilizes the strings defined in **strings.xml,** as shown in Listing 4.6.

Listing 4.5 **res/layout/main.xml**

```
<?xml version="1.0" encoding="utf-8"?>
<LinearLayout
    xmlns:android="http://schemas.android.com/apk/res/android"
    android:orientation="vertical"
    android:layout_width="fill_parent"
    android:layout_height="fill_parent">
    <TextView android:id="@+id/computation_status"
        android:layout_width="fill_parent"
        android:layout_height="wrap_content"
        android:text="@string/hello" android:textSize="36sp"
        android:textColor="#000" />
    <Button android:text="@string/action"
        android:id="@+id/action"
        android:layout_width="wrap_content"
        android:layout_height="wrap_content" />
</LinearLayout>
```

Listing 4.6 **res/layout/strings.xml**

```
<?xml version="1.0" encoding="utf-8"?>
<resources>
    <string name="hello">Hello World, HandlerUpdateUi!</string>
    <string name="app_name">HandlerUpdateUi</string>
    <string name="action">Press to Start</string>
    <string name="start">Starting...</string>
    <string name="first">First Done</string>
    <string name="second">Second Done</string>
</resources>
```

The steps to update the UI from a background thread are

1. Initialize a handle to the UI object that updates by the background thread. (Here, it is called `av`.)

2. Define a runnable function (here, it is called `mUpdateResults`) that updates the UI as needed.
3. Declare a handler to handle the messages between threads. (Here, it is called `mHandler`.)
4. In the background thread, set flags as appropriate to communicate the change in status. (Here, the `text_string` and `background_color` are to be changed.)
5. In the background thread, have the handler post the UI update function to the main thread.

The activity with these steps is shown in Listing 4.7.

Listing 4.7 **src/com/cookbook/handler_ui/HandlerUpdateUi.java**

```
package com.cookbook.handler_ui;

import android.app.Activity;
import android.graphics.Color;
import android.os.Bundle;
import android.os.Handler;
import android.view.View;
import android.widget.Button;
import android.widget.TextView;

public class HandlerUpdateUi extends Activity {
    TextView av; //UI reference
    int text_string = R.string.start;
    int background_color = Color.DKGRAY;

    final Handler mHandler = new Handler();
    // Create runnable for posting results to the UI thread
    final Runnable mUpdateResults = new Runnable() {
        public void run() {
            av.setText(text_string);
            av.setBackgroundColor(background_color);
        }
    };

    @Override
    public void onCreate(Bundle savedInstanceState) {
        super.onCreate(savedInstanceState);
        setContentView(R.layout.main);
        av = (TextView) findViewById(R.id.computation_status);

        Button actionButton = (Button) findViewById(R.id.action);
        actionButton.setOnClickListener(new View.OnClickListener() {
```

```
            public void onClick(View view) {
                do_work();
            }
        });
    }

    //example of a computationally intensive action with UI updates
    private void do_work() {
        Thread thread = new Thread(new Runnable() {
            public void run() {
                text_string=R.string.start;
                background_color = Color.DKGRAY;
                mHandler.post(mUpdateResults);

                computation(1);
                text_string=R.string.first;
                background_color = Color.BLUE;
                mHandler.post(mUpdateResults);

                computation(2);
                text_string=R.string.second;
                background_color = Color.GREEN;
                mHandler.post(mUpdateResults);
            }
        });
        thread.start();
    }

    final static int SIZE=1000; //large enough to take some time
    double tmp;
    private void computation(int val) {
        for(int ii=0; ii<SIZE; ii++)
            for(int jj=0; jj<SIZE; jj++)
                tmp=val*Math.log(ii+1)/Math.log1p(jj+1);
    }
}
```

Text Manipulation

In views that incorporate text, such as `TextView`, `EditText`, and `Button`, the text is represented in the XML layout file by the `android:text` element. As discussed in the beginning of this chapter, it is good practice to initialize this with a string defined in the strings

XML file, so that all strings are contained in a single place. Therefore, a way to add text to an UI element, such as `TextView`, looks like the following:

```
<TextView android:text="@string/myTextString"
        android:id="@+id/my_text_label"
        android:layout_width="wrap_content"
        android:layout_height="wrap_content" />
```

The default font depends on Android device and user preferences. To specify the exact font, use the elements shown in Table 4.3.

Table 4.3 **Useful TextView Attributes with Default Values in Bold in the Last Column**

TextView Attribute	XML Element	Java Method	Possible and Default Values
Display string	android:text	setText(CharSequence)	Any string
Font size	android:textSize	setTextSize(float)	Any dimension
Font color	android:textColor	setTextColor(int)	Any color
Background color	N/A	setBackgroundColor(int)	Any color
Font style	android:textStyle	setTypeface(Typeface)	bold italic bold italic
Font type	android:typeface	setTypeface(Typeface)	**normal** sans serif monospace
Text placement in display area	android:gravity	setGravity(int)	top bottom **left** right (more...)

Recipe: Setting and Changing Text Attributes

This recipe changes the color of displayed text when a button is clicked. It can easily be extended to change the font size or style instead, as discussed at the end of this recipe.

The main layout is simply a `TextView` and `Button` arranged in a vertical `LinearLayout`, as shown in Listing 4.8. The text is identified as `mod_text` and displays the string `changed_text` defined in the **strings.xml** file, as shown in Listing 4.9. The button is identified as `change` and displays the string `button_text` from the strings XML file.

Listing 4.8 **res/layout/main.xml**

```
<?xml version="1.0" encoding="utf-8"?>
<LinearLayout xmlns:android="http://schemas.android.com/apk/res/android"
    android:orientation="vertical"
        android:layout_width="fill_parent"
        android:layout_height="fill_parent">
        <TextView android:text="@string/changed_text"
                android:textSize="48sp"
                android:id="@+id/mod_text"
                android:layout_width="wrap_content"
                android:layout_height="wrap_content" />
        <Button android:text="@string/button_text"
                android:textSize="48sp"
                android:id="@+id/change"
                android:layout_width="wrap_content"
                android:layout_height="wrap_content" />
</LinearLayout>
```

Listing 4.9 **res/values/strings.xml**

```
<?xml version="1.0" encoding="utf-8"?>
<resources>
    <string name="app_name">ChangeFont</string>
    <string name="changed_text">Rainbow Connection</string>
    <string name="button_text">Press to change the font color</string>
</resources>
```

The activity shown in Listing 4.10 utilizes the **main.xml** layout and identifies the `TextView` handle to the `mod_text` ID. Then the button's `OnClickListener` is overriden to set the text color described in Table 4.3. The possible color resources are defined in a global **colors.xml** file, as shown in Listing 4.11. As defined, the colors are red, green, and blue, but they are named functionally as the start, mid, and last. This provides an easy way to change the colors later without needing to change their handle names.

Listing 4.10 **src/com/cookbook/change_font/ChangeFont.java**

```
package com.cookbook.change_font;

import android.app.Activity;
import android.os.Bundle;
import android.view.View;
import android.widget.Button;
import android.widget.TextView;

public class ChangeFont extends Activity {
    TextView tv;
    private int color_vals[]={R.color.start, R.color.mid, R.color.last};
    int idx=0;
```

```
    /** Called when the activity is first created. */
    @Override
    public void onCreate(Bundle savedInstanceState) {
        super.onCreate(savedInstanceState);
        setContentView(R.layout.main);
        tv = (TextView) findViewById(R.id.mod_text);

        Button changeFont = (Button) findViewById(R.id.change);
        changeFont.setOnClickListener(new View.OnClickListener() {
            public void onClick(View view) {
                tv.setTextColor(getResources().getColor(color_vals[idx]));
                idx = (idx+1)%3;
            }
        });
    }
}
```

Listing 4.11 **res/values/colors.xml**

```
<?xml version="1.0" encoding="utf-8"?>
<resources>
       <color name="start">#f00</color>
       <color name="mid">#0f0</color>
       <color name="last">#00f</color>
</resources>
```

This recipe can be modified to change the text size (or text style) easily. For example, the `color_vals[]` would change to `size_vals[]` and point to the `R.dimen` resources:

```
private int size_vals[]={R.dimen.small, R.dimen.medium, R.dimen.large};
tv.setTextSize(getResources().getDimension(size_vals[idx]));
```

Also, instead of the **colors.xml** file, the **dimens.xml** file would be used, as shown in Listing 4.12.

Listing 4.12 **Example of Similar Usage for the dimens.xml File**

```
<?xml version="1.0" encoding="utf-8"?>
<resources>
       <dimen name="small">12sp</dimen>
       <dimen name="medium">24sp</dimen>
       <dimen name="large">48sp</dimen>
</resources>
```

To use this recipe to change the text string instead, the `color_vals[]` would change to `text_vals[]` and point to the `R.string` resources as follows:

```
private int text_vals[]={R.string.first_text,
                         R.string.second_text, R.string.third_text};
tv.setText(getBaseContext().getString(text_vals[idx]));
```

The **strings.xml** file would then be used, as shown in Listing 4.13.

Listing 4.13 **Example of Similar Usage for the strings.xml File**

```
<?xml version="1.0" encoding="utf-8"?>
<resources>
    <string name="app_name">ChangeFont</string>
    <string name="changed_text">Rainbow Connection</string>
    <string name="button_text">Press To Change the Font Color</string>
    <string name="first_text">First</string>
    <string name="second_text">Second</string>
    <string name="third_text">Third</string>
</resources>
```

Recipe: Providing Text Entry

The `EditText` class provides a simple view for user input. It can be declared just like a `TextView` with the most useful attributes shown in Table 4.4. Although each does have a corresponding Java method, it is less illuminating to show those here.

Table 4.4 **Useful EditText Attributes in Addition to Those in Table 4.3. Again the Default Values Are in Bold in the Last Column.**

EditText Attribute	XML Element	Possible and **Default** Values
Minimum number of lines to display	`android:minLines`	Any integer
Maximum number of lines to display	`android:maxLines`	Any integer
Hint text to show when display empty	`android:hint`	Any string

Input type	`android:inputType`	**text**
		`textCapSentences`
		`textAutoCorrect`
		`textAutoComplete`
		`textEmailAddress`
		`textNoSuggestions`
		`textPassword`
		`number`
		`phone`
		`date`
		`time`
		(more...)

For example, using the following XML code in a layout file shows a text entry window with **"Type text here"** displayed in grayed out text as a hint. On devices without a keyboard or on those where the keyboard is hidden, selecting the Edit window brings up the soft keyboard for text entry, as shown in Figure 4.8.

```
<EditText android:id="@+id/text_result"
  android:inputType="text"
          android:textSize="30sp"
          android:hint="Type text here"
          android:layout_width="fill_parent"
          android:layout_height="wrap_content" />
```

Figure 4.8 Text entry with soft keyboard.

By using `android:inputType="phone"` or `="textEmailAddress"`, the soft keyboard for phone number entry or the soft keyboard for email address entry display when the user selects the Input window. These are shown in Figure 4.9 with appropriately changed `hint` text.

Figure 4.9 Examples of utilizing different soft keyboards when inputText is set as "phone" or "textEmailAddress".

One more note: The text entry method can be specified as shown in Table 4.4 to automatically capitalize each sentence as typed, automatically correct mistyped words, or turn off word suggestions during typing. Control over these choices might be useful depending on the text entry situation.

Recipe: Creating a Form

A form is a graphical layout with areas that can take text input or selection. For text input, an `EditText` object can be used. After it is declared, some Java code needs to capture the text entry at run-time. This is done as shown in Listing 4.14. Note that the content of the text entry `textResult` in this example should not be modified. A copy of the content can be made in case modification is needed.

Listing 4.14 **Capturing Text from an EditText Object**

```
CharSequence phoneNumber;
EditText textResult = (EditText) findViewById(R.id.text_result);
textResult.setOnKeyListener(new OnKeyListener() {
    public boolean onKey(View v, int keyCode, KeyEvent event) {
        // register the text when "enter" is pressed
        if ((event.getAction() == KeyEvent.ACTION_DOWN) &&
            (keyCode == KeyEvent.KEYCODE_ENTER)) {
          // grab the text for use in the activity
          phoneNumber = textResult.getText();
          return true;
        }
        return false;
    }
});
```

Returning `true` from the `onKey` method indicates to the super function that the key press event was consumed (utilized), and there is no need to process further.

To provide user selection of different options normally used in forms, the use of standard widgets such as checkboxes, radio buttons, and drop-down selection menus are implemented using widgets as shown in the next section.

Other Widgets: From Buttons to Seek Bars

The Android system provides some standard graphical widgets that developers can utilize to create a cohesive user experience across applications. The most common ones are

- `Button`—A rectangular graphic that registers when the screen is touched within its bounds. It can contain user-provided text or images.
- `CheckBox`—A button with a checkmark graphic and description text that can be toggled on or off when touched. The `ToggleButton` is similar and also discussed here.
- `RadioButton`—A button with a dot graphic that can be selected when touched, but cannot then be turned off. Multiple radio buttons can be grouped together into a `RadioGroup`, which allows only one radio button of the group to be selected at a time.
- `Spinner`—A button showing the current selection and an arrow graphic to denote a drop-down menu. When the spinner is touched, the list of possible values displays and when a new selection is made, it is displayed in the spinner.
- `ProgressBar`—A bar that lights up to visually indicate the percentage of progress (and optionally secondary progress) in an operation. It is not interactive. If a quantitative measure of progress cannot be determined, it can be set in indeterminate mode, which shows a rotating circular motion instead.

- SeekBar—An interactive progress bar that allows progress to be dragged and changed. This is useful to show media playback, for example. It can show how much of the media has been played, and a user can drag to move to an earlier or later place in the file.

The following recipes provide some practical examples of these widgets.

Recipe: Using Image Buttons in a Table Layout

Buttons were introduced in Chapter 2. Like any view, a background image can be added to a button using the android:background attribute. However, using the special ImageButton widget provides some additional layout flexibility. It specifies an image using the android:src attribute as follows:

```
<ImageButton android:id="@+id/imagebutton0"
             android:src="@drawable/android_cupcake"
             android:layout_width="wrap_content"
             android:layout_height="wrap_content" />
```

When used in this way, the image shows on top of a button widget. The ImageButton inherits image placement from the ImageView widget using android:scaleType. Possible values and how they modify a given image are illustrated in Figure 4.10.

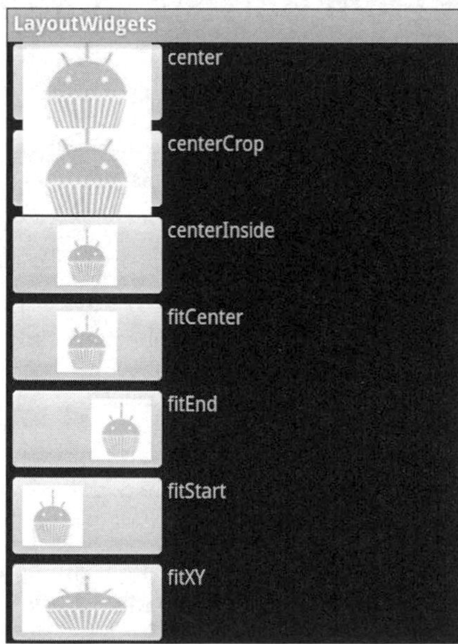

Figure 4.10 Example results of android:scaleType for image views.

In addition, some other possible manipulations used with image buttons are

- Using `android:padding` to keep buttons from overlapping or to add space between them
- Setting `android:background` to `null` (which is `@null` in the XML layout file) to hide the button and show only the image

When the button is hidden, by default, there is no visual feedback that an image button was pressed. This can be rectified by creating a drawable XML file that contains just a selector element:

```
<?xml version="1.0" encoding="utf-8"?>
<selector xmlns:android="http://schemas.android.com/apk/res/android">
    <item android:drawable="@drawable/myImage_pressed"
          android:state_pressed="true" />
    <item android:drawable="@drawable/myImage_focused"
          android:state_focused="true" />
    <item android:drawable="@drawable/myImage_normal" />
</selector>
```

This specifies three different images depending on whether the button is pressed, in focus, or just a normal state. The three different images for these cases should also reside in the drawable resource directory (such as **res/drawable-mdpi/**). Then, the selector file can be specified as the `android:src` of an `ImageButton`.

When multiple image buttons are placed together in a layout, it is often useful to utilize the table layout, which is also shown in this recipe. The `TableLayout` view group is similar to a `LinearLayout` with vertical orientation. Then, multiple rows can be specified using the `TableRow` view group for each row. The example layout shown in Listing 4.15 specifies an `ImageButton` and `TextView` view in each row, producing the screen layout shown in Figure 4.11.

Listing 4.15 **res/layout/ibutton.xml**

```
<?xml version="1.0" encoding="utf-8"?>
<TableLayout
    xmlns:android="http://schemas.android.com/apk/res/android"
    android:layout_width="fill_parent"
    android:layout_height="fill_parent">
    <TableRow>
        <ImageButton android:id="@+id/imagebutton0"
            android:src="@drawable/android_cupcake"
            android:scaleType="fitXY"
            android:background="@null"
            android:padding="5dip"
            android:layout_width="wrap_content"
            android:layout_height="90dip" />
        <TextView android:text="Cupcake"
```

```
            android:layout_width="wrap_content"
            android:layout_height="wrap_content" />
    </TableRow>
    <TableRow>
        <ImageButton android:id="@+id/imagebutton1"
            android:src="@drawable/android_donut"
            android:scaleType="fitXY"
            android:background="@null"
            android:padding="5dip"
            android:layout_width="wrap_content"
            android:layout_height="90dip" />
        <TextView android:text="Donut"
            android:layout_width="wrap_content"
            android:layout_height="wrap_content" />
    </TableRow>
    <TableRow>
        <ImageButton android:id="@+id/imagebutton2"
            android:src="@drawable/android_eclair"
            android:scaleType="fitXY"
            android:background="@null"
            android:padding="5dip"
            android:layout_width="wrap_content"
            android:layout_height="90dip" />
        <TextView android:text="Eclair"
            android:layout_width="wrap_content"
            android:layout_height="wrap_content" />
    </TableRow>
    <TableRow>
        <ImageButton android:id="@+id/imagebutton3"
            android:src="@drawable/android_froyo"
            android:scaleType="fitXY"
            android:background="@null"
            android:padding="5dip"
            android:layout_width="wrap_content"
            android:layout_height="90dip" />
        <TextView android:text="FroYo"
            android:layout_width="wrap_content"
            android:layout_height="wrap_content" />
    </TableRow>
    <TableRow>
        <ImageButton android:id="@+id/imagebutton4"
            android:src="@drawable/android_gingerbread"
            android:scaleType="fitXY"
            android:background="@null"
            android:padding="5dip"
            android:layout_width="wrap_content"
            android:layout_height="90dip" />
        <TextView android:text="Gingerbread"
```

```
            android:layout_width="wrap_content"
            android:layout_height="wrap_content" />
    </TableRow>
</TableLayout>
```

Figure 4.11 `TableLayout` of `ImageButtons` and `TextViews`.

Recipe: Using Check Boxes and Toggle Buttons

Check boxes have a predetermined checkmark graphic, colors for selection, and colors for behavior when pressed. This provides a unifying look and feel across Android applications. However, if a custom graphic to denote selection is required, the `setButtonDrawable()` method can be used.

Sticking with the check box example here, the `CheckBox` widget needs to be declared in a layout file, as shown in Listing 4.16. The `android:text` attribute displays as a label after the checkbox. For illustration, a few text views are also added to the layout.

Listing 4.16 **res/layout/ckbox.xml**

```
<?xml version="1.0" encoding="utf-8"?>
<LinearLayout
       xmlns:android="http://schemas.android.com/apk/res/android"
       android:orientation="vertical"
       android:layout_width="fill_parent"
```

```
        android:layout_height="fill_parent">
    <CheckBox android:id="@+id/checkbox0"
            android:text="Lettuce"
            android:layout_width="wrap_content"
            android:layout_height="wrap_content" />
    <CheckBox android:id="@+id/checkbox1"
            android:text="Tomato"
            android:layout_width="wrap_content"
            android:layout_height="wrap_content" />
    <CheckBox android:id="@+id/checkbox2"
            android:text="Cheese"
            android:layout_width="wrap_content"
            android:layout_height="wrap_content" />
    <TextView android:text="Lettuce, Tomato, Cheese choices:"
            android:layout_width="wrap_content"
            android:layout_height="wrap_content" />
    <TextView android:id="@+id/status"
            android:layout_width="wrap_content"
            android:layout_height="wrap_content" />
</LinearLayout>
```

The views in the layout file can be associated with view instances in the Java file, as shown in Listing 4.17. Here, a private inner class is used to register the toppings of a sandwich. All three checkboxes have an `onClickListener`, which keeps track of the changes to the toppings, and this is updated to the text view as an example. The final output with some sample selections is shown in Figure 4.12.

Listing 4.17 **src/com/cookbook/layout_widgets/CheckBoxExample.java**

```
package com.cookbook.layout_widgets;

import android.app.Activity;
import android.os.Bundle;
import android.view.View;
import android.view.View.OnClickListener;
import android.widget.CheckBox;
import android.widget.TextView;

public class CheckBoxExample extends Activity {
    private TextView tv;

    @Override
    public void onCreate(Bundle savedInstanceState) {
        super.onCreate(savedInstanceState);
        setContentView(R.layout.ckbox);
        tv = (TextView) findViewById(R.id.status);

        class Toppings {private boolean LETTUCE, TOMATO, CHEESE;}
```

```
        final Toppings sandwichToppings = new Toppings();
        final CheckBox checkbox[] = {
                (CheckBox) findViewById(R.id.checkbox0),
                (CheckBox) findViewById(R.id.checkbox1),
                (CheckBox) findViewById(R.id.checkbox2)};


        checkbox[0].setOnClickListener(new OnClickListener() {
            @Override
            public void onClick(View v) {
                if (((CheckBox) v).isChecked()) {
                    sandwichToppings.LETTUCE = true;
                } else {
                    sandwichToppings.LETTUCE = false;
                }
                tv.setText(""+sandwichToppings.LETTUCE + " "
                        +sandwichToppings.TOMATO + " "
                        +sandwichToppings.CHEESE + " ");
            }
        });
        checkbox[1].setOnClickListener(new OnClickListener() {
            @Override
            public void onClick(View v) {
                if (((CheckBox) v).isChecked()) {
                    sandwichToppings.TOMATO = true;
                } else {
                    sandwichToppings.TOMATO = false;
                }
                tv.setText(""+sandwichToppings.LETTUCE + " "
                        +sandwichToppings.TOMATO + " "
                        +sandwichToppings.CHEESE + " ");
            }
        });
        checkbox[2].setOnClickListener(new OnClickListener() {
            @Override
            public void onClick(View v) {
                if (((CheckBox) v).isChecked()) {
                    sandwichToppings.CHEESE = true;
                } else {
                    sandwichToppings.CHEESE = false;
                }
                tv.setText(""+sandwichToppings.LETTUCE + " "
                        +sandwichToppings.TOMATO + " "
                        +sandwichToppings.CHEESE + " ");
            }
        });
    }
}
```

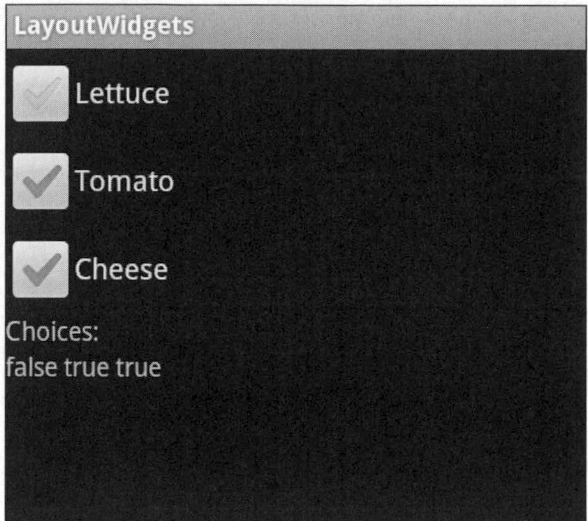

Figure 4.12 Checkbox example showing unselected and selected widgets.

Toggle buttons are similar to checkboxes, but use a different graphic. In addition, the text is incorporated into the button rather than put alongside. Listing 4.16 (and Listing 4.17 for that matter) can be modified to replace each `CheckBox` with a `ToggleButton`:

```
<ToggleButton android:id="@+id/ToggleButton0"
              android:textOff="No Lettuce"
              android:textOn="Lettuce"
              android:layout_width="wrap_content"
              android:layout_height="wrap_content" />
```

Note the `android:text` element is replaced by an `android:textOff` (defaults to `"OFF"` if not specified) and `android:textOn` (defaults to `"ON"` if not specified) element for display depending on the selection state of the toggle button. An example output is shown in Figure 4.13.

Recipe: Using Radio Buttons

A radio button is like a checkbox that cannot be unchecked. Selecting one radio button unselects a previously selected one. Usually a group of radio buttons is put into a `RadioGroup` view group that ensures only one button of the collection is selected at a time. This is shown in the layout file in Listing 4.18.

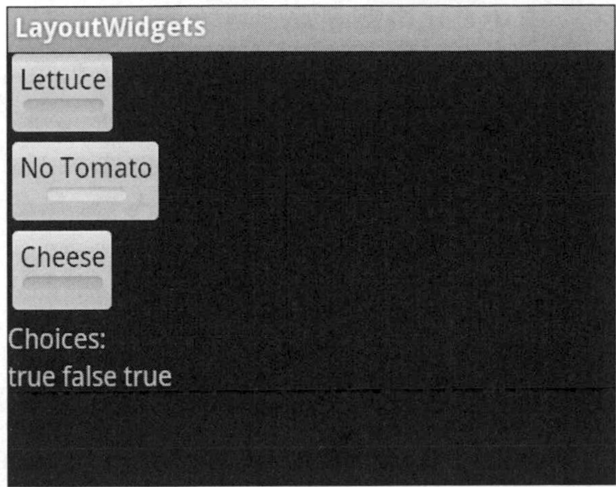

Figure 4.13 ToggleButton example with unselected and selected widgets.

Listing 4.18 **res/layout/rbutton.xml**

```
<?xml version="1.0" encoding="utf-8"?>
<LinearLayout
xmlns:android="http://schemas.android.com/apk/res/android"
        android:layout_width="wrap_content"
        android:layout_height="wrap_content">
        <RadioGroup android:id="@+id/RadioGroup01"
                android:layout_width="wrap_content"
                android:layout_height="wrap_content">
                <RadioButton android:text="Republican"
                        android:id="@+id/RadioButton02"
                        android:layout_width="wrap_content"
                        android:layout_height="wrap_content" />
                <RadioButton android:text="Democrat"
                        android:id="@+id/RadioButton03"
                        android:layout_width="wrap_content"
                        android:layout_height="wrap_content" />
                <RadioButton android:text="Independent"
                        android:id="@+id/RadioButton01"
                        android:layout_width="wrap_content"
                        android:layout_height="wrap_content" />
        </RadioGroup>
</LinearLayout>
```

An example activity is similar to the previous recipe in Listing 4.17, but with `CheckBox` replaced by `RadioButton`. Listing 4.18's layout is shown in Figure 4.14.

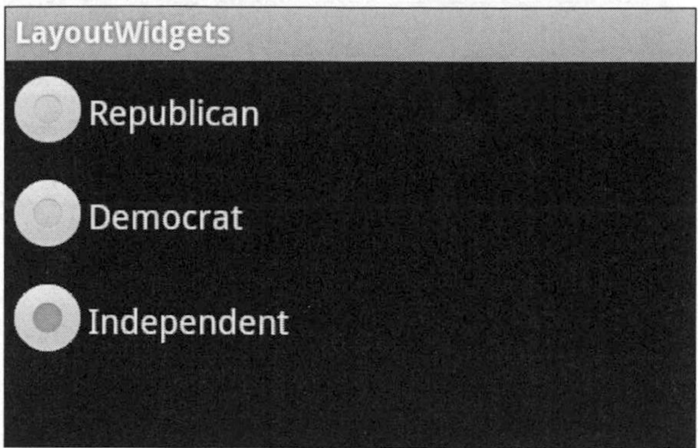

Figure 4.14 RadioGroup example showing three radio buttons.

Recipe: Creating a Drop-Down Menu

A drop-down menu is called a spinner. It is a widget defined in a normal screen layout such as the one shown in Listing 4.19.

Listing 4.19 **res/layout/spinner.xml**

```
<?xml version="1.0" encoding="utf-8"?>
<LinearLayout
        xmlns:android="http://schemas.android.com/apk/res/android"
        android:layout_width="wrap_content"
        android:layout_height="wrap_content">
        <Spinner android:id="@+id/spinner"
                 android:prompt="@string/ocean_prompt"
                 android:layout_width="wrap_content"
                 android:layout_height="wrap_content" />
</LinearLayout>
```

The title of the drop-down menu can be specified with the `android:prompt` attribute. It needs to be defined in a **strings.xml** file, for example:

```
<string name="ocean_prompt">Choose your favorite ocean</string>
```

The spinner also needs a separate layout defined for the drop-down menu appearance, such as Listing 4.20 for the **spinner_entry.xml**.

Listing 4.20 **res/layout/spinner_entry.xml**

```
<?xml version="1.0" encoding="utf-8"?>
<TextView
  xmlns:android="http://schemas.android.com/apk/res/android"
```

```
  android:gravity="center"
  android:textColor="#000"
  android:textSize="40sp"
  android:layout_width="fill_parent"
  android:layout_height="wrap_content">
</TextView>
```

Note the spinner entry layout is not limited to text, but can include images or any object supported in layouts.

The activity to call the spinner needs to declare an `Adapter` to fill the drop-down menu with the view from the spinner entry layout file. An example of such an activity is shown in Listing 4.21.

Listing 4.21 **src/com/cookbook/layout_widgets/SpinnerExample.java**

```
package com.cookbook.layout_widgets;

import android.app.Activity;
import android.os.Bundle;
import android.widget.ArrayAdapter;
import android.widget.Spinner;

public class SpinnerExample extends Activity {
    private static final String[] oceans = {
        "Pacific", "Atlantic", "Indian",
        "Arctic", "Southern" };

    @Override
    protected void onCreate(Bundle savedInstanceState) {
        super.onCreate(savedInstanceState);
        setContentView(R.layout.spinner);

        Spinner favoriteOcean = (Spinner) findViewById(R.id.spinner);

        ArrayAdapter<String> mAdapter = new
            ArrayAdapter<String>(this, R.layout.spinner_entry, oceans);
        mAdapter.setDropDownViewResource(R.layout.spinner_entry);
        favoriteOcean.setAdapter(mAdapter);
    }
}
```

In the previous example, the spinner entries are defined by the string array `oceans[]`, `which is passed to the ArrayAdapter constructor`. This implementation assumes the spinner entries do not change during run-time. To specify a more general case where spinner entries can be added or manipulated, `mAdapter` needs to be built using its `add()`

method. The bold part of code in the `onCreate()` method would then become the following:

```
Spinner favoriteOcean = (Spinner) findViewById(R.id.spinner);
ArrayAdapter<String> mAdapter = new
   ArrayAdapter<String>(this, R.layout.spinner_entry);
mAdapter.setDropDownViewResource(R.layout.spinner_entry);
for(int idx=0; idx<oceans.length; idx++)
   mAdapter.add(oceans[idx]);
favoriteOcean.setAdapter(mAdapter);
```

This `ArrayAdapter` allows the `add()`, `remove()`, and `clear()` methods to change the selection list during run-time, and `getView()` to improve performance speed by reusing layout views for each spinner entry.

Recipe: Using a Progress Bar

This recipe demonstrates the usage of a progress bar by taking Listing 4.7 from "*Recipe: Updating a Layout from a Separate Thread*," which used text to show progress in a computation, and it shows the progress graphically instead. This is done by adding a progress bar object to the layout, such as:

```
<ProgressBar android:id="@+id/ex_progress_bar"
         style="?android:attr/progressBarStyleHorizontal"
         android:layout_width="270px"
         android:layout_height="50px"
         android:progress="0"
         android:secondaryProgress="0" />
```

As the progress changes, the `android:progress` attribute can change to show a bright orange bar going across the screen. The optional `android:secondaryProgress` attribute shows a lighter colored orange bar that can be used to indicate a progress milestone, for example.

The activity to update the progress bar is shown in Listing 4.22. It is similar to Listing 4.7, but it uses a ProgressBar instead. Here the update results function updates the progress attribute from Java.

Listing 4.22 **src/com/cookbook/handler_ui/HandlerUpdateUi.java**

```
package com.cookbook.handler_ui;

import android.app.Activity;
import android.os.Bundle;
import android.os.Handler;
import android.view.View;
import android.widget.Button;
import android.widget.ProgressBar;
```

```
public class HandlerUpdateUi extends Activity {
    private static ProgressBar m_progressBar; //UI reference
    int percent_done = 0;

    final Handler mHandler = new Handler();
    // Create runnable for posting results to the UI thread
    final Runnable mUpdateResults = new Runnable() {
        public void run() {
            m_progressBar.setProgress(percent_done);
        }
    };

    @Override
    public void onCreate(Bundle savedInstanceState) {
        super.onCreate(savedInstanceState);
        setContentView(R.layout.main);
        m_progressBar = (ProgressBar) findViewById(R.id.ex_progress_bar);

        Button actionButton = (Button) findViewById(R.id.action);
        actionButton.setOnClickListener(new View.OnClickListener() {
            public void onClick(View view) {
                do_work();
            }
        });
    }

    //example of a computationally intensive action with UI updates
    private void do_work() {
        Thread thread = new Thread(new Runnable() {
            public void run() {
                percent_done = 0;
                mHandler.post(mUpdateResults);

                computation(1);
                percent_done = 50;
                mHandler.post(mUpdateResults);

                computation(2);
                percent_done = 100;
                mHandler.post(mUpdateResults);
            }
        });
        thread.start();
    }

    final static int SIZE=1000; //large enough to take some time
    double tmp;
```

```
    private void computation(int val) {
        for(int ii=0; ii<SIZE; ii++)
            for(int jj=0; jj<SIZE; jj++)
                tmp=val*Math.log(ii+1)/Math.log1p(jj+1);
    }
}
```

If the updates need to be shown more often, use the `postDelayed` method of the handler instead of the `post` method and add a `postDelayed` to the end of the runnable update results function (similar to what was used in "Scheduling a Runnable Task from the Main Thread recipe" in Chapter 3).

Recipe: Using a SeekBar

A seek bar is similar to a progress bar that can take user input to change the amount of progress. Current progress is indicated by a small sliding box called a thumb. A user can click and drag the thumb to visually indicate the new place to set the progress. The main activity is shown in Listing 4.23.

Listing 4.23 **src/com/cookbook/seekbar/SeekBarEx.java**

```
package com.cookbook.seekbar;

import android.app.Activity;
import android.os.Bundle;
import android.widget.SeekBar;

public class SeekBarEx extends Activity {
    private SeekBar m_seekBar;
    boolean advancing = true;

    @Override
    public void onCreate(Bundle savedInstanceState) {
        super.onCreate(savedInstanceState);
        setContentView(R.layout.main);

        m_seekBar = (SeekBar) findViewById(R.id.SeekBar01);
        m_seekBar.setOnSeekBarChangeListener(new
                    SeekBar.OnSeekBarChangeListener() {
            public void onProgressChanged(SeekBar seekBar,
                    int progress, boolean fromUser) {
                if(fromUser) count = progress;
            }

            public void onStartTrackingTouch(SeekBar seekBar) {}
            public void onStopTrackingTouch(SeekBar seekBar) {}
        });
```

```
        Thread initThread = new Thread(new Runnable() {
            public void run() {
                show_time();
            }
        });
        initThread.start();
    }

    int count;
    private void show_time() {
        for(count=0; count<100; count++) {
            m_seekBar.setProgress(count);

            try {
                Thread.sleep(100);
            } catch (InterruptedException e) {
                e.printStackTrace();
            }
        }
    }
}
```

The widget declaration in the layout XML file is shown in Listing 4.24. Note that rather than use the default thumb button, a cupcake image is used, as shown in Figure 4.15.

Listing 4.24 **res/layout/main.xml**

```
<?xml version="1.0" encoding="utf-8"?>
<RelativeLayout
    xmlns:android="http://schemas.android.com/apk/res/android"
    android:layout_width="fill_parent"
    android:layout_height="fill_parent">
    <TextView android:layout_width="fill_parent"
        android:layout_height="wrap_content"
        android:textSize="24sp" android:text="Drag the cupcake"
        android:layout_alignParentTop="true" />
    <SeekBar android:id="@+id/SeekBar01"
        android:layout_centerInParent="true"
        android:layout_width="fill_parent"
        android:layout_height="wrap_content"
        android:thumb="@drawable/pink_cupcake_no_bg" />
</RelativeLayout>
```

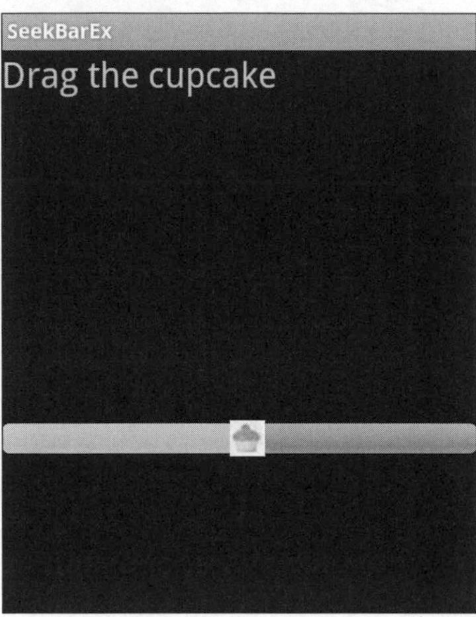

Figure 4.15 Seek bar with a custom picture of a cupcake as the thumb.

5

User Interface Events

The two aspects of a user interface are screen layout and event handling. Chapter 4, "User Interface Layout," discussed how layouts are made up of `View` objects, such as text and buttons. This chapter shows how to handle events from a user, such as physical key presses, touch events, and menu navigation. It also shows how to utilize a few advanced user interface (UI) libraries, namely gestures and 3D graphics.

Event Handlers and Event Listeners

Most user interaction with an Android device is captured by the system and sent to a corresponding callback method. For example, if the physical Back button is pressed, the `onBackPressed()` method is called. These events can be handled by extending the class and overriding the methods, called *event handlers*.

User interaction with `View` or `ViewGroup` objects can also support *event listeners*. These are methods that wait for the registered event and then trigger the system to send the event information to the corresponding callback method. For example, the `setOnClickListener()` event listener can be registered for a button and when it is pressed, the `onClick()` method is called.

Event listeners are the preferred method when available because they avoid the class extension overhead. Furthermore, an Activity implementing an event listener gets a callback for *all* the layout objects it contains, allowing for more concise code. Both event listeners and event handlers are demonstrated in this chapter within the context of handling physical key press events and screen touch events.

Recipe: Intercepting a Physical Key Press

A standard Android device has multiple physical keys that can trigger events, as listed in Table 5.1.

Table 5.1 **The Possible Physical Keys on an Android Device**

Physical Key	KeyEvent	Description
Power button	`KEYCODE_POWER`	Turns on the device or wakes it from sleep; brings UI to the lock screen
BACK key	`KEYCODE_BACK`	Navigates to the previous screen
MENU key	`KEYCODE_MENU`	Shows the menu for the active application
HOME key	`KEYCODE_HOME`	Navigates to the home screen
SEARCH key	`KEYCODE_SEARCH`	Launches a search in the active application
Camera button	`KEYCODE_CAMERA`	Launches the camera
Volume button	`KEYCODE_VOLUME_UP` `KEYCODE_VOLUME_DOWN`	Controls volume of the media by context (voice when in a phone call, music when in media playback, or ringer volume)
DPAD	`KEYCODE_DPAD_CENTER` `KEYCODE_DPAD_UP` `KEYCODE_DPAD_DOWN` `KEYCODE_DPAD_LEFT` `KEYCODE_DPAD_RIGHT`	Directional pad on some devices
Trackball	-	Directional joystick on some devices
Keyboard	`KEYCODE_0, ..., KEYCODE_9, KEYCODE_A, ..., KEYCODE_Z`	Pull-out keyboard on some devices
Media button	`KEYCODE_HEADSETHOOK`	Headset Play/Pause button

The system first sends any KeyEvent to the appropriate callback method in the in-focus activity or view. These callback methods are

- `onKeyUp()`, `onKeyDown()`, `onKeyLongPress()`—Physical key press callbacks
- `onTrackballEvent()`, `onTouchEvent()`—Trackball and touchscreen press callbacks
- `onFocusChanged()`—Called when the view gains or loses focus

These can be overridden by the application to customize with different actions. For example, to turn off the camera button (to avoid accidental presses), just consume the event in the `onKeyDown()` callback method for the Activity. This is done by intercepting the method for the event `KeyEvent.KEYCODE_CAMERA` and returning `true`:

```
public boolean onKeyDown(int keyCode, KeyEvent event) {
    if (keyCode == KeyEvent.KEYCODE_CAMERA) {
        return true; // consume event, hence do nothing on camera button
    }
    return super.onKeyDown(keyCode, event);
}
```

By consuming the event, it does not get passed on to other Android components. There are a few exceptions to this:

- The Power button and HOME key are intercepted by the system and do not reach the application for customization.
- The BACK, MENU, HOME, and SEARCH keys should not intercept the KeyDown but instead the KeyUp. This coincides with Android 2.0 suggestions because these buttons might not be physical keys in other platforms.

Listing 5.1 shows a variety of examples of intercepting physical key presses, including the following:

- The Camera and DPAD left buttons are intercepted in `onKeyDown()` to show a message to the screen, and then it is consumed (by returning `true`).
- The Volume Up button is intercepted to show a message to the screen, but it is not consumed (returning `false`) and hence also actually increases the volume.
- The SEARCH key is intercepted in `onKeyDown()`, and the `startTracking()` method is used to track it through to the key up where a message is sent to the screen.
- The BACK key is intercepted in `onBackPressed()`.

A note on the latter: An Android guideline for usability is that the BACK key should generally not be customized. However, if needed for some reason in an activity or dialog, there is a separate callback method available with Application Programming Interface (API) level 5 (Eclair) and higher to intercept the BACK key: `onBackPressed()`.

For backward compatibility with earlier Software Development Kits (SDKs), the `KeyEvent.KEYCODE_BACK` can be intercepted, and the `onBackPressed()` method can be explicitly called for earlier SDKs, as shown in Listing 5.1. (Note, this code can only be compiled with Android 2.0 or higher due to the explicit mention of Eclair, but it is backward compatible at run-time on all devices.) To intercept the BACK key in a view (not shown here) requires using the `startTracking()` method, which is similar to the SEARCH key example in Listing 5.1.

Listing 5.1 **src/com/cookbook/PhysicalKeyPress.java**

```
package com.cookbook.physkey;
import android.app.Activity;
import android.os.Bundle;
import android.view.KeyEvent;
import android.widget.Toast;
```

```
public class PhysicalKeyPress extends Activity {
    @Override
    public void onCreate(Bundle savedInstanceState) {
        super.onCreate(savedInstanceState);
        setContentView(R.layout.main);
    }
    public boolean onKeyDown(int keyCode, KeyEvent event) {
        switch (keyCode) {
        case KeyEvent.KEYCODE_CAMERA:
            Toast.makeText(this, "Pressed Camera Button",
                    Toast.LENGTH_LONG).show();
            return true;
        case KeyEvent.KEYCODE_DPAD_LEFT:
            Toast.makeText(this, "Pressed DPAD Left Button",
                    Toast.LENGTH_LONG).show();
            return true;
        case KeyEvent.KEYCODE_VOLUME_UP:
            Toast.makeText(this, "Pressed Volume Up Button",
                    Toast.LENGTH_LONG).show();
            return false;
        case KeyEvent.KEYCODE_SEARCH:
            //example of tracking through to the KeyUp
            if(event.getRepeatCount() == 0)
                event.startTracking();
            return true;
        case KeyEvent.KEYCODE_BACK:
            // Make new onBackPressed compatible with earlier SDK's
            if (android.os.Build.VERSION.SDK_INT
                    < android.os.Build.VERSION_CODES.ECLAIR
                    && event.getRepeatCount() == 0) {
                onBackPressed();
            }
        }
        return super.onKeyDown(keyCode, event);
    }

    public void onBackPressed() {
        Toast.makeText(this, "Pressed BACK Key",
                    Toast.LENGTH_LONG).show();
    }

    public boolean onKeyUp(int keyCode, KeyEvent event) {
        if (keyCode == KeyEvent.KEYCODE_SEARCH && event.isTracking()
                && !event.isCanceled()) {
            Toast.makeText(this, "Pressed SEARCH Key",
                    Toast.LENGTH_LONG).show();
            return true;
```

```
        }
        return super.onKeyUp(keyCode, event);
    }
}
```

Recipe: Building Menus

A developer can implement three types of menus in Android, and this recipe creates an example of each:

- Options menu—The main menu for an Activity that displays when the MENU key is pressed. It contains an Icon menu and possibly an Expanded menu when the More menu item is selected.
- Context Menu—A floating list of menu items that displays when a view is long pressed.
- Submenu—A floating list of menu items that displays when a menu item is pressed.

The Options menu is created the first time the MENU key is pressed in an activity. This launches the `onCreateOptionsMenu()` method that usually contains Menu methods, such as:

```
menu.add(GROUP_DEFAULT, MENU_ADD, 0, "Add")
     .setIcon(R.drawable.icon);
```

The first argument of the `add()` method labels the group of the menu item. Groups of items can be manipulated together. The second argument is an integer ID that represents the menu item. It is passed to the callback function to determine which menu item was selected. The third argument is the order of the item in the menu. If it is not used, the order falls back to the order the items were added to the `Menu` object. The last argument is the text that displays with the menu item. It can be a `String` or a string resource such as `R.string.myLabel`. This is the only menu that also supports adding icons to the menu choices using the `setIcon()` method.

This method is called only once, and the menu does not need to be built again for the rest of the activity. However, the `onPrepareOptionsMenu()` can be used if any of the menu options need to change during run-time.

When an item from the options menu is clicked, the `onOptionsItemSelected()` method is called. This passes the selected item ID, and a switch statement can be used to determine which option was selected.

For this recipe, the options are to add a note, delete a note, or send a note. These are represented as simple mock functions that increment a counter (`itemNum`), decrement a counter, or show a `Toast` to the screen of the current counter value. To show an example of changing the menu options at run-time, the delete option is available only if a note has already been added in the past. This is done by grouping the delete option in a separate group and hiding the group when the `itemNum` is zero. The activity is shown in Listing 5.2.

Listing 5.2 **src/com/cookbook/building_menus/BuildingMenus.java**

```
package com.cookbook.building_menus;

import android.app.Activity;
import android.os.Bundle;
import android.view.ContextMenu;
import android.view.Menu;
import android.view.MenuItem;
import android.view.SubMenu;
import android.view.View;
import android.view.ContextMenu.ContextMenuInfo;
import android.widget.TextView;
import android.widget.Toast;

public class BuildingMenus extends Activity {
    private final int MENU_ADD=1, MENU_SEND=2, MENU_DEL=3;
    private final int GROUP_DEFAULT=0, GROUP_DEL=1;
    private final int ID_DEFAULT=0;
    private final int ID_TEXT1=1, ID_TEXT2=2, ID_TEXT3=3;
    private String[] choices = {"Press Me", "Try Again", "Change Me"};

    private static int itemNum=0;
    private static TextView bv;

    @Override
    public void onCreate(Bundle savedInstanceState) {
        super.onCreate(savedInstanceState);
        setContentView(R.layout.main);
        bv = (TextView) findViewById(R.id.focus_text);

        registerForContextMenu((View) findViewById(R.id.focus_text));
    }

    @Override
    public boolean onCreateOptionsMenu(Menu menu) {
        menu.add(GROUP_DEFAULT, MENU_ADD, 0, "Add")
            .setIcon(R.drawable.icon); //example of adding icon
        menu.add(GROUP_DEFAULT, MENU_SEND, 0, "Send");
        menu.add(GROUP_DEL, MENU_DEL, 0, "Delete");

        return super.onCreateOptionsMenu(menu);
    }
```

```
@Override
public boolean onPrepareOptionsMenu(Menu menu) {
    if(itemNum>0) {
        menu.setGroupVisible(GROUP_DEL, true);
    } else {
        menu.setGroupVisible(GROUP_DEL, false);
    }
    return super.onPrepareOptionsMenu(menu);
}

@Override
public boolean onOptionsItemSelected(MenuItem item) {
    switch(item.getItemId()) {
    case MENU_ADD:
        create_note();
        return true;
    case MENU_SEND:
        send_note();
        return true;
    case MENU_DEL:
        delete_note();
        return true;
    }
    return super.onOptionsItemSelected(item);
}

@Override
public void onCreateContextMenu(ContextMenu menu, View v,
        ContextMenuInfo menuInfo) {
    super.onCreateContextMenu(menu, v, menuInfo);
    if(v.getId() == R.id.focus_text) {
        SubMenu textMenu = menu.addSubMenu("Change Text");
        textMenu.add(0, ID_TEXT1, 0, choices[0]);
        textMenu.add(0, ID_TEXT2, 0, choices[1]);
        textMenu.add(0, ID_TEXT3, 0, choices[2]);
        menu.add(0, ID_DEFAULT, 0,  "Original Text");
    }
}

@Override
public boolean onContextItemSelected(MenuItem item) {
    switch(item.getItemId()) {
    case ID_DEFAULT:
        bv.setText(R.string.hello);
        return true;
    case ID_TEXT1:
    case ID_TEXT2:
    case ID_TEXT3:
```

```
            bv.setText(choices[item.getItemId()-1]);
            return true;
        }
        return super.onContextItemSelected(item);
    }

    void create_note() { // mock code to create note
        itemNum++;
    }
    void send_note() { // mock code to send note
        Toast.makeText(this, "Item: "+itemNum,
                Toast.LENGTH_SHORT).show();
    }
    void delete_note() { // mock code to delete note
        itemNum—;
    }
}
```

The activity in Listing 5.2 also shows an example of a context menu and submenu. A TextView `focus_text` is added to the layout, as shown in Listing 5.3, and registered for a context menu using the `registerForContextMenu()` function in the `onCreate()` method of the activity.

When the view is pressed and held, the `onCreateContextMenu()` method is called to build the context menu. Here, the `SubMenu` is implemented using the `addSubMenu()` method for the `Menu` instance. The submenu items are specified along with the main menu items, and the `onContextItemSelected()` method is called when an item from either menu is clicked. Here, the recipe shows a change of text based on the menu choice.

Listing 5.3 **res/layout/main.xml**

```
<?xml version="1.0" encoding="utf-8"?>
<LinearLayout xmlns:android="http://schemas.android.com/apk/res/android"
    android:orientation="vertical"
    android:layout_width="fill_parent"
    android:layout_height="fill_parent"
    >
<TextView android:id="@+id/focus_text"
    android:layout_width="fill_parent"
    android:layout_height="wrap_content"
    android:textSize="40sp"
    android:text="@string/hello"
    />
</LinearLayout>
```

Figures 5.1 and 5.2 show how the menus look for the different cases.

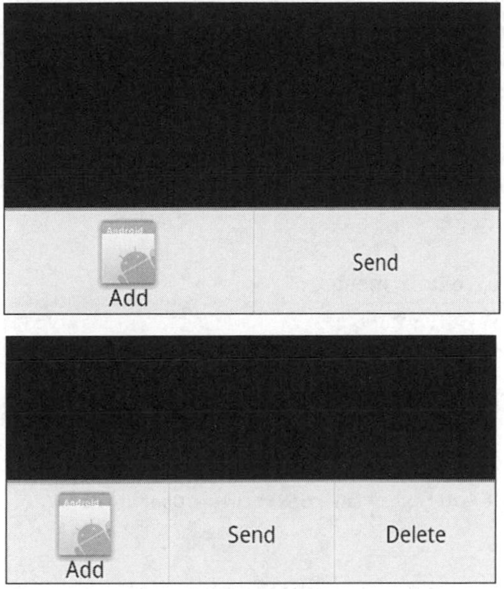

Figure 5.1 Options menu (top) and an added option at run-time (bottom).

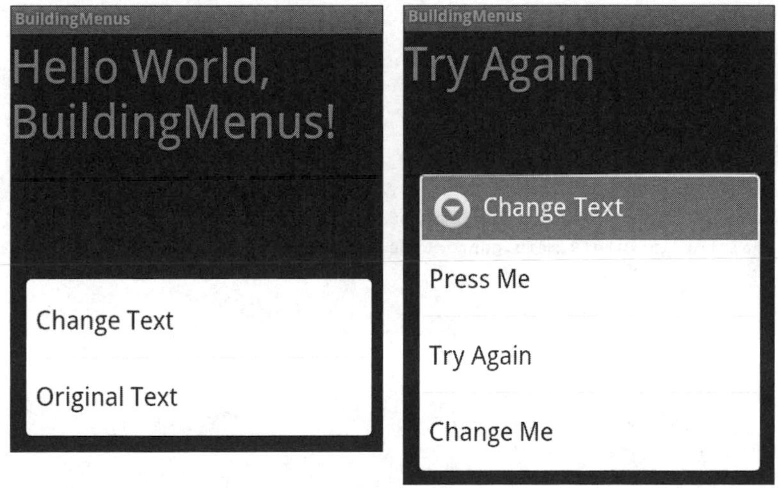

Figure 5.2 The Context menu that displays with a long click on the text (left) and the submenu for the Change Text option that provides three alternate strings for the text view (right).

Recipe: Defining Menus in XML

Menus can also be built in XML and inflated with the appropriate callback method from the previous recipe. This is a useful context for larger menus. Dynamic choices can still be handled in Java.

Menu files are usually kept in the **res/menu/** resources directory. For example, to make the context menu from the previous chapter, just create the XML file with nested menus, as shown in Listing 5.4.

Listing 5.4 **res/menu/context_menu.xml**

```
<?xml version="1.0" encoding="utf-8"?>
<menu xmlns:android="http://schemas.android.com/apk/res/android">
  <item android:id="@+id/submenu" android:title="Change Text">
  <menu xmlns:android="http://schemas.android.com/apk/res/android">
   <item android:id="@+id/text1" android:title="Press Me" />
   <item android:id="@+id/text2" android:title="Try Again" />
   <item android:id="@+id/text3" android:title="Change Me" />
  </menu>
  </item>
  <item android:id="@+id/orig" android:title="Original Text" />
</menu>
```

Then, inflate this XML in the creation of the menu, and reference the IDs from the item selection method. The two methods in Listing 5.2 that would be replaced are shown in Listing 5.5.

Listing 5.5 **Changed Methods in the Main Activity**

```
@Override
    public void onCreateContextMenu(ContextMenu menu, View v,
            ContextMenuInfo menuInfo) {
        super.onCreateContextMenu(menu, v, menuInfo);
        MenuInflater inflater = getMenuInflater();
        inflater.inflate(R.menu.context_menu, menu);
    }
@Override
    public boolean onContextItemSelected(MenuItem item) {
        switch(item.getItemId()) {
        case R.id.orig:
            bv.setText(R.string.hello);
            return true;
        case R.id.text1:
            bv.setText(choices[0]);
            return true;
        case R.id.text2:
            bv.setText(choices[1]);
```

```
            return true;
        case R.id.text3:
            bv.setText(choices[2]);
            return true;
        }
        return super.onContextItemSelected(item);
    }
```

Recipe: Utilizing the SEARCH Key

If an activity in the in-focus application is defined to be searchable, the SEARCH key invokes it. A menu choice or equivalent should always be a redundant way to call the searchable activity to accommodate devices without a SEARCH key. The menu choice simply needs a call to `onSearchRequested()`.

The searchable activity ideally should be declared as `singleTop` launch mode, as discussed in Chapter 2, "Application Basics: Activities and Intents." This enables multiple searches to take place without clogging the stack with multiple instances of the activity. The manifest file would have the following lines:

```
<activity android:name=".SearchDialogExample"
          android:launchMode="singleTop" >
  <intent-filter>
      <action android:name="android.intent.action.SEARCH" />
  </intent-filter>
  <meta-data android:name="android.app.searchable"
             android:resource="@xml/my_search"/>
</activity>
```

Here, the XML file referencing the detail is shown in Listing 5.6.

Listing 5.6 **res/xml/my_search.xml**

```
<?xml version="1.0" encoding="utf-8"?>
<searchable xmlns:android="http://schemas.android.com/apk/res/android"
   android:label="@string/app_name" android:hint="Search MyExample Here" >
</searchable>
```

This recipe provides a search interface. When the application starts, the simplest main activity is shown in Listing 5.7 with a default **main.xml** file.

Listing 5.7 **src/com/cookbook/search_diag/MainActivity.java**

```
package com.cookbook.search_diag;

import android.app.Activity;
import android.os.Bundle;
```

```
public class MainActivity extends Activity {
    @Override
    protected void onCreate(Bundle savedInstanceState) {
        super.onCreate(savedInstanceState);
        setContentView(R.layout.main);
    }
}
```

Then, if the SEARCH key is selected, the searchable activity is activated. The `onCreate()` method checks for whether the intent is an `ACTION_SEARCH`, and if it is, it acts on it. Listing 5.8 shows the main activity, which just displays the query to the screen.

Listing 5.8 **src/com/cookbook/search_diag/SearchDialogExample.java**

```
package com.cookbook.search_diag;

import android.app.Activity;
import android.app.SearchManager;
import android.content.Intent;
import android.os.Bundle;
import android.widget.Toast;

public class SearchDialogExample extends Activity {
    /** Called when the activity is first created. */
    @Override
    public void onCreate(Bundle savedInstanceState) {
        super.onCreate(savedInstanceState);
        setContentView(R.layout.main);
        Intent intent = getIntent();

        if (Intent.ACTION_SEARCH.equals(intent.getAction())) {
          String query = intent.getStringExtra(SearchManager.QUERY);
          Toast.makeText(this, "The QUERY: " + query,
                                        Toast.LENGTH_LONG).show();
        }
    }
}
```

Recipe: Reacting to Touch Events

Any interaction with the screen, be it a touch or a navigated selection using the trackball, is an interaction with the corresponding view at that location. Because the screen layout is a hierarchy of views, as described in Chapter 4, the system starts at the top of this hierarchy and passes the event down the tree until it is handled by a view. Some events, if not consumed, can continue to pass down the tree after being handled.

Listing 5.9 shows a button called `ex_button` that handles both a click and a long click (press and hold) by setting two event listeners. When the event occurs, the corresponding callback method is called and displays a `Toast` to the screen to show the method was triggered.

Listing 5.9 **src/com/cookbook/touch_examples/TouchExamples.java**

```
package com.cookbook.touch_examples;

import android.app.Activity;
import android.os.Bundle;
import android.view.View;
import android.view.View.OnClickListener;
import android.view.View.OnLongClickListener;
import android.widget.Button;
import android.widget.Toast;

public class TouchExamples extends Activity {
    @Override
    public void onCreate(Bundle savedInstanceState) {
        super.onCreate(savedInstanceState);
        setContentView(R.layout.main);
        Button ex = (Button) findViewById(R.id.ex_button);

        ex.setOnClickListener(new OnClickListener() {
            public void onClick(View v) {
                Toast.makeText(TouchExamples.this, "Click",
                        Toast.LENGTH_SHORT).show();
            }
        });
        ex.setOnLongClickListener(new OnLongClickListener() {
            public boolean onLongClick(View v) {
                Toast.makeText(TouchExamples.this, "LONG Click",
                        Toast.LENGTH_SHORT).show();
                return true;
            }
        });
    }
}
```

The layout providing the button is given in Listing 5.10.

Listing 5.10 **res/layout/main.xml**

```
<?xml version="1.0" encoding="utf-8"?>
<LinearLayout
    xmlns:android="http://schemas.android.com/apk/res/android"
```

```
    android:orientation="vertical"
    android:layout_width="fill_parent"
    android:layout_height="fill_parent">
    <Button android:id="@+id/ex_button"
        android:text="Press Me"
        android:layout_width="wrap_content"
        android:layout_height="wrap_content" />
</LinearLayout>
```

For compactness, this callback method is defined in place in Listing 5.9, but it can also be defined explicitly for readability and reusability:

```
View.OnClickListener myTouchMethod = new View.OnClickListener() {
    public void onClick(View v) {
        //insert relevant action here
    }
};
ex.setOnClickListener(myTouchMethod);
```

Another way is to have the activity implement the `OnClickListener` interface. Then, the method is at the activity level and avoids an extra class load:

```
public class TouchExamples extends Activity implements OnClickListener {
    @Override
    public void onCreate(Bundle savedInstanceState) {
        super.onCreate(savedInstanceState);
        setContentView(R.layout.main);
        Button ex = (Button) findViewById(R.id.ex_button);
        ex.setOnClickListener(this);
    }

    public void onClick(View v) {
        if(v.getId() == R.id.directory_button) {
            // insert relevant action here
        }
    }
}
```

This implementation of the `onClick()` method at the activity level helps to show how a parent view can handle touch events for multiple children.

Recipe: Listening for Fling Gestures

As discussed in the beginning of the chapter, each view has an `onTouchEvent()` method associated with it. In this recipe, it is overridden with a gesture detector that sets a gesture listener. The possible gestures in the `OnGestureListener` interface are

- `onDown()`—Notifies when a tap down event occurs
- `onFling()`—Notifies when a tap down, movement, and matching up event occurs
- `onLongPress()`—Notifies when a long press occurs
- `onScroll()`—Notifies when a scroll occurs
- `onShowPress()`—Notifies when a tap down occurs before any movement or release
- `onSingleTapUp()`—Notifies when a tap up event occurs

When only a subset of gestures are needed, the `SimpleOnGestureListener` class can be extended instead. It returns `false` for any of the previous methods not explicitly implemented.

A fling consists of two events: a touch down (the first `MotionEvent`) and a release (the second `MotionEvent`). Each motion event has a specified location on the screen given by an (x,y) coordinate pair, where x is the horizontal axis and y is the vertical axis. The (x,y) velocity of the event is also provided.

Listing 5.11 shows an activity that implements the `onFling()` method. When the movement is large enough (here, defined as 60 pixels), the event is consumed and appends the statement describing the event to the screen.

Listing 5.11 src/com/cookbook/fling_ex/FlingExample.java

```
package com.cookbook.fling_ex;

import android.app.Activity;
import android.os.Bundle;
import android.view.GestureDetector;
import android.view.MotionEvent;
import android.view.GestureDetector.SimpleOnGestureListener;
import android.widget.TextView;

public class FlingExample extends Activity {
    private static final int LARGE_MOVE = 60;
    private GestureDetector gestureDetector;
    TextView tv;

    @Override
    public void onCreate(Bundle savedInstanceState) {
        super.onCreate(savedInstanceState);
        setContentView(R.layout.main);
        tv = (TextView) findViewById(R.id.text_result);

        gestureDetector = new GestureDetector(this,
                new SimpleOnGestureListener() {
            @Override
            public boolean onFling(MotionEvent e1, MotionEvent e2,
                    float velocityX, float velocityY) {
```

```
            if (e1.getY() - e2.getY() > LARGE_MOVE) {
                tv.append("\nFling Up with velocity " + velocityY);
                return true;

            } else if (e2.getY() - e1.getY() > LARGE_MOVE) {
                tv.append("\nFling Down with velocity " + velocityY);
                return true;

            } else if (e1.getX() - e2.getX() > LARGE_MOVE) {
                tv.append("\nFling Left with velocity " + velocityX);
                return true;

            } else if (e2.getX() - e1.getX() > LARGE_MOVE) {
                tv.append("\nFling Right with velocity " + velocityX);
                return true;
            }

            return false;
        } });
    }

    @Override
    public boolean onTouchEvent(MotionEvent event) {
        return gestureDetector.onTouchEvent(event);
    }
}
```

The TextView that contains the descriptive text in the previous activity is defined in the main XML layout shown in Listing 5.12.

Listing 5.12 **res/layout/main.xml**

```
<?xml version="1.0" encoding="utf-8"?>
<LinearLayout
    xmlns:android="http://schemas.android.com/apk/res/android"
    android:orientation="vertical"
    android:layout_width="fill_parent"
    android:layout_height="fill_parent">
    <TextView android:id="@+id/text_result"
    android:layout_width="fill_parent"
    android:layout_height="fill_parent"
    android:textSize="16sp"
    android:text="Fling right, left, up, or down\n" />
</LinearLayout>
```

Recipe: Using Multitouch

A multitouch event is when more than one pointer (such as a finger) touches the screen at the same time. This is identified by using a touch listener OnTouchListener, which receives multiple types of motion events:

- `ACTION_DOWN`—A press gesture has started with a primary pointer (finger).
- `ACTION_POINTER_DOWN`—A secondary pointer (finger) has gone down.
- `ACTION_MOVE`—A change in press location has changed during a press gesture.
- `ACTION_POINTER_UP`—A secondary pointer was released.
- `ACTION_UP`—A primary pointer was released, and the press gesture has completed.

This recipe displays an image to the screen and allows the multitouch events to zoom the image in or out. It also checks for single pointer events to drag the picture around the screen. This is shown in the activity in Listing 5.13. First, the activity implements the `OnTouchListener` that is set in the `onCreate()` method. When a touch event occurs, the `onTouch()` method checks the motion event and acts as follows:

- If a first pointer touches the screen, the touch state is declared to be a drag motion, and the touch-down position and `Matrix` are saved.
- If a second pointer touches the screen when the first pointer is still down, the distance between the two touch-down positions is calculated. As long as it is larger than some threshold (50 pixels here), the touch state is declared to be a zoom motion, and the distance and mid-point of the two events, as well as the `Matrix`, are saved.
- If a move occurs, the figure is translated for a single touch-down event and scaled for a multitouch event.
- If a pointer goes up, the touch state is declared to be no motion.

Listing 5.13 **src/com/cookbook/multitouch/MultiTouch.java**

```
package com.cookbook.multitouch;

import android.app.Activity;
import android.graphics.Matrix;
import android.os.Bundle;
import android.util.FloatMath;

import android.view.MotionEvent;
import android.view.View;
import android.view.View.OnTouchListener;
import android.widget.ImageView;
```

```
public class MultiTouch extends Activity implements OnTouchListener {
    // Matrix instances to move and zoom image
    Matrix matrix = new Matrix();
    Matrix eventMatrix = new Matrix();

    // possible touch states
    final static int NONE = 0;
    final static int DRAG = 1;
    final static int ZOOM = 2;
    int touchState = NONE;

    @Override
    public void onCreate(Bundle savedInstanceState) {
        super.onCreate(savedInstanceState);
        setContentView(R.layout.main);
        ImageView view = (ImageView) findViewById(R.id.imageView);
        view.setOnTouchListener(this);
    }

    final static float MIN_DIST = 50;
    static float eventDistance = 0;
    static float centerX =0, centerY = 0;
    @Override
    public boolean onTouch(View v, MotionEvent event) {
        ImageView view = (ImageView) v;

        switch (event.getAction() & MotionEvent.ACTION_MASK) {
        case MotionEvent.ACTION_DOWN:
            //primary touch event starts: remember touch down location
            touchState = DRAG;
            centerX = event.getX(0);
            centerY = event.getY(0);
            eventMatrix.set(matrix);
            break;

        case MotionEvent.ACTION_POINTER_DOWN:
            //secondary touch event starts: remember distance and center
            eventDistance = calcDistance(event);
            calcMidpoint(centerX, centerY, event);
            if (eventDistance > MIN_DIST) {
                eventMatrix.set(matrix);

                touchState = ZOOM;
            }
            break;
```

```
        case MotionEvent.ACTION_MOVE:
            if (touchState == DRAG) {
                //single finger drag, translate accordingly
                matrix.set(eventMatrix);
                matrix.setTranslate(event.getX(0) - centerX,
                                    event.getY(0) - centerY);

            } else if (touchState == ZOOM) {
                //multi-finger zoom, scale accordingly around center
                float dist = calcDistance(event);

                if (dist > MIN_DIST) {
                    matrix.set(eventMatrix);
                    float scale = dist / eventDistance;

                    matrix.postScale(scale, scale, centerX, centerY);
                }
            }

            // Perform the transformation
            view.setImageMatrix(matrix);
            break;

        case MotionEvent.ACTION_UP:
        case MotionEvent.ACTION_POINTER_UP:
            touchState = NONE;
            break;
        }

        return true;
    }

    private float calcDistance(MotionEvent event) {
        float x = event.getX(0) - event.getX(1);
        float y = event.getY(0) - event.getY(1);
        return FloatMath.sqrt(x * x + y * y);
    }

    private void calcMidpoint(float centerX, float centerY,
                              MotionEvent event) {
        centerX = (event.getX(0) + event.getX(1))/2;
        centerY = (event.getY(0) + event.getY(1))/2;
    }
}
```

The layout that specifies a picture to zoom is shown in Listing 5.14. For this recipe, it is taken as the **icon.png**, which is automatically created in Eclipse; however, it can be replaced by any picture.

Listing 5.14 **res/layout/main.xml**

```
<?xml version="1.0" encoding="utf-8"?>
<FrameLayout
      xmlns:android="http://schemas.android.com/apk/res/android"
      android:layout_width="fill_parent"
      android:layout_height="fill_parent" >
   <ImageView android:id="@+id/imageView"
         android:layout_width="fill_parent"
         android:layout_height="fill_parent"
         android:src="@drawable/icon"
         android:scaleType="matrix" >
   </ImageView>
</FrameLayout>
```

Advanced User Interface Libraries

Some user interface features require complex algorithmic computations. Optimizing this for an embedded system can sometimes be challenging and time-consuming. It is in a developer's best interest to leverage any available UI libraries. The following two recipes provide some illustrative examples to use as a starting point.

Recipe: Using Gestures

A gesture is a hand-drawn shape on a touch screen. The `android.gesture` package provides libraries to recognize and handle these in a simple way. First, every SDK has a sample program that can be used to build a collection of gestures in **platforms/android-2.0/samples/GestureBuilder/**. The Gesture Builder project can be imported and run on an Android device. It produces a file called **/sdcard/gestures,** which can be copied off of the device and used as a raw resource for this recipe.

As an example, a file of handwritten numbers can be generated as shown in Figure 5.3. Multiple gestures can have the same name, so providing different examples of the same gesture is useful to improve pattern recognition.

After this file is created for all numbers from 0 to 9 in all variants of interest, it can be copied to **res/raw/numbers,** for example. The layout is shown in Listing 5.15, and the main activity is shown in Listing 5.16. In the activity, the `GestureLibrary` is initialized with this raw resource.

This recipe adds a `GestureOverlayView` on top of the screen and implements an `OnGesturePerformedListener`. When a gesture is drawn, the gesture is passed to the `onGesturePerformed()` method, which compares it with all the gestures in the library and returns an ordered list of predictions starting with the most likely. Each prediction has the name as defined in the library and the score for how correlated the gesture is to the input gesture. As long as the first entry has a score greater than one, it is generally a match.

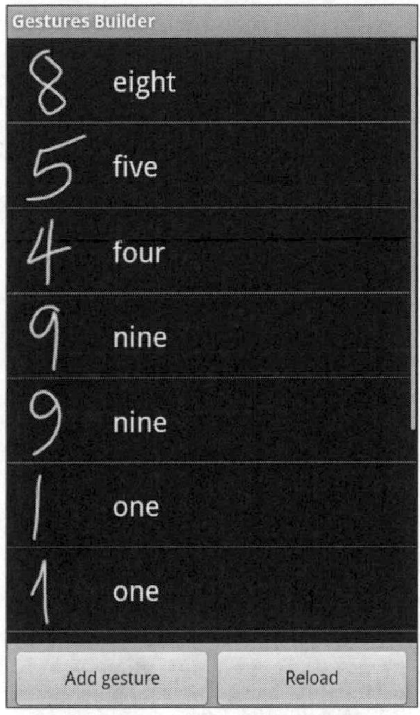

Figure 5.3 The Gesture Builder application, which comes with the Android SDK, can be used to create a gesture library.

Listing 5.15 **res/layout/main.xml**

```
<?xml version="1.0" encoding="utf-8"?>
<LinearLayout xmlns:android="http://schemas.android.com/apk/res/android"
    android:orientation="vertical"
    android:layout_width="fill_parent"
    android:layout_height="fill_parent"
    >
<TextView
    android:layout_width="fill_parent"
    android:layout_height="wrap_content"
    android:gravity="center_horizontal" android:textSize="20sp"
    android:text="Draw a number"
    android:layout_margin="10dip"/>
```

```
<android.gesture.GestureOverlayView
    android:id="@+id/gestures"
    android:layout_width="fill_parent"
    android:layout_height="0dip"
    android:layout_weight="1.0" />

<TextView android:id="@+id/prediction"
    android:layout_width="fill_parent"
    android:layout_height="wrap_content"
    android:gravity="center_horizontal" android:textSize="20sp"
    android:text=""
    android:layout_margin="10dip"/>
</LinearLayout>
```

For illustration, this recipe compiles all the predictions in a `String` and displays them on the screen. An example output is shown in Figure 5.4. This shows that even though a visual match is not complete, the partial number can match a library number well.

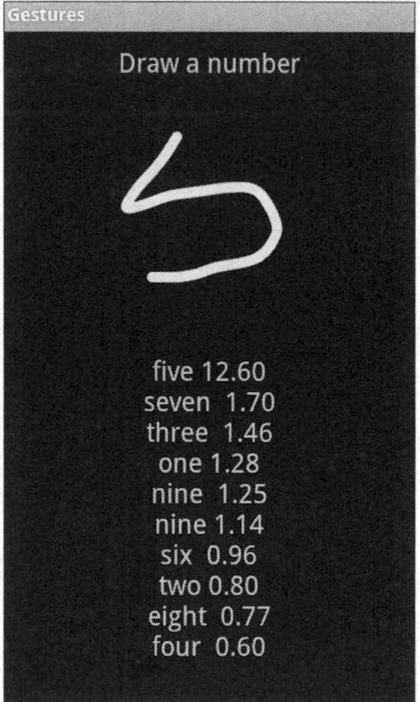

Figure 5.4 The gesture recognition example that shows prediction scores.

Listing 5.16 **src/com/cookbook/gestures/Gestures.java**

```
package com.cookbook.gestures;

import java.text.DecimalFormat;
import java.text.NumberFormat;
import java.util.ArrayList;

import android.app.Activity;
import android.gesture.Gesture;
import android.gesture.GestureLibraries;
import android.gesture.GestureLibrary;
import android.gesture.GestureOverlayView;
import android.gesture.Prediction;
import android.gesture.GestureOverlayView.OnGesturePerformedListener;
import android.os.Bundle;
import android.widget.TextView;

public class Gestures extends Activity
                      implements OnGesturePerformedListener {
    private GestureLibrary mLibrary;
    private TextView tv;

    @Override
    public void onCreate(Bundle savedInstanceState) {
        super.onCreate(savedInstanceState);
        setContentView(R.layout.main);
        tv = (TextView) findViewById(R.id.prediction);

        mLibrary = GestureLibraries.fromRawResource(this, R.raw.numbers);
        if (!mLibrary.load()) finish();

        GestureOverlayView gestures =
                         (GestureOverlayView) findViewById(R.id.gestures);
        gestures.addOnGesturePerformedListener(this);
    }

    public void onGesturePerformed(GestureOverlayView overlay,
                                   Gesture gesture) {
        ArrayList<Prediction> predictions = mLibrary.recognize(gesture);
        String predList = "";
        NumberFormat formatter = new DecimalFormat("#0.00");
        for(int i=0; i<predictions.size(); i++) {
            Prediction prediction = predictions.get(i);
            predList = predList + prediction.name + " "
                       + formatter.format(prediction.score) + "\n";
```

```
        }
        tv.setText(predList);
    }
}
```

Recipe: Drawing 3D Images

Android supports the Open Graphics Library for Embedded Systems (OpenGL ES). This recipe, based on an Android API Demo, shows how to create a three-dimensional pyramid shape using this library and have it bounce around the screen and spin as it reflects off the edges. The main activity requires two separate support classes: one to define the shape shown in Listing 5.17 and one to render the shape shown in Listing 5.18.

Listing 5.17 **src/com/cookbook/open_gl/Pyramid.java**

```
package com.cookbook.open_gl;

import java.nio.ByteBuffer;
import java.nio.ByteOrder;
import java.nio.IntBuffer;

import javax.microedition.khronos.opengles.GL10;

class Pyramid {
    public Pyramid() {
        int one = 0x10000;
        /* square base and point top to make a pyramid */
        int vertices[] = {
                -one, -one, -one,
                -one,  one, -one,
                one,  one,  -one,
                one,  -one,  -one,
                0, 0, one
        };

        /* purple fading to white at the top */
        int colors[] = {
                one, 0, one, one,
                one, 0, one, one,
                one, 0, one, one,
                one, 0, one, one,
                one, one, one, one
        };

        /* triangles of the vertices above to build the shape */
        byte indices[] = {
```

```
            0, 1, 2,  0, 2, 3, //square base
            0, 3, 4, // side 1
            0, 4, 1, // side 2
            1, 4, 2, // side 3
            2, 4, 3  // side 4
        };

        // Buffers to be passed to gl*Pointer() functions
        ByteBuffer vbb = ByteBuffer.allocateDirect(vertices.length*4);
        vbb.order(ByteOrder.nativeOrder());
        mVertexBuffer = vbb.asIntBuffer();
        mVertexBuffer.put(vertices);
        mVertexBuffer.position(0);

        ByteBuffer cbb = ByteBuffer.allocateDirect(colors.length*4);
        cbb.order(ByteOrder.nativeOrder());
        mColorBuffer = cbb.asIntBuffer();
        mColorBuffer.put(colors);
        mColorBuffer.position(0);

        mIndexBuffer = ByteBuffer.allocateDirect(indices.length);
        mIndexBuffer.put(indices);
        mIndexBuffer.position(0);
    }

    public void draw(GL10 gl) {
        gl.glFrontFace(GL10.GL_CW);
        gl.glVertexPointer(3, GL10.GL_FIXED, 0, mVertexBuffer);
        gl.glColorPointer(4, GL10.GL_FIXED, 0, mColorBuffer);
        gl.glDrawElements(GL10.GL_TRIANGLES, 18, GL10.GL_UNSIGNED_BYTE,
                          mIndexBuffer);
    }

    private IntBuffer   mVertexBuffer;
    private IntBuffer   mColorBuffer;
    private ByteBuffer  mIndexBuffer;
}
```

Note the pyramid has five vertices: four in a square base and one as the raised pointy top. It is important the vertices are in an order that can be traversed by a line across the figure (not just randomly listed). The center of the shape is at the origin `(0, 0, 0)`.

The five colors in RGBA form correspond with the vertices; the base vertices are defined as purple and the top vertex as white. The library gradates the colors to fill in the shape. Different colors or shading help provide a three-dimensional look.

The main `draw()` method is defined for triangle elements. The square base can be made of two triangles and each upper side is a triangle, which leads to 6 total triangles or 18 indices. The pyramid is shown in two different perspectives as it bounces around in Figure 5.5.

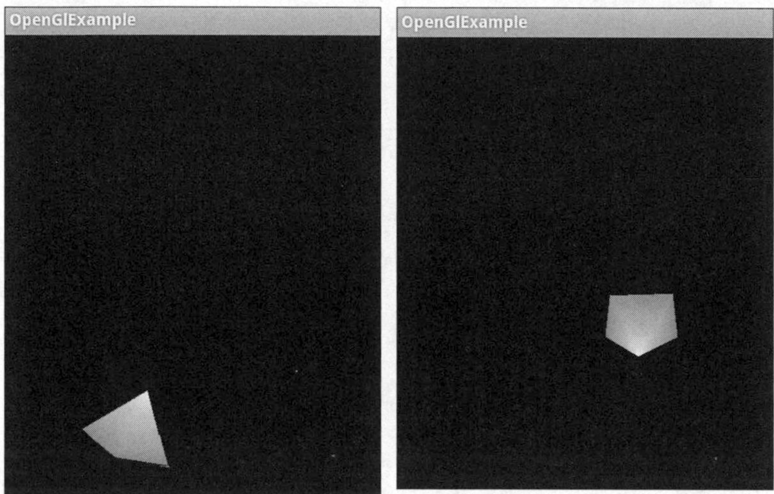

Figure 5.5 The rotating, bouncing pyramid created with OpenGL ES.

Then a separate class can be created to extend `GLSurfaceView.Renderer` to render this pyramid using the OpenGL ES library, as shown in Listing 5.18. Three methods need to be implemented:

- `onSurfaceCreated()`—One-time initialization of the OpenGL framework
- `onSurfaceChanged()`—Sets the projection at start-up or when the viewport is resized
- `onDrawFrame()`—Draws the graphic image every frame

Listing 5.18 **src/com/cookbook/open_gl/PyramidRenderer.java**

```
package com.cookbook.open_gl;

import javax.microedition.khronos.egl.EGLConfig;
import javax.microedition.khronos.opengles.GL10;

import android.opengl.GLSurfaceView;
```

```
/**
 * Render a tumbling Pyramid
 */

class PyramidRenderer implements GLSurfaceView.Renderer {
    public PyramidRenderer(boolean useTranslucentBackground) {
        mTranslucentBackground = useTranslucentBackground;
        mPyramid = new Pyramid();
    }

    public void onDrawFrame(GL10 gl) {
        /* clear the screen */
        gl.glClear(GL10.GL_COLOR_BUFFER_BIT | GL10.GL_DEPTH_BUFFER_BIT);

        /* draw a pyramid rotating */
        gl.glMatrixMode(GL10.GL_MODELVIEW);
        gl.glLoadIdentity();
        gl.glTranslatef(mCenter[0], mCenter[1], mCenter[2]);
        gl.glRotatef(mAngle,        0, 1, 0);
        gl.glRotatef(mAngle*0.25f,  1, 0, 0);

        gl.glEnableClientState(GL10.GL_VERTEX_ARRAY);
        gl.glEnableClientState(GL10.GL_COLOR_ARRAY);
        mPyramid.draw(gl);

        mAngle += mAngleDelta;

        /* draw it bouncing off the walls */
        mCenter[0] += mVel[0];
        mCenter[1] += mVel[1];

        if(Math.abs(mCenter[0])>4.0f) {
            mVel[0] = -mVel[0];
            mAngleDelta=(float) (5*(0.5-Math.random()));
        }
        if(Math.abs(mCenter[1])>6.0f) {
            mVel[1] = -mVel[1];
            mAngleDelta=(float) (5*(0.5-Math.random()));
        }
    }

    public void onSurfaceChanged(GL10 gl, int width, int height) {
        gl.glViewport(0, 0, width, height);

        /* Set a new projection when the viewport is resized */
        float ratio = (float) width / height;
```

```
        gl.glMatrixMode(GL10.GL_PROJECTION);
        gl.glLoadIdentity();
        gl.glFrustumf(-ratio, ratio, -1, 1, 1, 20);
    }

    public void onSurfaceCreated(GL10 gl, EGLConfig config) {
        gl.glDisable(GL10.GL_DITHER);

        /* one-time OpenGL initialization */
        gl.glHint(GL10.GL_PERSPECTIVE_CORRECTION_HINT,
                GL10.GL_FASTEST);

        if (mTranslucentBackground) {
            gl.glClearColor(0,0,0,0);
        } else {
            gl.glClearColor(1,1,1,1);
        }
        gl.glEnable(GL10.GL_CULL_FACE);
        gl.glShadeModel(GL10.GL_SMOOTH);
        gl.glEnable(GL10.GL_DEPTH_TEST);
    }
    private boolean mTranslucentBackground;
    private Pyramid mPyramid;
    private float mAngle, mAngleDelta=0;
    private float mCenter[]={0,0,-10};
    private float mVel[]={0.025f, 0.03535227f, 0f};
}
```

The dynamics of the bouncing ball are captured in the `onDrawFrame()` method. The screen is cleared for the new image, and then the pyramid center is set to `mCenter[]`. The screen is defined as the origin, so the starting point of `(0, 0, -10)` sets the shape back from right up against the screen. At each update, the shape is rotated by `mAngleDelta` and translates by `mVel[]`. The `mVel` in the x- and y-direction are set differently enough to provide a nice diversity of bouncing around the walls. When the shape reaches the edge of the screen, the velocity sign is switched to have it bounce back.

Finally, the main activity must set the content view to the OpenGL ES object, as shown in Listing 5.19. The shape movement can be paused and resumed along with the activity.

Listing 5.19 **src/com/cookbook/open_gl/OpenGlExample.java**

```
package com.cookbook.open_gl;

import android.app.Activity;
import android.opengl.GLSurfaceView;
import android.os.Bundle;
```

```
/* Wrapper activity demonstrating the use of GLSurfaceView, a view
 * that uses OpenGL drawing into a dedicated surface. */
public class OpenGlExample extends Activity {
    @Override
    protected void onCreate(Bundle savedInstanceState) {
        super.onCreate(savedInstanceState);

        // Set our Preview view as the Activity content
        mGLSurfaceView = new GLSurfaceView(this);
        mGLSurfaceView.setRenderer(new PyramidRenderer(true));
        setContentView(mGLSurfaceView);
    }

    @Override
    protected void onResume() {
        super.onResume();
        mGLSurfaceView.onResume();
    }

    @Override
    protected void onPause() {
        super.onPause();
        mGLSurfaceView.onPause();
    }

    private GLSurfaceView mGLSurfaceView;
}
```

6

Multimedia Techniques

The Android platform provides comprehensive multimedia functionality. This chapter introduces techniques to manipulate images, record and play back audio, and record and play back video. Most decoders are supported by Android for reading multimedia, but only a subset of encoders is available for creating multimedia. Media framework support in Android 2.2 is summarized in Table 6.1. In particular, note the absence of a lossless compressed audio format. This will change in future releases.

Table 6.1 **The Supported Media Types in Android 2.2 for Reading and Writing**

Media Type	Compression	Android Native Codec Support	Formats
Image	None (raw)	View	BMP
	Lossless	View	GIF, PNG
	Lossy	Save/View	JPEG
Audio (Music)	None (raw)	Record/Play	PCM
	None (raw)	Play	WAVE
	Lossless	No support	For example, FLAC
	Lossy	Play	MP3, MP4, AAC, HE-AACv1, HE-AACv2, Ogg Vorbis
	Midi	Play	MID, XMF, RTTTL, RTX, OTA, IMY
Audio (Speech)	Lossy	Record/Play	AMR-NB
	Lossy	Play	AMR-WB
Video	Nearly Lossless	Play	H.264
	Lossy	Record/Play	H.263, MPEG-4 SP

An application that records any type of media requires setting the appropriate permission in the AndroidManifest XML file (one or both of the following):

```
<uses-permission android:name="android.permission.RECORD_AUDIO"/>
<uses-permission android:name="android.permission.RECORD_VIDEO"/>
```

Images

Images local to an application are usually put in the **res/drawable/** directory, as discussed in Chapter 4, "User Interface Layout," and are packaged with the application. They can be accessed with the appropriate resource identifier, such as `R.drawable.my_picture`. Images on the Android device filesystem can be accessed using the normal Java classes, such as an `InputStream`. However, the preferred method in Android to read an image into memory for manipulation is to use the built-in class `BitmapFactory`.

`BitmapFactory` creates `Bitmap` objects from files, streams, or byte-arrays. For the two previous examples:

```
Bitmap myBitmap1 = BitmapFactory.decodeResource(getResources(),
                                                  R.drawable.my_picture);
Bitmap myBitmap2 = BitmapFactory.decodeFile(filePath);
```

After the image is in memory, it can be manipulated using the bitmap methods, such as `getPixel()` and `setPixel()`. However, most images are too large to manipulate full scale on an embedded device. Instead, consider subsampling the image:

```
Bitmap bm = Bitmap.createScaledBitmap(myBitmap2, 480, 320, false);
```

This avoids `OutOfMemory` run-time errors.

Recipe: Loading an Image for Manipulation

This recipe shows an example of an image cut into four pieces and scrambled before being displayed to the screen. It also shows how to create a selectable list of images.

When a picture is taken on the device, it is put in the **DCIM/Camera/** directory, which is used as an example image directory in this recipe. The image directory is passed to the `ListFiles` activity, which lists all files and returns the one chosen by the user.

The chosen picture is then loaded into memory for manipulation. If the file is too large, it can be subsampled as it is loaded to save memory; just replace the single bolded statement in `onActivityResult` with the following:

```
BitmapFactory.Options options = new BitmapFactory.Options();
options.inSampleSize = 4;
Bitmap ImageToChange= BitmapFactory.decodeFile(tmp, options);
```

An `inSampleSize` of four creates an image 1/16th the size of the original (four times smaller in each of the pixel dimensions). The limit can be adaptive based on the original image size.

Another method to save memory is to resize the bitmap in memory before manipulations. This is done using the `createScaledBitmap()` method, as shown in this recipe. Listing 6.1 shows the main activity.

Listing 6.1 **src/com/cookbook/image_manip/ImageManipulation.java**

```
package com.cookbook.image_manip;

import android.app.Activity;
import android.content.Intent;
import android.graphics.Bitmap;
import android.graphics.BitmapFactory;
import android.os.Bundle;
import android.os.Environment;
import android.widget.ImageView;

public class ImageManipulation extends Activity {
    static final String CAMERA_PIC_DIR = "/DCIM/Camera/";
    ImageView iv;

    @Override
    public void onCreate(Bundle savedInstanceState) {
        super.onCreate(savedInstanceState);
        setContentView(R.layout.main);
        iv = (ImageView) findViewById(R.id.my_image);

        String ImageDir = Environment.getExternalStorageDirectory()
                        .getAbsolutePath() + CAMERA_PIC_DIR;

        Intent i = new Intent(this, ListFiles.class);
        i.putExtra("directory", ImageDir);
        startActivityForResult(i,0);
    }

    @Override
    protected void onActivityResult(int requestCode,
            int resultCode, Intent data) {
        super.onActivityResult(requestCode, resultCode, data);
        if(requestCode == 0 && resultCode==RESULT_OK) {
            String tmp = data.getExtras().getString("clickedFile");
            Bitmap ImageToChange= BitmapFactory.decodeFile(tmp);
            process_image(ImageToChange);
        }
    }

    void process_image(Bitmap image) {
        Bitmap bm = Bitmap.createScaledBitmap(image, 480, 320, false);
```

```
        int width = bm.getWidth();
        int height = bm.getHeight();
        int x= width>>1;
        int y= height>>1;
        int[] pixels1 = new int[(width*height)];
        int[] pixels2 = new int[(width*height)];
        int[] pixels3 = new int[(width*height)];
        int[] pixels4 = new int[(width*height)];
        bm.getPixels(pixels1, 0, width, 0, 0, width>>1, height>>1);
        bm.getPixels(pixels2, 0, width, x, 0, width>>1, height>>1);
        bm.getPixels(pixels3, 0, width, 0, y, width>>1, height>>1);
        bm.getPixels(pixels4, 0, width, x, y, width>>1, height>>1);
        if(bm.isMutable()) {
            bm.setPixels(pixels2, 0, width, 0, 0, width>>1, height>>1);
            bm.setPixels(pixels4, 0, width, x, 0, width>>1, height>>1);
            bm.setPixels(pixels1, 0, width, 0, y, width>>1, height>>1);
            bm.setPixels(pixels3, 0, width, x, y, width>>1, height>>1);
        }
        iv.setImageBitmap(bm);
    }
}
```

The associated main layout is shown in Listing 6.2.

Listing 6.2 **res/layout/main.xml**

```
<?xml version="1.0" encoding="utf-8"?>
<LinearLayout
    xmlns:android="http://schemas.android.com/apk/res/android"
    android:orientation="vertical"
    android:layout_width="fill_parent"
    android:layout_height="fill_parent">
    <TextView android:layout_width="fill_parent"
        android:layout_height="wrap_content"
        android:textSize="30sp"
        android:text="Scrambled Picture" />
    <ImageView android:id="@+id/my_image"
        android:layout_width="wrap_content"
        android:layout_height="wrap_content" />
</LinearLayout>
```

The secondary activity to list the files in a given directory is shown in Listing 6.3. A `File` object is created based on the directory `String` passed to the activity. If it is a directory, the files are sorted into reverse chronological order by specifying a new `compare()` method based on the `lastModified()` flag of the files.

If instead an alphabetical list is desired, the `sort()` method can be used. (This is in the `ListFiles` activity, too, but commented out.) The list is then built and displayed on the screen using a separate layout file `R.layout.file_row`, which is shown in Listing 6.4.

Listing 6.3 **src/com/cookbook/image_manip/ListFiles.java**

```
package com.cookbook.image_manip;

import java.io.File;
import java.util.ArrayList;
import java.util.Arrays;
import java.util.Comparator;
import java.util.List;

import android.app.ListActivity;
import android.content.Intent;
import android.os.Bundle;
import android.view.View;
import android.widget.ArrayAdapter;
import android.widget.ListView;

public class ListFiles extends ListActivity {
    private List<String> directoryEntries = new ArrayList<String>();

    @Override
    public void onCreate(Bundle savedInstanceState) {
        super.onCreate(savedInstanceState);
        Intent i = getIntent();
        File directory = new File(i.getStringExtra("directory"));

        if (directory.isDirectory()){
            File[] files = directory.listFiles();

            //sort in descending date order
            Arrays.sort(files, new Comparator<File>(){
                public int compare(File f1, File f2) {
                    return -Long.valueOf(f1.lastModified())
                            .compareTo(f2.lastModified());
                }
            });

            //fill list with files
            this.directoryEntries.clear();
            for (File file : files){
                this.directoryEntries.add(file.getPath());
            }
```

```
            ArrayAdapter<String> directoryList
                = new ArrayAdapter<String>(this,
                    R.layout.file_row, this.directoryEntries);

            //alphabetize entries
            //directoryList.sort(null);
            this.setListAdapter(directoryList);
        }
    }

    @Override
    protected void onListItemClick(ListView l, View v, int pos, long id) {
        File clickedFile = new File(this.directoryEntries.get(pos));
        Intent i = getIntent();
        i.putExtra("clickedFile", clickedFile.toString());
        setResult(RESULT_OK, i);
        finish();
    }
}
```

The associated layout file for the `ListFiles` activity is shown in Listing 6.4. The AndroidManifest XML file must declare both the activities, as shown in Listing 6.5. An example of the output is shown in Figure 6.1.

Listing 6.4 **res/layout/file_row.xml**

```
<?xml version="1.0" encoding="utf-8"?>
<TextView
    xmlns:android="http://schemas.android.com/apk/res/android"
    android:layout_width="fill_parent"
    android:layout_height="wrap_content"
    android:textSize="20sp"
    android:padding="3pt"
/>
```

Listing 6.5 **AndroidManifest.xml**

```
<?xml version="1.0" encoding="utf-8"?>
<manifest xmlns:android="http://schemas.android.com/apk/res/android"
      package="com.cookbook.image_manip"
      android:versionCode="1" android:versionName="1.0">
    <application android:icon="@drawable/icon"
                 android:label="@string/app_name">
        <activity android:name=".ImageManipulation"
```

```
                android:label="@string/app_name">
            <intent-filter>
              <action android:name="android.intent.action.MAIN" />
              <category android:name="android.intent.category.LAUNCHER" />
            </intent-filter>
        </activity>
         <activity android:name=".ListFiles"
             android:screenOrientation="portrait"
             android:label="Choose a File">
            <intent-filter>
              <action android:name="android.intent.action.VIEW" />
              <category android:name="android.intent.category.DEFAULT" />
            </intent-filter>
        </activity>
    </application>
    <uses-sdk android:minSdkVersion="5" />
</manifest>
```

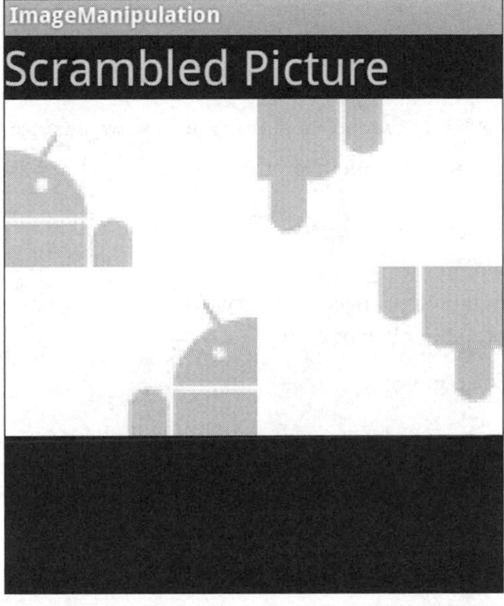

Figure 6.1 Example of the Android image getting scrambled.

Audio

There are two distinct frameworks for recording and playing audio. The choice on which to use depends on the application:

- MediaPlayer/MediaRecorder—This is the standard method to manipulate audio, but must be file- or stream-based data. Creates its own thread for processing. `SoundPool` utilizes this framework.
- AudioTrack/AudioRecorder—Provides direct access to raw audio. Useful to manipulate audio in memory, write to the buffer while already playing, or any other usage that does not require a file or stream. It does not create its own thread for processing.

These methods are shown in the following section in various recipes.

Recipe: Choosing and Playing Back Audio Files

The `MediaRecorder` and `MediaPlayer` classes are used to record and play back either audio or video. This recipe focuses on audio, and the usage is straightforward. For playback, the steps are

1. Create an instance of the `MediaPlayer`:

   ```
   MediaPlayer m_mediaPlayer = new MediaPlayer();
   ```

2. Specify the source of media. It can be created from a raw resource:

   ```
   m_mediaPlayer = MediaPlayer.create(this, R.raw.my_music);
   ```

   Another option is to set as a file from the filesystem (which then also needs a prepare statement):

   ```
   m_mediaPlayer.setDataSource(path);
   m_mediaPlayer.prepare();
   ```

   In any case, these statements need to be surrounded by a try-catch block because the specified resource might not exist.

3. Start playback of the audio:

   ```
   m_mediaPlayer.start();
   ```

4. When the playback is done, stop the `MediaPlayer` and release the instance to free up resources:

   ```
   m_mediaPlayer.stop();
   m_mediaPlayer.release();
   ```

This recipe utilizes the same `ListFiles` activity shown in Listing 6.3 and 6.4 to create a selectable list of audio files to choose from for playback. It is assumed that audio files are in the **/sdcard/music/** directory of the Android device, but this is configurable.

When the `ListFiles` activity returns a file, it is initialized as the `MediaPlayer` media source, and the method `startMP()` is called. This starts the `MediaPlayer` and sets the button text to show **"Pause."** Similarly, the `pauseMP()` method pauses the `MediaPlayer` and sets the button text to show **"Play."** At any time, the user can click the button to pause or continue the playback of the music.

In general, the `MediaPlayer` creates its own background thread and does not pause when the main activity pauses. This is reasonable behavior for a music player, but in general, the developer might want control over this. Therefore, for illustration purposes, in this recipe, the music playback is paused and resumed along with the main activity by overriding the `onPause()` and `onResume()` methods. This is shown in Listing 6.6.

Listing 6.6 **src/com/cookbook/audio_ex/AudioExamples.java**

```
package com.cookbook.audio_ex;

import android.app.Activity;
import android.content.Intent;
import android.media.MediaPlayer;
import android.os.Bundle;
import android.os.Environment;
import android.view.View;
import android.widget.Button;

public class AudioExamples extends Activity {
    static final String MUSIC_DIR = "/music/";
    Button playPauseButton;

    private MediaPlayer m_mediaPlayer;

    @Override
    protected void onCreate(Bundle savedInstanceState) {
        super.onCreate(savedInstanceState);

        setContentView(R.layout.main);
        playPauseButton = (Button) findViewById(R.id.play_pause);

        m_mediaPlayer= new MediaPlayer();

        String MusicDir = Environment.getExternalStorageDirectory()
        .getAbsolutePath() + MUSIC_DIR;

        //Show a list of Music files to choose
        Intent i = new Intent(this, ListFiles.class);
        i.putExtra("directory", MusicDir);
        startActivityForResult(i,0);

        playPauseButton.setOnClickListener(new View.OnClickListener() {
            public void onClick(View view) {
                if(m_mediaPlayer.isPlaying()) {
```

```
                    //stop and give option to start again
                    pauseMP();
                } else {
                    startMP();
                }
            }
        });
    }

    @Override
    protected void onActivityResult(int requestCode,
                                    int resultCode, Intent data) {
        super.onActivityResult(requestCode, resultCode, data);
        if(requestCode == 0 && resultCode==RESULT_OK) {
            String tmp = data.getExtras().getString("clickedFile");

            try {
                m_mediaPlayer.setDataSource(tmp);
                m_mediaPlayer.prepare();
            } catch (Exception e) {
                e.printStackTrace();
            }
            startMP();
        }
    }

    void pauseMP() {
        playPauseButton.setText("Play");
        m_mediaPlayer.pause();
    }

    void startMP() {
        m_mediaPlayer.start();
        playPauseButton.setText("Pause");
    }

    boolean needToResume = false;
    @Override
    protected void onPause() {
        if(m_mediaPlayer != null && m_mediaPlayer.isPlaying()) {
            needToResume = true;
            pauseMP();
        }
        super.onPause();
    }
```

```
    @Override
    protected void onResume() {
        super.onResume();
        if(needToResume && m_mediaPlayer != null) {
            startMP();
        }
    }
}
```

The associated main XML layout with the play/pause button is shown in Listing 6.7.

Listing 6.7 **res/layout/main.xml**

```
<?xml version="1.0" encoding="utf-8"?>
<LinearLayout
    xmlns:android="http://schemas.android.com/apk/res/android"
    android:orientation="vertical"
    android:layout_width="fill_parent"
    android:layout_height="fill_parent">
    <Button android:id="@+id/play_pause"
        android:text="Play"
        android:textSize="20sp"
        android:layout_width="wrap_content"
        android:layout_height="wrap_content" />
</LinearLayout>
```

Recipe: Recording Audio Files

Recording audio using `MediaRecorder` is similar to playback from the previous recipe, except a few more things need to be specified (note, `DEFAULT` can also be used and is the same as the first choice in these lists):

- `MediaRecorder.AudioSource`:
    - `MIC`—Built-in microphone
    - `VOICE_UPLINK`—Transmitted audio during voice call
    - `VOICE_DOWNLINK`—Received audio during voice call
    - `VOICE_CALL`—Both uplink and downlink audio during voice call
    - `CAMCORDER`—Microphone associated with camera if available
    - `VOICE_RECOGNITION`—Microphone tuned for voice recognition if available
- `MediaRecorder.OutputFormat`:
    - `THREE_GPP`—3GPP media file format
    - `MPEG_4`—MPEG4 media file format
    - `AMR_NB`—Adaptive multirate narrowband file format

- MediaRecorder.AudioEncoder:
    - AMR_NB—Adaptive multirate narrowband vocoder

The steps to record audio are

1. Create an instance of the MediaRecorder:
```
MediaRecorder m_Recorder = new MediaRecorder();
```
2. Specify the source of media, for example the microphone:
```
m_Recorder.setAudioSource(MediaRecorder.AudioSource.MIC);
```
3. Set the output file format and encoding, such as:
```
m_Recorder.setOutputFormat(MediaRecorder.OutputFormat.THREE_GPP);
m_Recorder.setAudioEncoder(MediaRecorder.AudioEncoder.AMR_NB);
```
4. Set the path for the file to be saved:
```
m_Recorder.setOutputFile(path);
```
5. Prepare and start the recording:
```
m_Recorder.prepare();
m_Recorder.start();
```

These steps for audio recording can be used just as they were in the previous recipe for playback.

Recipe: Manipulating Raw Audio

The MediaRecorder/MediaPlayer framework is useful for most audio uses, but to manipulate raw audio straight from the microphone, process it without saving to a file, and/or play back raw audio, use AudioRecord/AudioTrack instead. First, set the permission in the AndroidManifest XML file:

```
<uses-permission android:name="android.permission.RECORD_AUDIO" />
```

Then, the steps to record are

1. Create an AudioRecord instance, specifying the following to the constructor:
    - Audio source—Use one of the MediaRecorder.AudioSource choices described in the previous recipe; for example, use MediaRecorder.AudioSource.MIC.
    - Sampling frequency in Hz—Use 44100 for CD-quality audio or half-rates such as 22050 or 11025 (which are sufficient for voice).
    - Channel configuration—Use AudioFormat.CHANNEL_IN_STEREO to record stereo sound and CHANNEL_IN_MONO to record mono sound.
    - Audio encoding—Use either AudioFormat.ENCODING_PCM_8BIT for 8-bit quantization or AudioFormat.ENCODING_PCM_16BIT for 16-bit.

- Buffer size in Bytes—This is the total size of allotted memory in static mode or the size of chunks used in streaming mode. This must be at least `getMinBufferSize()` bytes.

2. Start recording from the `AudioRecord` instance.
3. Read audio data to memory `audioData[]` using one of the following methods:
```
read(short[] audioData, int offsetInShorts, int sizeInShorts)
read(byte[] audioData, int offsetInBytes, int sizeInBytes)
read(ByteBuffer audioData, int sizeInBytes)
```
4. Stop recording.

For example, the following is suitable to record voice from the built-in microphone to a memory buffer `myRecordedAudio`, which can be declared a `short[]` (for instance, 16 bits each sample). Note that 11,025 samples per second and a buffer size of 10,000 samples means this recording is a little less than a second long:

```
short[] myRecordedAudio = new short[10000];
AudioRecord audioRecord = new AudioRecord(
          MediaRecorder.AudioSource.MIC, 11025,
          AudioFormat.CHANNEL_IN_MONO,
          AudioFormat.ENCODING_PCM_16BIT, 10000);
audioRecord.startRecording();
audioRecord.read(myRecordedAudio, 0, 10000);
audioRecord.stop();
```

Then, the steps to playback are

1. Create an `AudioTrack` instance specifying the following to the constructor:

   - Stream type—Use `AudioManager.STREAM_MUSIC` for capturing from the microphone or playback to the speaker. Other choices are `STREAM_VOICE_CALL`, `STREAM_SYSTEM`, `STREAM_RING`, and `STREAM_ALARM`.
   - Sampling frequency in Hz—This has the same meaning as during recording.
   - Channel configuration—Use `AudioFormat.CHANNEL_OUT_STEREO` to play back stereo sound. There are many other choices such as `CHANNEL_OUT_MONO` and `CHANNEL_OUT_5POINT1` (for surround sound).
   - Audio encoding—This has the same meaning as recording.
   - Buffer size in Bytes—This is the size of chunks of data to play at a time.
   - Buffer mode—Use `AudioTrack.MODE_STATIC` for short sounds that can fully fit in memory, avoiding transfer overheads. Otherwise, use `AudioTrack.MODE_STREAM` to write data to hardware in buffer chunks.

2. Start playback from the `AudioTrack` instance.
3. Write memory `audioData[]` to hardware using one of the following methods:
   `write(short[] audioData, int offsetInShorts, int sizeInShorts)`
   `write(byte[] audioData, int offsetInBytes, int sizeInBytes)`
4. Stop playback (optional).

For example, the following is suitable to play back the voice data in the previous record example:

```
AudioTrack audioTrack = new AudioTrack(
            AudioManager.STREAM_MUSIC, 11025,
            AudioFormat.CHANNEL_OUT_MONO,
            AudioFormat.ENCODING_PCM_16BIT, 4096,
            AudioTrack.MODE_STREAM);
audioTrack.play();
audioTrack.write(myRecordedAudio, 0, 10000);
audioTrack.stop();
```

This recipe utilizes these two methods to record audio to memory and play it back. The layout specifies two buttons on the screen: one to record audio and another to play back that recorded audio, as declared in the main layout file shown in Listing 6.8.

Listing 6.8 **res/layout/main.xml**

```
<?xml version="1.0" encoding="utf-8"?>
<LinearLayout xmlns:android="http://schemas.android.com/apk/res/android"
    android:orientation="vertical"
    android:layout_width="fill_parent"
    android:layout_height="fill_parent">
    <TextView android:id="@+id/status"
        android:text="Ready" android:textSize="20sp"
        android:layout_width="wrap_content"
        android:layout_height="wrap_content" />
    <Button android:id="@+id/record"
        android:text="Record for 5 seconds"
        android:textSize="20sp" android:layout_width="wrap_content"
        android:layout_height="wrap_content" />
    <Button android:id="@+id/play"
        android:text="Play" android:textSize="20sp"
        android:layout_width="wrap_content"
        android:layout_height="wrap_content" />
</LinearLayout>
```

The main activity shown in Listing 6.9 first creates an `OnClickListener` for these buttons to record or play back the in-memory audio buffer. The `onClick()` callback method creates the appropriate background thread because neither `AudioTrack` or `AudioRecord` should be run in the UI thread. For illustration, two different methods of creating the thread are shown: The `record_thread()` has a local thread with the UI updated through a `Handler`, and the play thread utilizes the main activity's `run()` method.

The buffer is kept in memory. For illustration, the recording is kept to 5 seconds.

Listing 6.9 **src/com/cookbook/audio_ex/AudioExamplesRaw.java**

```
package com.cookbook.audio_ex;

import android.app.Activity;
import android.media.AudioFormat;
import android.media.AudioManager;
import android.media.AudioRecord;
import android.media.AudioTrack;
import android.media.MediaRecorder;
import android.os.Bundle;
import android.os.Handler;
import android.util.Log;
import android.view.View;
import android.widget.Button;
import android.widget.TextView;

public class AudioExamplesRaw extends Activity implements Runnable {
    private TextView statusText;

    public void onCreate(Bundle savedInstanceState) {
        super.onCreate(savedInstanceState);
        setContentView(R.layout.main);

        statusText = (TextView) findViewById(R.id.status);

        Button actionButton = (Button) findViewById(R.id.record);
        actionButton.setOnClickListener(new View.OnClickListener() {
            public void onClick(View view) {
                record_thread();
            }
        });

        Button replayButton = (Button) findViewById(R.id.play);
        replayButton.setOnClickListener(new View.OnClickListener() {
            public void onClick(View view) {
                Thread thread = new Thread(AudioExamplesRaw.this);
                thread.start();
            }
        });
    }
```

```
String text_string;
final Handler mHandler = new Handler();
// Create runnable for posting
final Runnable mUpdateResults = new Runnable() {
    public void run() {
        updateResultsInUi(text_string);
    }
};

private void updateResultsInUi(String update_txt) {
    statusText.setText(update_txt);
}

private void record_thread() {
    Thread thread = new Thread(new Runnable() {
        public void run() {
            text_string = "Starting";
            mHandler.post(mUpdateResults);

            record();

            text_string = "Done";
            mHandler.post(mUpdateResults);
        }
    });
    thread.start();
}

private int audioEncoding = AudioFormat.ENCODING_PCM_16BIT;
int frequency = 11025; //Hz
int bufferSize = 50*AudioTrack.getMinBufferSize(frequency,
        AudioFormat.CHANNEL_OUT_MONO, audioEncoding);
// Create new AudioRecord object to record the audio.
public AudioRecord audioRecord = new AudioRecord(
        MediaRecorder.AudioSource.MIC,
        frequency, AudioFormat.CHANNEL_IN_MONO,
        audioEncoding, bufferSize);
// Create new AudioTrack object w/same parameters as AudioRecord obj
public AudioTrack audioTrack = new AudioTrack(
        AudioManager.STREAM_MUSIC, frequency,
        AudioFormat.CHANNEL_OUT_MONO,
        audioEncoding, 4096,
        AudioTrack.MODE_STREAM);
short[] buffer = new short[bufferSize];
```

```
    public void record() {
        try {
            audioRecord.startRecording();
            audioRecord.read(buffer, 0, bufferSize);
            audioRecord.stop();
        } catch (Throwable t) {
            Log.e("AudioExamplesRaw","Recording Failed");
        }
    }

    public void run() { //play audio using runnable Activity
        audioTrack.play();
        //this alone works: audioTrack.write(buffer, 0, bufferSize);
        //but for illustration showing another way to play using a loop:
        int i=0;
        while(i<bufferSize) {
            audioTrack.write(buffer, i++, 1);
        }
        return;
    }

    @Override
    protected void onPause() {
        if(audioTrack!=null) {
            if(audioTrack.getPlayState()==AudioTrack.PLAYSTATE_PLAYING) {
                audioTrack.pause();
            }
        }
        super.onPause();
    }
}
```

Recipe: Using Sound Resources Efficiently

To keep the smaller memory requirements of compressed audio files but also the benefit of lower-latency playback of raw audio files, the `SoundPool` class can be used. This uses the `MediaPlayer` service to decode audio and provides methods to repeat sound buffers and also speed them up or slow them down.

Usage is similar to other sound recipes: initialize, load a resource, play, and release. However, note that the `SoundPool` launches a background thread, so a `play()` right after a `load()` might not produce sound if the resource does not have time to load. Similarly, a `release()` called right after a `play()` releases the resource before it can be played. Therefore, it is best to tie `SoundPool` resources to activity lifecycle events (such as `onCreate` and `onPause`) and tie the playback of `SoundPool` resources to a user-generated event (such as a button press or advancement in a game).

Using the same layout file as in Listing 6.7, the main activity of this recipe is shown in Listing 6.10. A button press triggers the `SoundPool` to repeat a drum beat eight times (the initial time plus seven repeats). Also, the rate alternates from half-speed to double-speed between button presses. Up to ten streams can play at once, which means ten quick button presses can launch ten drum beats playing simultaneously.

Listing 6.10 **src/com/cookbook/audio_ex/AudioExamplesSP.java**

```
package com.cookbook.audio_ex;

import android.app.Activity;
import android.media.AudioManager;
import android.media.SoundPool;
import android.os.Bundle;
import android.view.View;
import android.widget.Button;

public class AudioExamplesSP extends Activity {
    static float rate = 0.5f;
    @Override
    protected void onCreate(Bundle savedInstanceState) {
        super.onCreate(savedInstanceState);

        setContentView(R.layout.main);
        Button playDrumButton = (Button) findViewById(R.id.play_pause);

        final SoundPool mySP = new
                         SoundPool(10, AudioManager.STREAM_MUSIC, 0);
        final int soundId = mySP.load(this, R.raw.drum_beat, 1);

        playDrumButton.setOnClickListener(new View.OnClickListener() {
            public void onClick(View view) {
                rate = 1/rate;
                mySP.play(soundId, 1f, 1f, 1, 7, rate);
            }
        });
    }
}
```

Recipe: Adding Media and Updating Paths

After an application creates a newly recorded audio file, it can be registered with the system as available for use. This is done using the `MediaStore` class. For example, after an audio file `myFile` is saved, Listing 6.11 shows how to register it as a possible ringtone, notification, and alarm, but not to be seen by an MP3 player (because `IS_MUSIC` is `false`).

Listing 6.11 **Example of Registering an Audio File to the System**

```
//reload MediaScanner to search for media and update paths
sendBroadcast(new Intent(Intent.ACTION_MEDIA_MOUNTED,
            Uri.parse("file://"
                      + Environment.getExternalStorageDirectory())));
ContentValues values = new ContentValues();
values.put(MediaStore.MediaColumns.DATA, myFile.getAbsolutePath());
values.put(MediaStore.MediaColumns.TITLE, myFile.getName());
values.put(MediaStore.MediaColumns.TIMESTAMP,
                                        System.currentTimeMillis());
values.put(MediaStore.MediaColumns.MIME_TYPE,
                                        recorder.getMimeContentType());
values.put(MediaStore.Audio.Media.ARTIST, SOME_ARTIST_HERE);
values.put(MediaStore.Audio.Media.IS_RINGTONE, true);
values.put(MediaStore.Audio.Media.IS_NOTIFICATION, true);
values.put(MediaStore.Audio.Media.IS_ALARM, true);
values.put(MediaStore.Audio.Media.IS_MUSIC, false);
ContentResolver contentResolver = new ContentResolver();
Uri base = MediaStore.Audio.INTERNAL_CONTENT_URI;
Uri newUri = contentResolver.insert(base, values);
String path = contentResolver.getDataFilePath(newUri);
```

Here `ContentValues` is used to declare some standard properties of the file, such as `TITLE`, `TIMESTAMP`, and `MIME_TYPE`, and `ContentResolver` is used to create an entry in the `MediaStore` content database with the file's path automatically added.

Video

Recording and playback of video files utilizes the `MediaPlayer/MediaRecorder` framework in a similar way to the audio examples discussed previously. For completeness, the steps are included here. First, if video is recorded, set the permission in the AndroidManifest XML file:

```
<uses-permission android:name="android.permission.RECORD_VIDEO" />
```

Then, the specification has different choices from the audio examples (note, `DEFAULT` can also be used and is the same as the first choice in these lists):

- `MediaRecorder.VideoSource`:
  - `CAMERA`—Built-in camera
- `MediaRecorder.OutputFormat`:
  - `THREE_GPP`—3GPP media file format
  - `MPEG_4`—MPEG4 media file format
- `MediaRecorder.VideoEncoder`:
  - `H263`—`H.263 video codec`
  - `H264`—`H.264 video codec`
  - `MPEG_4_SP`—`MPEG4 Simple Profile`

The steps to record video are

1. Create an instance of the `MediaRecorder`:
   ```
   MediaRecorder m_Recorder = new MediaRecorder();
   ```
2. Specify the source of media, which currently is only the camera:
   ```
   m_Recorder.setVideoSource(MediaRecorder.VideoSource.CAMERA);
   ```
3. Set the output file format and encoding:
   ```
   m_Recorder.setOutputFormat(MediaRecorder.OutputFormat.THREE_GPP);
   m_Recorder.setAudioEncoder(MediaRecorder.AudioEncoder.H263);
   ```
4. Set the path for the file to be saved:
   ```
   m_Recorder.setOutputFile(path);
   ```
5. Prepare and start the recording:
   ```
   m_Recorder.prepare();
   m_Recorder.start();
   ```

For playback, the steps are

1. Create an instance of the `MediaPlayer`:
   ```
   MediaPlayer m_mediaPlayer = new MediaPlayer();
   ```
2. Specify the source of media. It can be created from a raw resource:
   ```
   m_mediaPlayer = MediaPlayer.create(this, R.raw.my_video);
   ```
   Another option is to set as a file from the filesystem (which then also needs a prepare statement):
   ```
   m_mediaPlayer.setDataSource(path);
   m_mediaPlayer.prepare();
   ```
   In any case, these statements need to be surrounded by a try-catch block because the specified resource might not exist.

3. Start playback of the video:

   ```
   m_mediaPlayer.start();
   ```

4. When the playback is done, stop the MediaPlayer instance and release it to free up resources:

   ```
   m_mediaPlayer.stop();
   m_mediaPlayer.release();
   ```

7

Hardware Interface

Android devices have multiple different types of hardware that are built in and accessible to developers. Sensors, such as a camera, accelerometer, magnetometer, pressure sensor, temperature sensor, and proximity sensor, are available on most devices. Telephony, Bluetooth, and other wireless connections are also accessible to the developer in some form. This chapter shows how to leverage these hardware Application Programming Interfaces (API) to enrich an application's experience. Note that these recipes are best run on actual Android devices because the emulator might not provide accurate or realistic behavior of hardware interfaces.

Camera

The camera is the most visible and most used sensor in an Android device. It is a selling point for most consumers, and the capabilities are getting better with each generation. Image-processing applications normally work on an image after it is taken, but other applications, such as augmented reality, utilize the camera in real-time with overlays.

There are two ways to access the camera from an application. The first is by declaring an implicit intent as described in Chapter 2, "Application Basics: Activities and Intents." The implicit intent launches the default camera interface:

```
Intent intent = new Intent("android.media.action.IMAGE_CAPTURE");
startActivity(intent);
```

The second way leverages the `Camera` class, which provides more flexibility in the settings. This creates a custom camera interface, which is the focus of the examples that follow. Camera hardware access requires explicit permission in the AndroidManifest XML file:

```
<uses-permission android:name="android.permission.CAMERA" />
```

This is implied in the following section.

Recipe: Customizing the Camera

Control of the camera is abstracted into various components in the Android system:

- `Camera` class—Accesses the camera hardware
- `Camera.Parameters` class—Specifies the camera parameters such as picture size, picture quality, flash modes, and method to assign Global Positioning System (GPS) location
- Camera Preview methods—Sets the camera output display and toggles streaming video preview to the display
- `SurfaceView` class—Dedicates a drawing surface at the lowest level of the view hierarchy as a placeholder to display the camera preview

Before describing how these are tied together, the layout structure is introduced. The main layout is shown in Listing 7.1 and includes a `SurfaceView` to hold the camera output.

Listing 7.1 **res/layout/main.xml**

```
<LinearLayout
    xmlns:android="http://schemas.android.com/apk/res/android"
    android:layout_width="fill_parent"
    android:layout_height="fill_parent"
    android:orientation="vertical">

   <SurfaceView android:id="@+id/surface"
        android:layout_width="fill_parent"
        android:layout_height="fill_parent">
    </SurfaceView>

</LinearLayout>
```

A control interface can be added on top of this view by using a separate layout, as shown in Listing 7.2. This layout contains a button at the bottom, center of the screen to take a picture.

Listing 7.2 **res/layout/cameraoverlay.xml**

```
<LinearLayout xmlns:android="http://schemas.android.com/apk/res/android"
    android:layout_width="fill_parent"
    android:layout_height="fill_parent"
    android:orientation="vertical"
    android:gravity="bottom"
    android:layout_gravity="bottom">

    <LinearLayout
    xmlns:android="http://schemas.android.com/apk/res/android"
        android:layout_width="fill_parent"
```

```
        android:layout_height="wrap_content"
        android:orientation="horizontal"
        android:gravity="center_horizontal">
            <Button
            android:id="@+id/button"
            android:layout_width="wrap_content"
            android:layout_height="wrap_content"
            android:text="take picture"
            />
    </LinearLayout>
</LinearLayout>
```

The main activity involves multiple functionalities. First, the layout is set up as follows:

1. The window settings are changed to be translucent and full screen. (In this instance, they hide the title and notification bar.)

2. The `SurfaceView` defined in the previous layout (`R.id.surface`) is then filled by the camera preview. Each `SurfaceView` contains a `SurfaceHolder` for access and control over the surface. The activity is added as the `SurfaceHolder`'s callback and the type is set to `SURFACE_TYPE_PUSH_BUFFERS`, which means it creates a "push" surface and the object does not own the buffer. This makes video streaming more efficient.

3. A `LayoutInflater` is declared to inflate another layout (**cameraoverlay.xml**) over the original (**main.xml**) layout.

Next, the activity sets a trigger for taking a picture:

1. An `OnClickListener` is added on the button from the `cameraoverlay` layout, so when clicked, it takes a picture (`mCamera.takePicture()`).

2. The `takePicture()` method needs three methods to be defined:.

    - `ShutterCallback()` to define any effects needed after the picture is taken, such as a sound to let the user know that picture has been captured.

    - A `PictureCallback()` for raw picture data if hardware has enough memory to support this feature. (Otherwise. the data might return as null.)

    - A second `PictureCallback()` for the compressed picture data. This calls the local method `done()` to save the picture.

Then, the activity saves any pictures that were taken:

1. The compressed picture byte array is saved to a local variable `tempdata` for manipulation. The `BitmapFactory` is used to decode the `ByteArray` into a `Bitmap` Object.

2. The media content provider is used to save the bitmap and return a URL. If this main activity were called by another activity, this URL would be the return information to the caller activity to retrieve the image.
3. After this process, `finish()` is called to kill the activity.

Finally, the activity sets up a response to a change in the surface view:

1. A `SurfaceHolder.CallBack` interface is implemented. This requires three methods to be overridden:
   - `surfaceCreated()`—Called when the surface is first created. Initialize objects here.
   - `surfaceChanged()`—Called after surface creation and when the surface changes (for example, format or size).
   - `surfaceDestroyed()`—Called between removing the surface from the view of the user and destroying the surface. This is used for memory cleanup.
2. The parameters for the camera are changed when the surface is changed (such as the `PreviewSize` based on the surface size).

These functionalities are in the complete activity shown in Listing 7.3.

Listing 7.3 **src/com/cookbook/hardware/CameraApplication.java**

```
package com.cookbook.hardware;

import android.app.Activity;
import android.content.Intent;
import android.graphics.Bitmap;
import android.graphics.BitmapFactory;
import android.graphics.PixelFormat;
import android.hardware.Camera;
import android.hardware.Camera.PictureCallback;
import android.hardware.Camera.ShutterCallback;
import android.os.Bundle;
import android.provider.MediaStore.Images;
import android.util.Log;
import android.view.LayoutInflater;
import android.view.SurfaceHolder;
import android.view.SurfaceView;
import android.view.View;
import android.view.Window;
import android.view.WindowManager;
import android.view.View.OnClickListener;
import android.view.ViewGroup.LayoutParams;
import android.widget.Button;
import android.widget.Toast;
```

```
public class CameraApplication extends Activity
                            implements SurfaceHolder.Callback {
    private static final String TAG = "cookbook.hardware";
    private LayoutInflater mInflater = null;
    Camera mCamera;
    byte[] tempdata;
    boolean mPreviewRunning = false;
    private SurfaceHolder mSurfaceHolder;
    private SurfaceView mSurfaceView;
    Button takepicture;

    @Override
    public void onCreate(Bundle savedInstanceState) {
        super.onCreate(savedInstanceState);

        getWindow().setFormat(PixelFormat.TRANSLUCENT);
        requestWindowFeature(Window.FEATURE_NO_TITLE);
        getWindow().setFlags(WindowManager.LayoutParams.FLAG_FULLSCREEN,
                WindowManager.LayoutParams.FLAG_FULLSCREEN);

        setContentView(R.layout.main);

        mSurfaceView = (SurfaceView)findViewById(R.id.surface);
        mSurfaceHolder = mSurfaceView.getHolder();
        mSurfaceHolder.addCallback(this);
        mSurfaceHolder.setType(SurfaceHolder.SURFACE_TYPE_PUSH_BUFFERS);

        mInflater = LayoutInflater.from(this);
        View overView = mInflater.inflate(R.layout.cameraoverlay, null);
        this.addContentView(overView,
                new LayoutParams(LayoutParams.FILL_PARENT,
                        LayoutParams.FILL_PARENT));
        takepicture = (Button) findViewById(R.id.button);
        takepicture.setOnClickListener(new OnClickListener(){
            public void onClick(View view){
                mCamera.takePicture(mShutterCallback,
                        mPictureCallback, mjpeg);
            }
        });
    }

    ShutterCallback mShutterCallback = new ShutterCallback(){
        @Override
        public void onShutter() {}
    };
    PictureCallback mPictureCallback = new PictureCallback() {
```

```
    public void onPictureTaken(byte[] data, Camera c) {}
};
PictureCallback mjpeg = new PictureCallback() {
    public void onPictureTaken(byte[] data, Camera c) {
        if(data !=null) {
            tempdata=data;
            done();
        }
    }
};

void done() {
    Bitmap bm = BitmapFactory.decodeByteArray(tempdata,
                                          0, tempdata.length);
    String url = Images.Media.insertImage(getContentResolver(),
            bm, null, null);
    bm.recycle();
    Bundle bundle = new Bundle();
    if(url!=null) {
        bundle.putString("url", url);

        Intent mIntent = new Intent();
        mIntent.putExtras(bundle);
        setResult(RESULT_OK, mIntent);
    } else {
        Toast.makeText(this, "Picture can not be saved",
                       Toast.LENGTH_SHORT).show();
    }
    finish();
}
@Override
public void surfaceChanged(SurfaceHolder holder, int format,
                           int w, int h) {
    Log.e(TAG, "surfaceChanged");
    try {
        if (mPreviewRunning) {
            mCamera.stopPreview();
            mPreviewRunning = false;
        }

        Camera.Parameters p = mCamera.getParameters();
        p.setPreviewSize(w, h);

        mCamera.setParameters(p);
        mCamera.setPreviewDisplay(holder);
        mCamera.startPreview();
```

```
                mPreviewRunning = true;
            } catch(Exception e) {
                Log.d("",e.toString());
            }
        }

        @Override
        public void surfaceCreated(SurfaceHolder holder) {
            Log.e(TAG, "surfaceCreated");
            mCamera = Camera.open();
        }

        @Override
        public void surfaceDestroyed(SurfaceHolder holder) {
            Log.e(TAG, "surfaceDestroyed");
            mCamera.stopPreview();
            mPreviewRunning = false;
            mCamera.release();
            mCamera=null;
        }
    }
```

Note the camera preview from the camera hardware is not standardized, and some Android devices might show the preview sideways. In this case, simply add the following to the `onCreate()` method of the `CameraPreview` activity:

```
this.setRequestedOrientation(ActivityInfo.SCREEN_ORIENTATION_LANDSCAPE);
```

Other Sensors

The proliferation of small and low-power Micro-Electro-Mechanical Systems (MEMS) is becoming more evident. Smart-phones are becoming an aggregator of sensors, and the push for sensor accuracy by smart-phone manufacturers is driving the need for better performing devices.

As discussed in Chapter 1, "Overview of Android," each Android phone has a selection of different sensors. The standard two are a three-axis accelerometer to determine device tilt and a three-axis magnetometer to determine compass direction. Other devices that might be integrated are temperature sensor, proximity sensor, light sensor, and gyroscope. Currently supported sensors in the Android Software Development Kit (SDK) are listed in Table 7.1.

Table 7.1 **The Sensors Accessible from the Android SDK**

Sensor Type	Description
`TYPE_ACCELEROMETER`	Measures acceleration in meters/sec^2
`TYPE_ALL`	Describes sensor types and is a constant
`TYPE_GYROSCOPE`	Measures orientation based on angular momentum
`TYPE_LIGHT`	Measures ambient light in lux
`TYPE_MAGNETIC_FIELD`	Measures magnetic field in micro-Tesla
`TYPE_PRESSURE`	Measures air pressure
`TYPE_PROXIMITY`	Measures distance of blocking object in centimeters
`TYPE_TEMPERATURE`	Measures temperature in degrees Celsius

The `getSensorList()` method lists all the available sensors in a particular device. A `SensorManager manages all sensors.` It provides various sensor event listeners with two callback functions—`onSensorChanged()` and `onAccuracyChanged()`—that are used to listen for sensor value and accuracy changes.

Recipe: Getting a Device's Rotational Attitude

Ideally, the accelerometer measures the Earth's gravitational field as G=9.8 meters/sec^2, and the magnetometer measures the Earth's magnetic field that ranges from H=30μT to 60μT depending on the location in the world. These two vectors are enough to implement a simple textbook estimation of rotation, as used in the `getRotationMatrix()` method. This recipe shows how to use this information.

The coordinate system of the device (also known as the body) frame is defined as:

- x-axis in the direction of the short side of the screen (along the menu keys)
- y-axis in the direction of the long side of the screen
- z-axis pointing out of the screen

The coordinate system of the world (also known as inertial) frame is defined as:

- The x-axis is the cross-product of the y-axis with the z-axis.
- The y-axis is tangential to the ground and points toward the North Pole.
- The z-axis points perpendicular to the ground toward the sky.

These two systems are aligned when the device is flat on a table with the screen facing up and pointing north. In this case, the accelerometer measures (0, 0, G) in the x-, y-, and z-directions. At most locations, the magnetic field of the Earth points slightly toward the ground at an angle θ and even when the device points north is given by (0, H cos(θ), -H sin(θ)).

As the device tilts and rotates, `SensorManager.getRotationMatrix()` provides the 3x3 rotation matrix `R[]` to get from the device coordinate system to the world coordinate system and 3x3 inclination matrix `I[]` (rotation around the x-axis) to get from the true magnetic field direction to the ideal case (0, H, 0).

Note that if the device has its own acceleration or is near a strong magnetic field, the values measured do not necessarily reflect the proper reference frame of the Earth.

Another way to express the rotation is using `SensorManager.getOrientation()`. This provides the rotation matrix `R[]` and the attitude vector `attitude[]`:

- `attitude[0]`—Azimuth (in radians) is the rotation angle around the world-frame z-axis required to have the device facing north. It takes values between -PI and PI, with 0 representing north and PI/2 representing east.
- `attitude[1]`—Pitch (in radians) is the rotation angle around the world-frame x-axis required to have the device face straight up along the long dimension of the screen. It takes values between -PI and PI with 0 representing device face up, and PI/2 means it points toward the ground.
- `attitude[2]`—Roll (in radians) is the rotation angle around the world-frame y-axis required to have the device face straight up along the short dimension of the screen. It takes values between -PI and PI with 0 representing device face up, and PI/2 means it points toward the right.

This recipe displays the attitude information to the screen. The layout provides a text with ID `attitude`, as shown in Listing 7.4.

Listing 7.4 **res/layout/main.xml**

```
<?xml version="1.0" encoding="utf-8"?>
<LinearLayout xmlns:android="http://schemas.android.com/apk/res/android"
    android:orientation="vertical"
    android:layout_width="fill_parent"
    android:layout_height="fill_parent"
    >
<TextView android:id="@+id/attitude"
    android:layout_width="fill_parent"
    android:layout_height="wrap_content"
    android:text="Azimuth, Pitch, Roll"
    />
</LinearLayout>
```

The main activity is shown in Listing 7.5. The accelerometer and magnetometer are registered to return data to the sensor listener. The SensorEventListener then assigns values based on which sensor triggered the callback. The attitude information is determined based on the rotation matrix, converted from radians to degrees, and displayed on the screen. Note the refresh rate of the sensors can take on different values as follows:

- `SENSOR_DELAY_FASTEST`—Fastest update rate possible (ranges from 8ms to approximately 30ms depending on device)
- `SENSOR_DELAY_GAME`—Update rate suitable for games (approximately 40ms)
- `SENSOR_DELAY_NORMAL`—The default; update rate suitable for screen orientation changes (approximately 200ms)
- `SENSOR_DELAY_UI`—Update rate suitable for the user interface (approximately 350ms)

Listing 7.5 **src/com/cookbook/orientation/OrientationMeasurements.java**

```
package com.cookbook.orientation;

import android.app.Activity;
import android.hardware.Sensor;
import android.hardware.SensorEvent;
import android.hardware.SensorEventListener;
import android.hardware.SensorManager;
import android.os.Bundle;
import android.widget.TextView;

public class OrientationMeasurements extends Activity {
    private SensorManager myManager = null;
    TextView tv;

    @Override
    public void onCreate(Bundle savedInstanceState) {
        super.onCreate(savedInstanceState);
        setContentView(R.layout.main);
        tv = (TextView) findViewById(R.id.attitude);
        // Set Sensor Manager
        myManager = (SensorManager)getSystemService(SENSOR_SERVICE);
        myManager.registerListener(mySensorListener,
                myManager.getDefaultSensor(Sensor.TYPE_ACCELEROMETER),
                SensorManager.SENSOR_DELAY_GAME);
        myManager.registerListener(mySensorListener,
                myManager.getDefaultSensor(Sensor.TYPE_MAGNETIC_FIELD),
                SensorManager.SENSOR_DELAY_GAME);
    }

    float[] mags = new float[3];
    float[] accels = new float[3];
    float[] RotationMat = new float[9];
    float[] InclinationMat = new float[9];
    float[] attitude = new float[3];
```

```
    final static double RAD2DEG = 180/Math.PI;
    private final SensorEventListener mySensorListener
                                 = new SensorEventListener() {
        @Override
        public void onSensorChanged(SensorEvent event)
        {
            int type = event.sensor.getType();

            if(type == Sensor.TYPE_MAGNETIC_FIELD) {
                mags = event.values;
            }
            if(type == Sensor.TYPE_ACCELEROMETER) {
                accels = event.values;
            }

            SensorManager.getRotationMatrix(RotationMat,
                    InclinationMat, accels, mags);
            SensorManager.getOrientation(RotationMat, attitude);
            tv.setText("Azimuth, Pitch, Roll:\n"
                    + attitude[0]*RAD2DEG + "\n"
                    + attitude[1]*RAD2DEG + "\n"
                    + attitude[2]*RAD2DEG);
        }

        public void onAccuracyChanged(Sensor sensor, int accuracy) {}
    };
}
```

For consistent data, it is good practice to avoid putting computationally intensive code into the `onSensorChanged()` method. Also note that the `SensorEvent` is reused for subsequent sensor data. Therefore, for precise data, it is good practice to use the `clone()` method on event values, for example:

```
accels = event.values.clone();
```

This ensures that if the `accels` data is used elsewhere in the class, it does not keep changing as the sensors continue sampling.

Recipe: Using the Temperature and Light Sensor

The temperature sensor is used to determine temperature of the phone for internal hardware calibration. The light sensor measures ambient light and is used to automatically adjust the brightness of the screen.

These sensors are not available on all phones, but if they exist, the developer can use them for alternative reasons. The code to read the values from these sensors is shown in Listing 7.6. It can be added to the activity in the previous recipe to see the result.

Listing 7.6 **Example Code to Access the Temperature and Light Sensors**

```
private final SensorEventListener mTListener
                                  = new SensorEventListener(){
    @Override
    public void onAccuracyChanged(Sensor sensor, int accuracy) {}

    @Override
    public void onSensorChanged(SensorEvent event) {
        Log.v("test Temperature",
               "onSensorChanged:"+event.sensor.getName());
        if(event.sensor.getType()==Sensor.TYPE_TEMPERATURE){
            tv2.setText("Temperature:"+event.values[0]);
        }
    }

};

private final SensorEventListener mLListener
                                  = new SensorEventListener(){
    @Override
    public void onAccuracyChanged(Sensor sensor, int accuracy) {}

    @Override
    public void onSensorChanged(SensorEvent event) {
        Log.v("test Light",
              "onSensorChanged:"+event.sensor.getName());
        if(event.sensor.getType()==Sensor.TYPE_LIGHT){
            tv3.setText("Light:"+event.values[0]);
        }
    }

};

sensorManager.registerListener(mTListener, sensorManager
                    .getDefaultSensor(Sensor.TYPE_TEMPERATURE),
                     SensorManager.SENSOR_DELAY_FASTEST);
sensorManager.registerListener(mLListener, sensorManager
                    .getDefaultSensor(Sensor.TYPE_LIGHT),
                     SensorManager.SENSOR_DELAY_FASTEST);
```

Telephony

The Android telephony API provides a way to monitor basic phone information, such as the network type, connection state, and utilities for manipulating phone number strings.

Recipe: Utilizing the Telephony Manager

The telephony API has a TelephonyManager class, which is an Android system service, to access information about the telephony services on the device. Some of the telephony information is permission protected, so access must be declared in the AndroidManifest XML file:

```
<uses-permission android:name="android.permission.READ_PHONE_STATE" />
```

The main activity is shown in Listing 7.7.

Listing 7.7 **src/com/cookbook/hardware.telephony/TelephonyApp.java**

```
package com.cookbook.hardware.telephony;

import android.app.Activity;
import android.os.Bundle;
import android.telephony.TelephonyManager;
import android.widget.TextView;

public class TelephonyApp extends Activity {
    TextView tv1;
    TelephonyManager telManager;
    @Override
    public void onCreate(Bundle savedInstanceState) {
        super.onCreate(savedInstanceState);
        setContentView(R.layout.main);
        tv1 =(TextView) findViewById(R.id.tv1);
        telManager = (TelephonyManager)
                     getSystemService(TELEPHONY_SERVICE);

        StringBuilder sb = new StringBuilder();
        sb.append("deviceid:")
          .append(telManager.getDeviceId()).append("\n");
        sb.append("device Software Ver:")
          .append(telManager.getDeviceSoftwareVersion()).append("\n");
        sb.append("Line number:")
          .append(telManager.getLine1Number()).append("\n");
        sb.append("Network Country ISO:")
          .append(telManager.getNetworkCountryIso()).append("\n");
        sb.append("Network Operator:")
          .append(telManager.getNetworkOperator()).append("\n");
        sb.append("Network Operator Name:")
          .append(telManager.getNetworkOperatorName()).append("\n");
        sb.append("Sim Country ISO:")
          .append(telManager.getSimCountryIso()).append("\n");
        sb.append("Sim Operator:")
          .append(telManager.getSimOperator()).append("\n");
        sb.append("Sim Operator Name:")
          .append(telManager.getSimOperatorName()).append("\n");
        sb.append("Sim Serial Number:")
          .append(telManager.getSimSerialNumber()).append("\n");
```

```
        sb.append("Subscriber Id:")
          .append(telManager.getSubscriberId()).append("\n");
        sb.append("Voice Mail Alpha Tag:")
          .append(telManager.getVoiceMailAlphaTag()).append("\n");
        sb.append("Voice Mail Number:")
          .append(telManager.getVoiceMailNumber()).append("\n");
        tv1.setText(sb.toString());
    }
}
```

The main layout XML file is shown in Listing 7.8 and outputs the screen shown in Figure 7.1.

Listing 7.8 **res/layout/main.xml**

```
<?xml version="1.0" encoding="utf-8"?>
<LinearLayout xmlns:android="http://schemas.android.com/apk/res/android"
    android:orientation="vertical"
    android:layout_width="fill_parent"
    android:layout_height="fill_parent"
    >
<TextView
    android:id="@+id/tv1"
    android:layout_width="fill_parent"
    android:layout_height="wrap_content"
    android:text="@string/hello"
    />
</LinearLayout>
```

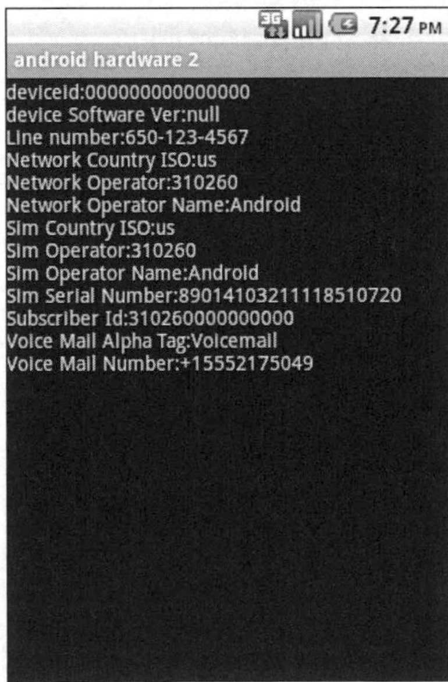

Figure 7.1 Output using the TelephonyManager class.

Recipe: Listening for Phone States

The `PhoneStateListener` class provides information about the different telephony states on the device, including network service state, signal strength, and message waiting indicator (voicemail). Some require an explicit permission as shown in Table 7.2.

Table 7.2 **The Possible Phone State Listener Events and Required Permissions**

Phone State Listener	Description	Permission
`LISTEN_CALL_FORWARDING_INDICATOR`	Listen for call forward indicator changes	`READ_PHONE_STATE`
`LISTEN_CALL_STATE`	Listen for call state changes	`READ_PHONE_STATE`
`LISTEN_CELL_LOCATION`	Listen for cell location changes	`ACCESS_COARSE_LOCATION`
`LISTEN_DATA_ACTIVITY`	Listen for direction of data traffic on cellular changes	`READ_PHONE_STATE`
`LISTEN_DATA_CONNECTION_STATE`	Listen for data connection state changes	None
`LISTEN_MESSAGE_WAITING_INDICATOR`	Listen for message waiting indicator changes	`READ_PHONE_STATE`
`LISTEN_NONE`	Remove listeners	None
`LISTEN_SERVICE_STATE`	Listen for network service state changes	None
`LISTEN_SIGNAL_STRENGTHS`	Listen for network signal strength changes	None

For example, to listen for an incoming call, the `TelephonyManager` needs to register a listener for the `PhoneStateListener.LISTEN_CALL_STATE` event. The three possible call states are

- `CALL_STATE_IDLE`—Device not being used for a phone call
- `CALL_STATE_RINGING`—Device receiving a call
- `CALL_STATE_OFFHOOK`—Call in progress

This recipe lists the phone call state changes as they occur. By using the Logcat tool (discussed in Chapter 12, "Debugging"), these different states can be seen when an incoming call or outgoing call occurs.

The main activity is shown in Listing 7.9. It creates a new inner class extending the `PhoneStateListener`, which overrides the `onCallStateChanged` method to catch the phone call state changes. Other methods that can be overridden are `onCallForwardingIndicator()`, `onCellLocationChanged()`, and `onDataActivity()`.

Listing 7.9 **src/com/cookbook/hardware.telephony/HardwareTelephony.java**

```
package com.cookbook.hardware.telephony;

import android.app.Activity;
import android.os.Bundle;
import android.telephony.PhoneStateListener;
import android.telephony.TelephonyManager;
import android.util.Log;
import android.widget.TextView;

public class HardwareTelephony extends Activity {
    TextView tv1;
    TelephonyManager telManager;
    @Override
    public void onCreate(Bundle savedInstanceState) {
        super.onCreate(savedInstanceState);
        setContentView(R.layout.main);
        tv1 =(TextView) findViewById(R.id.tv1);
        telManager = (TelephonyManager)
                     getSystemService(TELEPHONY_SERVICE);

        telManager.listen(new TelListener(),
                          PhoneStateListener.LISTEN_CALL_STATE);
    }

    private class TelListener extends PhoneStateListener {
        public void onCallStateChanged(int state, String incomingNumber) {
            super.onCallStateChanged(state, incomingNumber);
```

```
            Log.v("Phone State", "state:"+state);
            switch (state) {
                case TelephonyManager.CALL_STATE_IDLE:
                    Log.v("Phone State",
                            "incomingNumber:"+incomingNumber+" ended");
                    break;
                case TelephonyManager.CALL_STATE_OFFHOOK:
                    Log.v("Phone State",
                            "incomingNumber:"+incomingNumber+" picked up");
                    break;
                case TelephonyManager.CALL_STATE_RINGING:
                    Log.v("Phone State",
                            "incomingNumber:"+incomingNumber+" received");
                    break;
                default:
                    break;
            }
        }
    }
}
```

Recipe: Dialing a Phone Number

To make a phone call from an application, the following permission needs to be added to the AndroidManifest XML file:

```
<uses-permission android:name="android.permission.CALL_PHONE" />
```

The act of making a call can either use the `ACTION_CALL` or `ACTION_DIALER` implicit intent. When using the `ACTION_DIALER` intent, the phone dialer user interface is displayed with the specified phone number ready to call. This is created using:

```
startActivity(new Intent(Intent.ACTION_CALL,
  Uri.parse("tel:15102345678")));
```

When using the `ACTION_CALL` intent, the phone dialer is not shown and the specified phone number is just dialed. This is created using:

```
startActivity(new Intent(Intent.ACTION_DIAL,
  Uri.parse("tel:15102345678")));
```

Bluetooth

Bluetooth from the IEEE standard 802.15.1 is an open, wireless protocol for exchanging data between devices over short distances. A common example is from a phone to a headset, but other applications can include proximity tracking. To communicate between devices using Bluetooth, four steps need to be performed:

1. Turn on Bluetooth for the device.
2. Find paired or available devices in a valid range.
3. Connect to devices.
4. Transfer data between devices.

To use the Bluetooth Service, the application needs to have `BLUETOOTH` permission to receive and transmit and `BLUETOOTH_ADMIN` permission to manipulate Bluetooth settings or initiate device discovery. These require the following lines in the AndroidManifest XML file:

```
<uses-permission android:name="android.permission.BLUETOOTH" />
<uses-permission android:name="android.permission.BLUETOOTH_ADMIN" />
```

All the Bluetooth API functionality resides in the `android.bluetooth` package. There are five main classes that provide the features:

- `BluetoothAdapter`—Represents the Bluetooth radio interface that is used to discover devices and instantiate Bluetooth connections
- `BluetoothClass`—Describes the general characteristics of the Bluetooth device
- `BluetoothDevice`—Represents a remote Bluetooth device
- `BluetoothSocket`—Represents the socket or connection point for data exchange with another Bluetooth device
- `BluetoothServerSocket`—Represents an open socket listening for incoming requests

These are discussed in detail in the following recipes.

Recipe: Turning on Bluetooth

Bluetooth is initialized using the `BluetoothAdapter` class. The `getDefaultAdapter()` method retrieves information about the Bluetooth radio interface. If `null` is returned, it means the device does not support Bluetooth:

```
BluetoothAdapter myBluetooth = BluetoothAdapter.getDefaultAdapter();
```

Activate Bluetooth using this `BluetoothAdapter` instance to query the status. If not enabled, the Android built-in activity `ACTION_REQUEST_ENABLE` can be used to ask the user to start Bluetooth:

```
if(!myBluetooth.isEnabled()) {
    Intent enableIntent = new Intent(BluetoothAdapter
                                .ACTION_REQUEST_ENABLE);
    startActivity(enableIntent);
}
```

Recipe: Discovering Bluetooth Devices

After Bluetooth is activated, to discover paired or available Bluetooth devices, use the `BluetoothAdapter` instance's `startdiscovery()` method as an asynchronous call. This requires registering a `BroadcastReceiver` to listen for `ACTION_FOUND` events that tell the application whenever a new remote Bluetooth device is discovered. This is shown in the example code in Listing 7.10.

Listing 7.10 **Example Code for Discovering Bluetooth Devices**

```
private final BroadcastReceiver mReceiver = new BroadcastReceiver() {
    public void onReceive(Context context, Intent intent) {
        String action = intent.getAction();
        // When discovery finds a device
        if (BluetoothDevice.ACTION_FOUND.equals(action)) {
            // Get the BluetoothDevice object from the Intent
            BluetoothDevice device = intent.getParcelableExtra(
                                    BluetoothDevice.EXTRA_DEVICE);
            Log.v("BlueTooth Testing",device.getName() + "\n"
                  + device.getAddress());
        }
    }
};

IntentFilter filter = new IntentFilter(BluetoothDevice.ACTION_FOUND);
registerReceiver(mReceiver, filter);
myBluetooth.startDiscovery();
```

The broadcast receiver can also listen for `ACTION_DISCOVERY_STARTED` events and `ACTION_DISCOVERY_FINISHED` events that tell the application when the discovery starts and ends.

For other Bluetooth devices to discover the current device, the application can enable discoverability using the `ACTION_REQUEST_DISCOVERABLE` intent. This activity displays another dialog on top of the application to ask users whether or not they want to make the current device discoverable:

```
Intent discoverableIntent
       = new Intent(BluetoothAdapter.ACTION_REQUEST_DISCOVERABLE);
startActivity(discoverableIntent);
```

Recipe: Pairing with Bonded Bluetooth Devices

Bonded Bluetooth devices are those that have already paired with the current devices sometime in the past. When pairing two Bluetooth devices, one connects as a server and the other as the client using the `BluetoothSocket` and `BluetoothServerSocket` classes. To get the bonded Bluetooth devices, the `BluetoothAdapter` instance's method `getBondedDevices()` can be used:

```
Set<BluetoothDevice> pairedDevices = mBluetoothAdapter.getBondedDevices();
```

Recipe: Opening a Bluetooth Socket

To establish a Bluetooth connection with another device, the application needs to implement either the client-side or server-side socket. After the server and client are bonded, there is a connected Bluetooth socket for each device on the same RFCOMM (Bluetooth transport protocol). However, the client device and service device obtain the Bluetooth socket in different ways. The server receives the Bluetooth socket instance when an incoming connection is accepted. The client receives the instance when it opens an RFCOMM channel to the server.

Server-side initialization uses the generic client-server programming model with applications requiring an open socket for accepting incoming requests (similar to TCP). The interface `BluetoothServerSocket` should be used to create a server listening port. After the connection is accepted, a `BluetoothSocket` is returned and can be used to manage the connection.

The `BluetoothServerSocket` can be obtained from the `BluetoothAdapter` instance's method `listenUsingRfcommWithServiceRecord()`. After obtaining the socket, the `accept()` method starts listening for a request and returns only when either a connection has been accepted or an exception has occurred. The `BluetoothSocket` then returns when `accept()` returns a valid connection. Finally, the `close()` method should be called to release the server socket and its resources because RFCOMM allows only one connected client per channel at a time. This does not close the connected `BluetoothSocket`. The following excerpt shows how these steps are done:

```
BluetoothServerSocket myServerSocket
    = myBluetoothAdapter.listenUsingRfcommWithServiceRecord(name, uuid);
myServerSocket.accept();
myServerSocket.close();
```

Note that the `accept()` method is a blocking call and so it should not be implemented inside the main thread. It is better idea to implement this inside a working thread, as shown in Listing 7.11.

Listing 7.11 **Example of Establishing a Bluetooth Socket**

```
private class AcceptThread extends Thread {
    private final BluetoothServerSocket mmServerSocket;

    public AcceptThread() {
        // Use a temporary object that is later assigned
        // to mmServerSocket, because mmServerSocket is final
        BluetoothServerSocket tmp = null;
        try {
            // MY_UUID is the app's UUID string, also used by the client
          tmp = mAdapter.listenUsingRfcommWithServiceRecord(NAME,MY_UUID);
        } catch (IOException e) { }
        mmServerSocket = tmp;
    }

    public void run() {
        BluetoothSocket socket = null;
        // Keep listening until exception occurs or a socket is returned
        while (true) {
            try {
                socket = mmServerSocket.accept();
            } catch (IOException e) {
                break;
            }
            // If a connection was accepted
            if (socket != null) {
                // Do work to manage the connection (in a separate thread)
                manageConnectedSocket(socket);
                mmServerSocket.close();
                break;
            }
        }
    }

    /** Will cancel the listening socket, and cause thread to finish */
    public void cancel() {
        try {
            mmServerSocket.close();
        } catch (IOException e) { }
    }
}
```

To implement the client device mechanism, the `BluetoothDevice` needs to be obtained from the remote device. Then the socket needs to be retrieved to make the connection. To retrieve the `BluetoothSocket`, use the `BluetoothDevice` method `createRfcommSocketToServiceRecord(UUID)` with the `UUID` used in `listenUsingRfcommWithServiceRecord`. After the socket is retrieved, the `connect()` method can be used to initiate a connection. This method is also blocking and should also be implemented in a separate thread, as shown in Listing 7.12.

Listing 7.12 Example of Connecting to a Bluetooth Socket

```
private class ConnectThread extends Thread {
    private final BluetoothSocket mmSocket;
    private final BluetoothDevice mmDevice;

    public ConnectThread(BluetoothDevice device) {
        // Use a temporary object that is later assigned to mmSocket,
        // because mmSocket is final
        BluetoothSocket tmp = null;
        mmDevice = device;

        // Get a BluetoothSocket to connect with the given BluetoothDevice
        try {
            // MY_UUID is the app's UUID string, also used by the server code
            tmp = device.createRfcommSocketToServiceRecord(MY_UUID);
        } catch (IOException e) { }
        mmSocket = tmp;
    }

    public void run() {
       // Cancel discovery because it will slow down the connection
        mAdapter.cancelDiscovery();

        try {
            // Connect the device through the socket. This will block
            // until it succeeds or throws an exception
            mmSocket.connect();
        } catch (IOException connectException) {
            // Unable to connect; close the socket and get out
            try {
                mmSocket.close();
            } catch (IOException closeException) { }
            return;
        }

        // Do work to manage the connection (in a separate thread)
        manageConnectedSocket(mmSocket);
    }
```

```
    /** Will cancel an in-progress connection, and close the socket */
    public void cancel() {
        try {
            mmSocket.close();
        } catch (IOException e) { }
    }
}
```

After the connection is established, the normal `InputStream` and `OutputStream` can be used to read and send data between the Bluetooth devices.

Recipe: Using Device Vibration

Device vibration is a common feature in all cellular phones. To control vibration on an Android device, a permission must be defined in the AndroidManifest XML file:

```
<uses-permission android:name="android.permission.VIBRATE" />
```

Then, using the device vibrator is just another Android system service provided by the framework. It can be accessed using the `Vibrator` class:

```
Vibrator myVib = (Vibrator) getSystemService(Context.VIBRATOR_SERVICE);
```

With a Vibrator instance, just call the `vibrate()` method to start device vibration:

```
myVib.vibrate(3000); //vibrate for 3 seconds
```

If needed, the `cancel()` method can be used to stop a vibration before it finishes:

```
myVib.cancel(); //cancel the vibration
```

It is also possible to vibrate a rhythmic pattern. This is specified as a vibration-pause sequence. For example:

```
long[] pattern = {2000,1000,5000};
 myVib.vibrate(pattern,1);
```

This causes the device to wait for 2 seconds, and then start a pattern of vibrating for 1 second, pausing for 5 seconds indefinitely. The second argument to the `vibrate()` method means the index into the pattern to start repeating at. This can be set to `-1` to cause no repeat of the pattern at all.

Recipe: Accessing the Wireless Network

Many applications utilize the network connectivity of the Android device. To better understand how to handle application behavior due to network changes, Android provides access to the underlying network state. This is done by broadcasting intents to notify application components of changes in network connectivity and offer control over network settings and connections.

Android provides a system service through the `ConnectivityManager` class to let developers monitor the connectivity state, set the preferred network connection, and manage connectivity failover. This is initialized as follows:

```
ConnectivityManager myNetworkManager
 = (ConnectivityManager) getSystemService(Context.CONNECTIVITY_SERVICE);
```

To use the connectivity manager, the appropriate permission is needed in the AndroidManifest XML file for the application:

```
<uses-permission android:name="android.permission.ACCESS_NETWORK_STATE" />
```

The connectivity manager does provide the two methods `getNetworkInfo()` and `getActiveNetworkInfo()` to obtain the details of the current network in a `NetworkInfo` class. However, a better way to monitor the network changes is to create a broadcast receiver, as shown in the following example:

```
private BroadcastReceiver mNetworkReceiver = new BroadcastReceiver(){
    public void onReceive(Context c, Intent i){
        Bundle b = i.getExtras();
        NetworkInfo ni = (NetworkInfo)
                        b.get(ConnectivityManager.EXTRA_NETWORK_INFO);
        if(ni.isConnected()){
            //do the operation
        }else{
            //announce the user the network problem
        }
    }
};
```

After a broadcast receiver is defined, it can be registered to listen for `ConnectivityManager.CONNECTIVITY_ACTION` intents:

```
this.registerReceiver(mNetworkReceiver,
            new IntentFilter(ConnectivityManager.CONNECTIVITY_ACTION));
```

The `mNetworkReceiver` defined previous extracts only the `NetworkInfo` from `ConnectivityManager.EXTRA_NETWORK_INFO`. However the connectivity manager has more information that can be exposed. The different types of information available are collected in Table 7.3.

Table 7.3 **The Possible Information from a Connectivity Manager**

Type of Information	Description
EXTRA_EXTRA_INFO	Contains additional information about network state
EXTRA_IS_FAILOVER	Returns `boolean` value if the current connection is the result of a failover network
EXTRA_NETWORK_INFO	Returns a `NetworkInfo` object
EXTRA_NO_CONNECTIVITY	Returns `boolean` value if there is no network connectivity
EXTRA_OTHER_NETWORK_INFO	Returns a `NetworkInfo` object about the available network for failover when the network is disconnected
EXTRA_REASON	Returns a `String` value that describes the reason of connection failure

The `ConnectivityManager` also provides the capability to control network hardware and failover preferences. The `setNetworkPreference()` method can be used to select a network type. To change the network, the application needs to set another permission in the AndroidManifest XML file:

```
<uses-permission android:name="android.permission.CHANGE_NETWORK_STATE" />
```

8

Networking

Network-based applications provide increased value for a user in that content can be dynamic and interactive. Networking enables multiple features from social networking to cloud computing.

This chapter focuses on short message service (SMS), Internet resource-based applications, and social networking applications. SMS is a communication service component that enables the exchange of short text messages between mobile phone devices. Internet resource-based applications rely on web content such as HTML (HyperText Markup Language), XML (eXtensible Markup Language), and JSON (JavaScript Object Notation). Social networking applications, such as Twitter, are important methods for people to connect with each other.

Using SMS

The Android framework provides full access to SMS functionality using the `SmsManager` class. Early versions of Android placed `SmsManager` in the `android.telephony.gsm` package. Since Android 1.5, where `SmsManager` supports both GSM and CDMA mobile telephony standards, the `SmsManager` is now placed in the `android.telephony` package.

Sending an SMS through the `SmsManager` is fairly straightforward. The steps are

1. Set the permission in the AndroidManifest XML file to send SMS:

```
<uses-permission android:name="android.permission.SEND_SMS">
```

2. Use the `SmsManager.getDefault()` static method to get an SMS manager instance:

```
SmsManager mySMS = SmsManager.getDefault();
```

3. Define the destination phone number for the message and message to send. Use the `sendTextMesssage()` method to send the SMS to another device:

```
String destination = "16501234567";
String msg = "Sending my first message";
mySMS.sendTextMessage(destination, null, msg, null, null);
```

This is sufficient to send an SMS message. However, the three additional parameters in the previous call set to `null` can be utilized as follows.

- The second parameter is the specific SMS service center to use. Set to null to use the default service center from the carrier.
- The fourth parameter is a `PendingIntent` to track if the SMS message was sent.
- The fifth parameter is a `PendingIntent` to track if the SMS message was received.

To use the fourth and fifth parameters, a send message and a delivered message intent need to be declared:

```
String SENT_SMS_FLAG = "SENT_SMS";
String DELIVER_SMS_FLAG = "DELIVER_SMS";

Intent sentIn = new Intent(SENT_SMS_FLAG);
PendingIntent sentPIn = PendingIntent.getBroadcast(this,0,sentIn,0);

Intent deliverIn = new Intent(SENT_SMS_FLAG);
PendingIntent deliverPIn
                   = PendingIntent.getBroadcast(this,0,deliverIn,0);
```

Then, a `BroadcastReceiver` needs to be registered for each `PendingIntent` to receive the result:

```
BroadcastReceiver sentReceiver = new BroadcastReceiver(){
    @Override public void onReceive(Context c, Intent in) {
        switch(getResultCode()){
            case Activity.RESULT_OK:
                //sent SMS message successfully;
                break;
            default:
                //sent SMS message failed
                break;
        }
    }
};
BroadcastReceiver deliverReceiver = new BroadcastReceiver(){
    @Override public void onReceive(Context c, Intent in) {
        //SMS delivered actions
    }
};

registerReceiver(sentReceiver, new IntentFilter(SENT_SMS_FLAG));
registerReceiver(deliverReceiver, new IntentFilter(DELIVER_SMS_FLAG));
```

Most SMSes are restricted to 140 characters per text message. To make sure the message is within this limitation, use the `divideMessage()` method that divides the text into fragments in the maximum SMS message size. Then, the method `sendMultipartTextMessage()`

should be used instead of the `sendTextMessage()` method. The only difference is the use of an `ArrayList` of messages and pending intents:

```
ArrayList<String> multiSMS = mySMS.divideMessage(msg);
ArrayList<PendingIntent> sentIns = new ArrayList<PendingIntent>();
ArrayList<PendingIntent> deliverIns = new ArrayList<PendingIntent>();

for(int i=0; i< multiSMS.size(); i++){
    sentIns.add(sentIn);
    deliverIns.add(deliverIn);
}

mySMS.sendMultipartTextMessage(destination, null,
                               multiSMS, sentIns, deliverIns);
```

Recipe: Autosend an SMS Based on a Received SMS

Because most SMS messages are not read by the recipient until hours later, this recipe sends an autoresponse SMS when an SMS is received. This is done by creating an Android service in the background that can receive incoming SMS. An alternative method is to register a broadcast receiver in the AndroidManifest XML file.

The application must declare permission to send and receive SMS in the AndroidManifest XML file, as shown in Listing 8.1. It also declares a main activity `SMSResponder` that creates the autoresponse and a service `ResponderService` to send the response when an SMS is received.

Listing 8.1 **AndroidManifest.xml**

```
<?xml version="1.0" encoding="utf-8"?>
<manifest xmlns:android="http://schemas.android.com/apk/res/android"
      package="com.cookbook.SMSResponder"
      android:versionCode="1"
      android:versionName="1.0">
    <application android:icon="@drawable/icon"
                 android:label="@string/app_name">
        <activity android:name=".SMSResponder"
                  android:label="@string/app_name">
            <intent-filter>
              <action android:name="android.intent.action.MAIN" />
              <category android:name="android.intent.category.LAUNCHER" />
            </intent-filter>
        </activity>
        <service android:enabled="true" android:name=".ResponderService">
        </service>
    </application>
```

```
    <uses-permission android:name="android.permission.RECEIVE_SMS"/>
    <uses-permission android:name="android.permission.SEND_SMS"/>
</manifest>
```

The main layout file shown in Listing 8.2 contains a `LinearLayout` with three views: a `TextView` to display the message used for the autoresponse, a button used to commit changes on the reply message inside the application, and `EditText` where the user can enter a reply message.

Listing 8.2 **res/layout/main.xml**

```
<?xml version="1.0" encoding="utf-8"?>
<LinearLayout xmlns:android="http://schemas.android.com/apk/res/android"
    android:orientation="vertical"
    android:layout_width="fill_parent"
    android:layout_height="fill_parent">
        <TextView android:id="@+id/display"
        android:layout_width="fill_parent"
        android:layout_height="wrap_content"
        android:text="@string/hello"
        android:textSize="18dp"
        />
        <Button android:id="@+id/submit"
        android:layout_width="wrap_content"
        android:layout_height="wrap_content"
        android:text="Change my response"
        />
        <EditText android:id="@+id/editText"
        android:layout_width="fill_parent"
        android:layout_height="fill_parent"
        />
</LinearLayout>
```

The main activity is shown in Listing 8.3. It starts the service that listens and autoresponds to SMS messages. It also allows the user to change the reply message and save it in a `SharedPreference` for future use.

Listing 8.3 **src/com/cookbook/SMSresponder/SMSResponder.java**

```
package com.cookbook.SMSresponder;

import android.app.Activity;
import android.content.Intent;
import android.content.SharedPreferences;
import android.content.SharedPreferences.Editor;
import android.os.Bundle;
```

```
import android.preference.PreferenceManager;
import android.util.Log;
import android.view.View;
import android.view.View.OnClickListener;
import android.widget.Button;
import android.widget.EditText;
import android.widget.TextView;

public class SMSResponder extends Activity {
    TextView tv1;
    EditText ed1;
    Button bt1;
    SharedPreferences myprefs;
    Editor updater;
    String reply=null;

    @Override
    public void onCreate(Bundle savedInstanceState) {
        super.onCreate(savedInstanceState);
        setContentView(R.layout.main);

        myprefs = PreferenceManager.getDefaultSharedPreferences(this);
        tv1 = (TextView) this.findViewById(R.id.display);
        ed1 = (EditText) this.findViewById(R.id.editText);
        bt1 = (Button) this.findViewById(R.id.submit);

        reply = myprefs.getString("reply",
               "Thank you for your message. I am busy now. "
               + "I will call you later");
        tv1.setText(reply);

        updater = myprefs.edit();
        ed1.setHint(reply);
        bt1.setOnClickListener(new OnClickListener() {
            public void onClick(View view) {
                updater.putString("reply", ed1.getText().toString());
                updater.commit();
                SMSResponder.this.finish();
            }
        });

        try {
            // start Service
            Intent svc = new Intent(this, ResponderService.class);
            startService(svc);
        }
```

```
        catch (Exception e) {
            Log.e("onCreate", "service creation problem", e);
        }
    }
}
```

The majority of code is contained in the service, as shown in Listing 8.4. It retrieves the `SharedPreferences` for this application first. Then it registers a broadcast receiver for listening to incoming and outgoing SMS messages. The broadcast receiver for outgoing SMS messages is not used here but shown for completeness.

The incoming SMS broadcast receiver uses a bundle to retrieve the protocol description unit (PDU), which contains the SMS text and any additional SMS meta-data, and parses it into an `Object` array. The method `createFromPdu()` converts the `Object` array into an `SmsMessage`. Then the method `getOriginatingAddress()` can be used to get the sender's phone number, and `getMessageBody()` can be used to get the text message.

In this recipe, after the sender address is retrieved, it calls the `respond()` method. This method tries to get the data stored inside the `SharedPreferences` for the autorespond message. If there is no data stored, it uses a default value. Then, it creates two `PendingIntents` for sent status and delivered status. The method `divideMessage()` is used to make sure the message is not oversized. After all the data is managed, it is sent using `sendMuiltTextMessage()`.

Listing 8.4 **src/com/cookbook/SMSresponder/ResponderService.java**

```
package com.cookbook.SMSresponder;

import java.util.ArrayList;

import android.app.Activity;
import android.app.PendingIntent;
import android.app.Service;
import android.content.BroadcastReceiver;
import android.content.Context;
import android.content.Intent;
import android.content.IntentFilter;
import android.content.SharedPreferences;
import android.os.Bundle;
import android.os.IBinder;
import android.preference.PreferenceManager;
import android.telephony.SmsManager;
import android.telephony.SmsMessage;
import android.util.Log;
import android.widget.Toast;

public class ResponderService extends Service {
```

```
//The Action fired by the Android-System when a SMS was received.
private static final String RECEIVED_ACTION =
                        "android.provider.Telephony.SMS_RECEIVED";
private static final String SENT_ACTION="SENT_SMS";
private static final String DELIVERED_ACTION="DELIVERED_SMS";

String requester;
String reply="";
SharedPreferences myprefs;

@Override
public void onCreate() {
    super.onCreate();
    myprefs = PreferenceManager.getDefaultSharedPreferences(this);

    registerReceiver(sentReceiver, new IntentFilter(SENT_ACTION));
    registerReceiver(deliverReceiver,
                     new IntentFilter(DELIVERED_ACTION));

    IntentFilter filter = new IntentFilter(RECEIVED_ACTION);
    registerReceiver(receiver, filter);

    IntentFilter attemptedfilter = new IntentFilter(SENT_ACTION);
    registerReceiver(sender,attemptedfilter);
}

private BroadcastReceiver sender = new BroadcastReceiver(){
    @Override
    public void onReceive(Context c, Intent i) {
        if(i.getAction().equals(SENT_ACTION)) {
            if(getResultCode() != Activity.RESULT_OK) {
                String reciptent = i.getStringExtra("recipient");
                requestReceived(reciptent);
            }
        }
    }
};
BroadcastReceiver sentReceiver = new BroadcastReceiver() {
    @Override public void onReceive(Context c, Intent in) {
        switch(getResultCode()) {
            case Activity.RESULT_OK:
                //sent SMS message successfully;
                smsSent();
                break;
            default:
                //sent SMS message failed
                smsFailed();
                break;
         }
```

```
        }
    };

    public void smsSent() {
        Toast.makeText(this, "SMS sent", Toast.LENGTH_SHORT);
    }
    public void smsFailed() {
        Toast.makeText(this, "SMS sent failed", Toast.LENGTH_SHORT);
    }
    public void smsDelivered() {
        Toast.makeText(this, "SMS delivered", Toast.LENGTH_SHORT);
    }

    BroadcastReceiver deliverReceiver = new BroadcastReceiver() {
        @Override public void onReceive(Context c, Intent in) {
            //SMS delivered actions
            smsDelivered();
        }
    };

    public void requestReceived(String f) {
        Log.v("ResponderService","In requestReceived");
        requester=f;
    }

    BroadcastReceiver receiver = new BroadcastReceiver() {
        @Override
        public void onReceive(Context c, Intent in) {
            Log.v("ResponderService","On Receive");
            reply="";
            if(in.getAction().equals(RECEIVED_ACTION)) {
                Log.v("ResponderService","On SMS RECEIVE");

                Bundle bundle = in.getExtras();
                if(bundle!=null) {
                    Object[] pdus = (Object[])bundle.get("pdus");
                    SmsMessage[] messages = new SmsMessage[pdus.length];
                    for(int i = 0; i<pdus.length; i++) {
                        Log.v("ResponderService","FOUND MESSAGE");
                        messages[i] =
                                SmsMessage.createFromPdu((byte[])pdus[i]);
                    }
                    for(SmsMessage message: messages) {
                        requestReceived(message.getOriginatingAddress());
                    }
                    respond();
                }
```

```
            }
        }
    };

    @Override
    public void onStart(Intent intent, int startId) {
        super.onStart(intent, startId);
    }

    public void respond() {
        Log.v("ResponderService","Responing to " + requester);
        reply = myprefs.getString("reply",
                        "Thank you for your message. I am busy now. "
                        + "I will call you later");
        SmsManager sms = SmsManager.getDefault();
        Intent sentIn = new Intent(SENT_ACTION);
        PendingIntent sentPIn = PendingIntent.getBroadcast(this,
                                                        0,sentIn,0);
        Intent deliverIn = new Intent(DELIVERED_ACTION);
        PendingIntent deliverPIn = PendingIntent.getBroadcast(this,
                                                        0,deliverIn,0);
        ArrayList<String> Msgs = sms.divideMessage(reply);
        ArrayList<PendingIntent> sentIns = new ArrayList<PendingIntent>();
        ArrayList<PendingIntent> deliverIns =
                                new ArrayList<PendingIntent>();

        for(int i=0; i< Msgs.size(); i++) {
            sentIns.add(sentPIn);
            deliverIns.add(deliverPIn);
        }

        sms.sendMultipartTextMessage(requester, null,
                                Msgs, sentIns, deliverIns);
    }

    @Override
    public void onDestroy() {
        super.onDestroy();
        unregisterReceiver(receiver);
        unregisterReceiver(sender);
    }

    @Override
    public IBinder onBind(Intent arg0) {
        return null;
    }
}
```

Using Web Content

To launch an Internet browser to display web content, the implicit intent `ACTION_VIEW` can be used as discussed in Chapter 2, "Application Basics: Activities and Intents," for example:

```
Intent i = new Intent(Intent.ACTION_VIEW);
i.setData(Uri.parse("http://www.google.com"));
startActivity(i);
```

It is also possible for developers to create their own web browser by using `WebView`, which is a `View` that displays web content. As with any view, it can occupy the full screen or only a portion of the layout in an activity. `WebView` uses WebKit, the open source browser engine used in Apple's Safari, to render web pages.

Recipe: Customizing a Web Browser

There are two ways to obtain a `WebView` object. It can be instantiated from the constructor:

```
WebView webview = new WebView(this);
```

Alternatively, a `WebView` can be used in a layout and declared in the activity:

```
WebView webView = (WebView) findViewById(R.id.webview);
```

After the object is retrieved, a web page can be displayed using the `loadURL()` method:

```
webview.loadUrl("http://www.google.com/");
```

The `WebSettings` class can be used to define the features of the browser. For example, network images can be blocked in the browser to reduce the data loading using `the setBlockNetworkImage()` method. The font size of the displayed web content can be set using the `setDefaultFontSize()` method. Some other commonly used settings are shown in the example:

```
WebSettings webSettings = webView.getSettings();
webSettings.setSaveFormData(false);
webSettings.setJavaScriptEnabled(true);
webSettings.setSavePassword(false);
webSettings.setSaveFormData(false);
webSettings.setJavaScriptEnabled(true);
webSettings.setSupportZoom(true);
```

Recipe: Using an HTTP GET

Besides launching a browser or using the `WebView` widget to include a WebKit-based browser control in an activity, developers might also want to create native Internet-based applications. This means the application relies on only the raw data from the Internet, such as images, media files, and XML data. Just the data of relevance can be loaded. This is important for creating social networking applications. Two packages are useful in Android to handle network communication: `java.net` and `android.net`.

In this recipe, the HTTP GET is used to retrieve XML or JSON data (see http://www.json.org/ for an overview). In particular, the Google search Representational State Transfer (REST) Application Programming Interface (API) is demonstrated, and the following query is used:

```
http://ajax.googleapis.com/ajax/services/search/web?v=1.0&q=
```

More information on Google Asynchronous Javascript And XML (AJAX) search can be found at http://code.google.com/apis/ajaxsearch/.

To search any topic, the topic just needs to be appended to the query. For example, to search information on the National Basketball Association (NBA), the following query returns JSON data:

```
http://ajax.googleapis.com/ajax/services/search/web?v=1.0&q=NBA
```

The activity needs Internet permission to run. So, the following should be added to the AndroidManifest XML file:

```
<uses-permission android:name="android.permission.INTERNET"/>
```

The main layout is shown in Listing 8.5. It has three views: `EditText` for user input of the search topic, `Button` to trigger the search, and `TextView` to display the search result.

Listing 8.5 **res/layout/main.xml**

```
<?xml version="1.0" encoding="utf-8"?>
<LinearLayout xmlns:android="http://schemas.android.com/apk/res/android"
    android:orientation="vertical"
    android:layout_width="fill_parent"
    android:layout_height="fill_parent"
    >
           <EditText
           android:id="@+id/editText"
           android:layout_width="fill_parent"
           android:layout_height="wrap_content"
           android:singleLine="true"
            />
            <Button
              android:id="@+id/submit"
            android:layout_width="wrap_content"
            android:layout_height="wrap_content"
            android:text="Search"
            />
            <TextView
            android:id="@+id/display"
            android:layout_width="fill_parent"
            android:layout_height="fill_parent"
            android:text="@string/hello"
            android:textSize="18dp"
            />
</LinearLayout>
```

The main activity is shown in Listing 8.6. It initiates the three layout elements in `onCreate()`. Inside the `OnClickListener` for the button, it calls the `SearchRequest()`. This composes the search item using the Google REST API URL and then initiates an URL class instance. The URL class instance is then used to get an `HttpURLConnection` instance.

The `HttpURLConnection` instance can retrieve the status of the connection. When the `HttpURLConnection` returns a result code of `HTTP_OK`, it means the whole HTTP transaction went through. Then, the JSON data returned from the HTTP transaction can be dumped into a string. This is done using an `InputStreamReader` passed to a `BufferReader` to read the data and create a `String` instance. After the result from HTTP is obtained, it uses another function `ProcessResponse()` to parse the JSON data. The detailed mechanism used requires an understanding of the incoming JSON data structure. In this case, the Google REST API provides all the result data under the results `JSONArray`. Figure 8.1 shows a screenshot of the search result for NBA.

Listing 8.6 **src/com/cookbook/internet/search/GoogleSearch.java**

```
package com.cookbook.internet.search;

import java.io.BufferedReader;
import java.io.IOException;
import java.io.InputStreamReader;
import java.net.HttpURLConnection;
import java.net.MalformedURLException;
import java.net.URL;
import java.security.NoSuchAlgorithmException;

import org.json.JSONArray;
import org.json.JSONException;
import org.json.JSONObject;

import android.app.Activity;
import android.os.Bundle;
import android.util.Log;
import android.view.View;
import android.view.View.OnClickListener;
import android.widget.Button;
import android.widget.EditText;
import android.widget.TextView;

public class GoogleSearch extends Activity {
    /** Called when the activity is first created. */
    TextView tv1;
    EditText ed1;
    Button bt1;
    static String url =
"http://ajax.googleapis.com/ajax/services/search/web?v=1.0&q=";
```

```
@Override
public void onCreate(Bundle savedInstanceState) {
    super.onCreate(savedInstanceState);
    setContentView(R.layout.main);
    tv1 = (TextView) this.findViewById(R.id.display);
    ed1 = (EditText) this.findViewById(R.id.editText);
    bt1 = (Button) this.findViewById(R.id.submit);

    bt1.setOnClickListener(new OnClickListener() {
        public void onClick(View view) {
                if(ed1.getText().toString()!=null) {
                    try{
                        ProcessResponse(
                          SearchRequest(ed1.getText().toString()));
                    } catch(Exception e) {
                        Log.v("Exception google search",
                              "Exception:"+e.getMessage());
                    }
                }
                ed1.setText("");
        }
    });
}

public String SearchRequest(String searchString)
                        throws MalformedURLException, IOException {
    String newFeed=url+searchString;
    StringBuilder response = new StringBuilder();
    Log.v("gsearch","gsearch url:"+newFeed);
    URL url = new URL(newFeed);

    HttpURLConnection httpconn
                          = (HttpURLConnection) url.openConnection();

    if(httpconn.getResponseCode()==HttpURLConnection.HTTP_OK) {
        BufferedReader input = new BufferedReader(
                new InputStreamReader(httpconn.getInputStream()),
                8192);
        String strLine = null;
        while ((strLine = input.readLine()) != null) {
            response.append(strLine);
        }
        input.close();
    }
    return response.toString();
}
```

```
    public void ProcessResponse(String resp) throws IllegalStateException,
                IOException, JSONException, NoSuchAlgorithmException {
        StringBuilder sb = new StringBuilder();
        Log.v("gsearch","gsearch result:"+resp);
        JSONObject mResponseObject = new JSONObject(resp);
        JSONObject responObject
                    = mResponseObject.getJSONObject("responseData");
        JSONArray array = responObject.getJSONArray("results");
        Log.v("gsearch","number of resultst:"+array.length());
        for(int i = 0; i<array.length(); i++) {
            Log.v("result",i+"] "+array.get(i).toString());
            String title = array.getJSONObject(i).getString("title");
            String urllink = array.getJSONObject(i)
                                .getString("visibleUrl");
            sb.append(title);
            sb.append("\n");
            sb.append(urllink);
            sb.append("\n");
        }
        tv1.setText(sb.toString());
    }
}
```

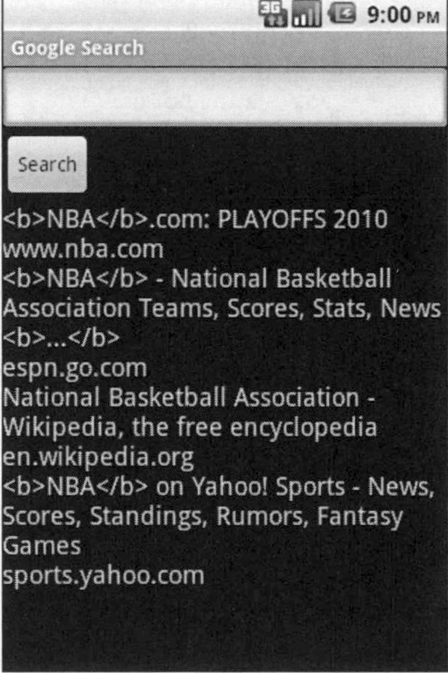

Figure 8.1 The search result from the Google REST API query.

Recipe: Using HTTP POST

Sometimes, raw binary data needs to be retrieved from the Internet such as an image, video, or audio file. This can be achieved using the HTTP POST protocol by using the `setRequestMethod()`, such as:

```
httpconn.setRequestMethod(POST);
```

Accessing data through the Internet can be time-consuming and unpredictable. Therefore, a separate thread should be spawned anytime network data is required.

In addition to the methods shown in Chapter 3, "Threads, Services, Receivers, and Alerts," there is a built-in Android class called `AsyncTask` that allows background operations to be performed and publishes results on the UI thread without needing to manipulate threads or handlers. So, the POST method can be implemented asynchronously with the following code:

```
private class mygoogleSearch extends AsyncTask<String, Integer, String> {

        protected String doInBackground(String... searchKey) {

            String key = searchKey[0];

            try {
                return SearchRequest(key);
            } catch(Exception e) {
                Log.v("Exception google search",
                      "Exception:"+e.getMessage());
                return "";
            }
        }

        protected void onPostExecute(String result) {
            try {
                ProcessResponse(result);
            } catch(Exception e) {
                Log.v("Exception google search",
                      "Exception:"+e.getMessage());
            }
        }
    }
```

This excerpt can be added to the end of the **GoogleSearch.java** activity in Listing 8.6. It provides the same result with one additional change to the code inside the button `OnClickListener` to:

```
new mygoogleSearch().execute(ed1.getText().toString());
```

Social Networking

Twitter is a social networking and microblogging service that enables its users to send and read messages known as tweets. Twitter is described as "SMS of the Internet," and indeed, each tweet cannot exceed 140 characters. Twitter users can follow other people's tweets or be followed by others.

Recipe: Integrating with Twitter

Some third-party libraries exist to assist in integrating Twitter into an Android application (from http://dev.twitter.com/pages/libraries#java):

- Twitter4J by Yusuke Yamamoto—An open-sourced, mavenized, and Google App Engine-safe Java library for the Twitter API, released under the BSD license
- java-twitter by DeWitt Clinton—Pure Java interface for the Twitter API
- jtwitter by Daniel Winterstein—Open-source pure Java interface to Twitter
- Twitter Client by Gist, Inc.—Java client to connect to the streaming API

For this recipe, the Twitter4J library by Yusuke Yamamoto is used, which has documentation at http://twitter4j.org/en/javadoc/overview-summary.html. The recipe enables users to log in to Twitter and make a tweet. At the same time, it retrieves any updated tweets and displays them to the screen.

There are two screens to specify: the login screen and update status screen (see Figure 8.2). Also on the update status screen under the `EditText` box, the latest status from the user account is displayed. The two activities (one for each screen) and Internet permissions need to be declared in the AndroidManifest XML file, as shown in Listing 8.7.

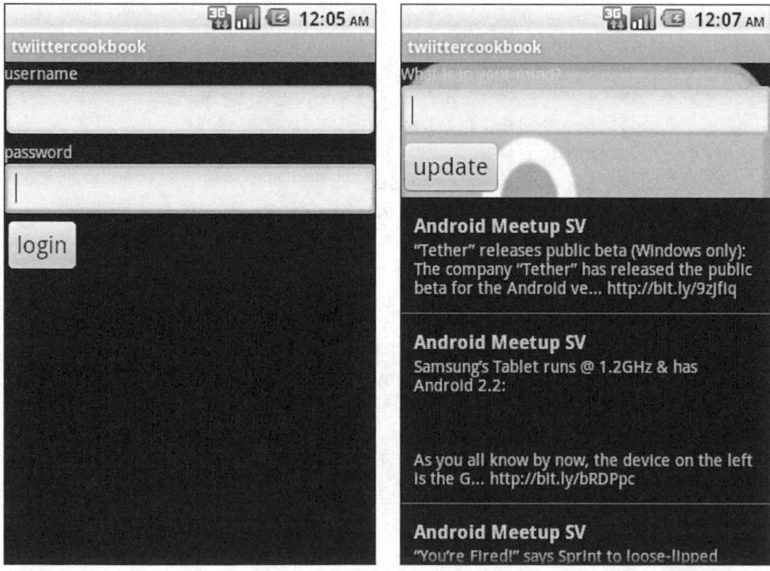

Figure 8.2 The login (left) and tweets (right) from the Twitter recipe.

Listing 8.7 **AndroidManifest.xml**

```
<?xml version="1.0" encoding="utf-8"?>
<manifest xmlns:android="http://schemas.android.com/apk/res/android"
      package="com.cookbook.twitter"
      android:versionCode="1"
      android:versionName="1.0">
    <application android:icon="@drawable/icon"
                 android:label="@string/app_name">
        <activity android:name=".TwitterCookBook"
                  android:label="@string/app_name">
            <intent-filter>
              <action android:name="android.intent.action.MAIN" />
              <category android:name="android.intent.category.LAUNCHER" />
            </intent-filter>
        </activity>
        <activity android:name=".UpdateAndList" />
    </application>
    <uses-permission android:name="android.permission.INTERNET"/>
</manifest>
```

The layout files needed are

- login.xml—The login screen, as shown in Listing 8.8
- main.xml—The screen to update the status and display the home status, as shown in Listing 8.9
- usertimelinerow.xml—The view for display of each status timeline, as shown in Listing 8.10

Listing 8.8 **res/layout/login.xml**

```
<?xml version="1.0" encoding="utf-8"?>
<LinearLayout xmlns:android="http://schemas.android.com/apk/res/android"
        android:orientation="vertical"
        android:layout_width="fill_parent"
        android:layout_height="fill_parent"
        >
        <TextView
            android:layout_width="fill_parent"
            android:layout_height="wrap_content"
            android:text="username"
        />
        <EditText
            android:id="@+id/userText"
            android:layout_width="fill_parent"
            android:layout_height="wrap_content"
            android:singleLine="true"
        />
```

```
        <TextView
            android:layout_width="fill_parent"
            android:layout_height="wrap_content"
            android:text="password"
        />
        <EditText
            android:id="@+id/passwordText"
            android:layout_width="fill_parent"
            android:layout_height="wrap_content"
            android:password="true"
            android:singleLine="true"
        />
        <Button
            android:id="@+id/loginButton"
            android:layout_width="wrap_content"
            android:layout_height="wrap_content"
            android:text="login"
            android:textSize="20dp"
        />
</LinearLayout>
```

Listing 8.9 **res/layout/main.xml**

```
<?xml version="1.0" encoding="utf-8"?>
<LinearLayout xmlns:android="http://schemas.android.com/apk/res/android"
        android:orientation="vertical"
        android:layout_width="fill_parent"
        android:layout_height="fill_parent"
        android:background="@drawable/twitter">
        <TextView
            android:layout_width="fill_parent"
            android:layout_height="wrap_content"
            android:text="What is in your mind?"
            />
        <EditText
            android:id="@+id/userStatus"
            android:layout_width="fill_parent"
            android:layout_height="wrap_content"
            />
        <Button
            android:id="@+id/updateButton"
            android:layout_width="wrap_content"
            android:layout_height="wrap_content"
            android:text="update"
            android:textSize="20dp"
            />
```

```
        <ListView
            android:layout_width="fill_parent"
            android:dividerHeight="1px"
            android:layout_height="fill_parent"
            android:id="list"
            />
</LinearLayout>
```

Listing 8.10 **res/layout/usertimelinerow.xml**

```
<?xml version="1.0" encoding="utf-8"?>
<LinearLayout android:layout_width="wrap_content"
        android:layout_height="wrap_content"
        android:orientation="vertical"
        android:layout_alignLeft="@+id/name"
        android:layout_below="@+id/name"
        xmlns:android="http://schemas.android.com/apk/res/android"
        android:padding="12dip">
        <TextView android:layout_width="wrap_content"
            android:layout_height="wrap_content" android:id="@+id/name"
            android:layout_marginRight="4dp" android:text="Diary Title "
            android:textStyle="bold" android:textSize="16dip"  />
        <TextView android:id="@+id/msg"
            android:layout_width="wrap_content"
            android:layout_height="wrap_content"
            android:text="Date Recorded"
            android:textSize="14dip" />
</LinearLayout>
```

The two activities needed are the login to Twitter activity and the update and list tweets activity. The login activity is shown in Listing 8.11. It contains an `EditText` object for username and password, `Button` object to submit the login data, `SharedPreferences` object to save the login information upon initial successful login, and `Twitter` object from the `twitter4j` library.

Upon startup, the application checks for login information from `SharedPreferences` and if available, it prepopulates the `EditText` boxes. When the user clicks on the `Button`, it initiates the `Twitter` object with the username and password from the `EditText` boxes. After the `Twitter` object is initiated, it tries to call `getFollowersIDs()` to verify if the login is valid. If the login is invalid, an exception is thrown, and in this example, it shows a `Toast` message for login failure.

Listing 8.11 **src/com/cookbook/twitter/TwitterCookBook.java**

```
package com.cookbook.twitter;

import twitter4j.Twitter;
import twitter4j.TwitterFactory;

import android.app.Activity;
import android.content.Intent;
import android.content.SharedPreferences;
import android.content.SharedPreferences.Editor;
import android.os.Bundle;
import android.preference.PreferenceManager;
import android.view.View;
import android.view.View.OnClickListener;
import android.widget.Button;
import android.widget.EditText;
import android.widget.Toast;

public class TwitterCookBook extends Activity {
    SharedPreferences myprefs;
    EditText userET, passwordET;
    Button loginBT;
    static Twitter twitter;

    @Override
    public void onCreate(Bundle savedInstanceState) {
        super.onCreate(savedInstanceState);
        myprefs = PreferenceManager.getDefaultSharedPreferences(this);
        final String username = myprefs.getString("username", null);
        final String password = myprefs.getString("password", null);
        setContentView(R.layout.login);
        userET = (EditText)findViewById(R.id.userText);
        passwordET = (EditText)findViewById(R.id.passwordText);
        loginBT = (Button)findViewById(R.id.loginButton);
        userET.setText(username);
        passwordET.setText(password);
        loginBT.setOnClickListener(new OnClickListener() {
            public void onClick(View v) {
                try {

                    twitter = new TwitterFactory()
                                 .getInstance(userET.getText().toString(),
                                         passwordET.getText().toString());
                    twitter.getFollowersIDs();
```

```
                    Intent i = new Intent(TwitterCookBook.this,
                                          UpdateAndList.class);
                    startActivity(i);

                    Editor ed = myprefs.edit();
                    ed.putString("username",userET.getText().toString());
                    ed.putString("password",
                                 passwordET.getText().toString());
                    ed.commit();
                    finish();

                } catch (Exception e) {
                    e.printStackTrace();
                    Toast.makeText(TwitterCookBook.this, "login failed!!",
                                   Toast.LENGTH_SHORT).show();
                }
            }
        });
    }
}
```

After the login is passed, the `UpdateAndList` activity is started. As shown in Listing 8.12, it contains an `EditText` object for the user to enter their tweet, a `Button` object to submit the tweet to the Twitter server, a `Twitter` object from the `twitter4j` library, a `ResponseList` of status for holding the data returned from the Twitter object, and a custom adapter for managing the status data.

The activity calls the `getHomeTimeline()` to retrieve the timeline status shown on the Twitter home page when a user logs in. Note that all Internet access function calls are placed inside an `AsyncTask` to avoid hanging the UI thread. The `getHomeTimeline()` method is called every time the user submits a tweet and updates the data adapter.

To hold status data in a `ListView` format, the activity is extended as `ListActivity`. Inside the `ListActivity`, a custom `BaseAdapter` called `UserTimeLineAdapter` is defined. This adapter uses `ResponseList<Status> userTimeLine` to display the data in `ListView`.

The `ListActivity` has two `AsyncTask` classes: `setup` and `loadstatus`. They both call the same operation `getHomeTimeLine()`. The only difference is that `setup` tries to initiate the adapter and set the `ListActivity` with `UserTimeLineAdapter`, whereas `loadstatus` just notifies the `UserTimeLineAdapter` that data is changed.

Listing 8.12 **src/com/cookbook/twitter/UpdateAndList.java**

```
package com.cookbook.twitter;

import twitter4j.ResponseList;
import twitter4j.Status;
import twitter4j.Twitter;
```

```
import android.app.ListActivity;
import android.content.Context;
import android.os.AsyncTask;
import android.os.Bundle;
import android.util.Log;
import android.view.LayoutInflater;
import android.view.View;
import android.view.ViewGroup;
import android.view.View.OnClickListener;
import android.widget.BaseAdapter;
import android.widget.Button;
import android.widget.EditText;
import android.widget.TextView;

public class UpdateAndList extends ListActivity {
    EditText userET;
    Button updateBT;
    Twitter twitter;
    ResponseList<Status> userTimeline;
    UserTimeLineAdapter myAdapter;

    @Override
    public void onCreate(Bundle savedInstanceState) {
        super.onCreate(savedInstanceState);
        setContentView(R.layout.main);
        userET = (EditText)findViewById(R.id.userStatus);

        updateBT = (Button)findViewById(R.id.updateButton);

        twitter = TwitterCookBook.twitter;
        setup stup = new setup();
        stup.execute();

        updateBT.setOnClickListener(new OnClickListener() {
            public void onClick(View v) {
                try {
                    twitter.updateStatus(userET.getText().toString());
                    loadstatus ldstatus = new loadstatus();
                    ldstatus.execute();
                    userET.setText("");
                } catch (Exception e) {
                    e.printStackTrace();
                }
            }
        });
    }
```

```
private class UserTimeLineAdapter extends BaseAdapter{
    private LayoutInflater mInflater;

    public UserTimeLineAdapter(Context context) {
        mInflater = LayoutInflater.from(context);
    }

    @Override
    public int getCount() {
        return userTimeline.size();
    }

    @Override
    public Status getItem(int i) {
        return userTimeline.get(i);
    }

    @Override
    public long getItemId(int i) {
        return i;
    }

    @Override
    public View getView(int arg0, View arg1, ViewGroup arg2) {
        final ViewHolder holder;
        View v = arg1;
        if ((v == null) || (v.getTag() == null)) {
                v = mInflater.inflate(R.layout.usertimelinerow, null);
                holder = new ViewHolder();
                holder.mName = (TextView)v.findViewById(R.id.name);
                holder.mStatus = (TextView)v.findViewById(R.id.msg);
                v.setTag(holder);
        } else {
            holder = (ViewHolder) v.getTag();
        }

        holder.status= getItem(arg0);
        holder.mName.setText(holder.status.getUser().getName());
        holder.mStatus.setText(holder.status.getText());

        v.setTag(holder);

        return v;
    }
```

```
    public class ViewHolder {
        Status status;
        TextView mName;
        TextView mStatus;
    }
}

private class setup extends AsyncTask<String, Integer, String> {

    protected String doInBackground(String... searchKey) {

        try{
            userTimeline = twitter.getHomeTimeline();
            return "";
        }catch(Exception e){
            Log.v("Exception Twitter query",
                  "Exception:"+e.getMessage());
            return "";

        }
    }

    protected void onPostExecute(String result) {
        try {
            myAdapter = new UserTimeLineAdapter(UpdateAndList.this);
            UpdateAndList.this.setListAdapter(myAdapter);
        } catch(Exception e) {
            Log.v("Exception Twitter query",
                  "Exception:"+e.getMessage());
        }
    }
}

private class loadstatus extends AsyncTask<String, Integer, String> {

    protected String doInBackground(String... searchKey) {

        try {
            userTimeline = twitter.getHomeTimeline();
            return "";
        } catch(Exception e) {
            Log.v("Exception Twitter query",
                  "Exception:"+e.getMessage());
            return "";
        }
```

```
        }

        protected void onPostExecute(String result) {
            try {
                myAdapter.notifyDataSetChanged();
            } catch(Exception e) {
                Log.v("Exception twitter query",
                      "Exception:"+e.getMessage());
            }
        }
    }
}
```

9

Data Storage Methods

Complicated and robust Android applications often need to utilize some type of data storage. Depending on the situation, different data storage methods are available to the developer:

- Shared Preferences for lightweight usage, such as saving application settings and the user interface (UI) state
- A built-in SQLite database for more complicated usage, such as saving application records
- The standard Java flat file storage methods: `InputFileStream` and `OutputFileStream`

These are discussed in this chapter. Also discussed is the Content Provider Android component that is used to share data between applications. It should be noted that another basic data storage method managed by the Android system, the `onSaveInstanceState()` and `onRestoreInstanceState()` pair, was already discussed in Chapter 2, "Application Basics: Activities and Intents." The optimal method to use depends on the situation, as discussed in each case that follows.

Shared Preferences

`SharedPreferences` is an interface that an application can use to quickly and efficiently save data in name-values pairs, similar to a Bundle. The information is stored in an XML file on the Android device. For example, if the application `com.cookbook.datastorage` creates a shared preference, the Android system creates a new XML file under the **/data/data/com.cookbook.datastorage/shared_prefs** directory. Shared preferences are usually used for saving application settings such as user settings, theme, and other general application properties. It can also save login information such as username, password, auto-login flag and remember-user flag. The shared preferences data is accessible by every component of the application which created it.

Recipe: Creating and Retrieving Shared Preferences

The shared preferences for an activity can be accessed using the `getPreferences()` method, which specifies the operating mode for the default preferences file. If instead multiple preference files are needed, each can be specified using the `getSharedPreferences()` method. If the shared preferences XML file exists in the data directory, it is opened; otherwise, it is created. The operating mode provides control over the different kinds of access permission to the preferences:

- `MODE_PRIVATE`—Only the calling application has access to the XML file.
- `MODE_WORLD_READABLE`—All applications can read the XML file.
- `MODE_WORLD_WRITEABLE`—All applications can write to the XML file.

After a `SharedPreferences` object is retrieved, an `Editor` object is needed to write the name-value pairs to the XML file using the `put()` method. Currently, there are five primitive types supported: `int`, `long`, `float`, `String`, and `boolean`. The following code shows how to create and store shared preferences data:

```
SharedPreferences prefs = getSharedPreferences("myDataStorage",
                                               MODE_PRIVATE);
Editor mEditor = prefs.edit();
mEditor.putString("username","datastorageuser1");
mEditor.putString("password","password1234");
mEditor.commit();
```

The following shows how to retrieve shared preferences data:

```
SharedPreferences prefs = getSharedPreferences("myDataStorage",
                                               MODE_PRIVATE);
String username = prefs.getString("username", "");
String password = prefs.getString("password", "");
```

Recipe: Using the Preferences Framework

Android provides a standardized framework for setting preferences across all applications. The framework uses category preferences and screens to group related settings. `PreferenceCategory` is used to declare a set of preferences into one category. `PreferenceScreen` presents a group of preferences in a new screen.

This recipe uses the preferences defined in the XML file in Listing 9.1. A `PreferenceScreen` is the root element with two `EditTextPreference` elements for username and password. Other possible elements are `CheckBoxPreference`, `RingtonePreference`, and `DialogPreference`. The Android system then generates a UI to manipulate the preferences, as shown in Figure 9.1. These preferences are stored in shared preferences, which means they can be retrieved by calling `getPreferences()`.

Listing 9.1 **res/xml/preferences.xml**

```
<?xml version="1.0" encoding="utf-8"?>
<PreferenceScreen xmlns:android="http://schemas.android.com/apk/res/android">
  <EditTextPreference android:title="User Name"
                      android:key="username"
                      android:summary="Please provide user
name"></EditTextPreference>
  <EditTextPreference android:title="Password"
                      android:password="true"
                      android:key="password"
                      android:summary="Please enter your
password"></EditTextPreference>
</PreferenceScreen>
```

Then, an activity extending the `PreferenceActivity` calls the `addPreferencesFromResource()` method to include these preferences in the activity, as shown in Listing 9.2.

Listing 9.2 **src/com/cookbook/datastorage/MyPreferences.java**

```
package com.cookbook.datastorage;

import android.os.Bundle;
import android.preference.PreferenceActivity;

public class MyPreferences extends PreferenceActivity {

  @Override
  public void onCreate(Bundle savedInstanceState) {
    super.onCreate(savedInstanceState);

    addPreferencesFromResource(R.xml.preferences);
  }
}
```

The main activity merely needs to launch the `PreferenceActivity` when needed (for example, when the Menu button is pressed). Listing 9.3 shows the simple example of showing the preferences upon startup of the activity.

Listing 9.3 **src/com/cookbook/datastorage/DataStorage.java**

```
package com.cookbook.datastorage;

import android.app.Activity;
import android.content.Intent;
import android.os.Bundle;

public class DataStorage extends Activity {
    /** Called when the activity is first created. */
    @Override
    public void onCreate(Bundle savedInstanceState) {
        super.onCreate(savedInstanceState);
        setContentView(R.layout.main);
        Intent i = new Intent(this, MyPreferences.class);
        startActivity(i);
    }
}
```

The AndroidManifest XML file needs to include all activities, including the new `PreferenceActivity`, as shown in Listing 9.4.

Listing 9.4 **AndroidManifest.xml**

```
<?xml version="1.0" encoding="utf-8"?>
<manifest xmlns:android="http://schemas.android.com/apk/res/android"
      package="com.cookbook.datastorage"
      android:versionCode="1"
      android:versionName="1.0">
    <application android:icon="@drawable/icon" android:label="@string/app_name">
        <activity android:name=".DataStorage"
                  android:label="@string/app_name">
            <intent-filter>
                <action android:name="android.intent.action.MAIN" />
                <category android:name="android.intent.category.LAUNCHER"
            />
            </intent-filter>
        </activity>
        <activity android:name=".MyPreferences" />
    </application>
    <uses-sdk android:minSdkVersion="7" />
</manifest>
```

This creates the preferences screen shown in Figure 9.1.

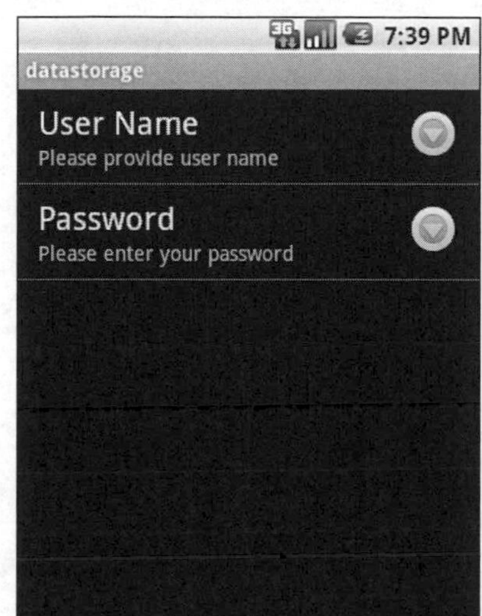

Figure 9.1 The preferences UI generated by the Android system from an XML preferences file.

Recipe: Changing the UI Based on Stored Data

The `DataStorage` activity of the previous recipe can be extended to check the shared preferences when loading, altering the behavior accordingly. In this recipe, if a username and password is already saved in the SharedPreferences file, a login page is displayed. After a successful login, the activity can successfully continue. If no login information is on file, the activity continues directly.

The **main.xml** layout file can be modified to be a login page, as shown in Listing 9.5. This uses two `EditText` objects for username and password, as covered in Chapter 4, "User Interface Layout."

Listing 9.5 **res/layout/main.xml**

```
<?xml version="1.0" encoding="utf-8"?>
<LinearLayout xmlns:android="http://schemas.android.com/apk/res/android"
    android:orientation="vertical"
    android:layout_width="fill_parent"
    android:layout_height="fill_parent">
    <TextView
        android:layout_width="fill_parent"
        android:layout_height="wrap_content"
```

```
        android:text="username"
    />
    <EditText
        android:id="@+id/userText"
        android:layout_width="fill_parent"
        android:layout_height="wrap_content"
    />
    <TextView
        android:layout_width="fill_parent"
        android:layout_height="wrap_content"
        android:text="password"
    />
    <EditText
        android:id="@+id/passwordText"
        android:layout_width="fill_parent"
        android:layout_height="wrap_content"
        android:password="true"
    />
    <Button
        android:id="@+id/loginButton"
        android:layout_width="wrap_content"
        android:layout_height="wrap_content"
        android:text="login"
        android:textSize="20dp"
    />
</LinearLayout>
```

The main activity `DataStorage`, as shown in Listing 9.6, is modified to first read the `username` and `password` data from the SharedPreferences instance. If these data are not set, the application launches the `MyPreferences` activity (Listing 9.2) directly to set the preferences. If these data are set, then the application displays the login layout **main.xml** shown in Figure 9.2. The button has an `onClickListener` that verifies whether the login information matches the username and password from the `SharedPreferences` file. A successful login enables the application to continue on, which in this case, just launches the `MyPreferences` activity. Any login attempt shows a Toast message of success or failure for illustration purposes.

Listing 9.6 **src/com/cookbook/datastorage/DataStorage.java**

```
package com.cookbook.datastorage;

import android.app.Activity;
import android.content.Intent;
import android.content.SharedPreferences;
import android.os.Bundle;
import android.preference.PreferenceManager;
import android.view.View;
```

```
import android.view.View.OnClickListener;
import android.widget.Button;
import android.widget.EditText;
import android.widget.Toast;

public class DataStorage extends Activity {
    SharedPreferences myprefs;
    EditText userET, passwordET;
    Button loginBT;
    @Override
    public void onCreate(Bundle savedInstanceState) {
        super.onCreate(savedInstanceState);
        myprefs = PreferenceManager.getDefaultSharedPreferences(this);
        final String username = myprefs.getString("username", null);
        final String password = myprefs.getString("password", null);
        if (username != null && password != null){
            setContentView(R.layout.main);
            userET = (EditText)findViewById(R.id.userText);
            passwordET = (EditText)findViewById(R.id.passwordText);
            loginBT = (Button)findViewById(R.id.loginButton);
            loginBT.setOnClickListener(new OnClickListener() {
                public void onClick(View v) {
                    try {
                        if(username.equals(userET.getText().toString())
                           && password.equals(
                                        passwordET.getText().toString())) {
                            Toast.makeText(DataStorage.this,
                                           "login passed!!",
                                           Toast.LENGTH_SHORT).show();
                            Intent i = new Intent(DataStorage.this,
                                                  myPreferences.class);
                            startActivity(i);
                        } else {
                            Toast.makeText(DataStorage.this,
                                           "login failed!!",
                                           Toast.LENGTH_SHORT).show();
                        }
                    } catch (Exception e) {
                        e.printStackTrace();
                    }
                }
            });
        } else {
            Intent i = new Intent(this, MyPreferences.class);
            startActivity(i);
        }
    }
}
```

Figure 9.2 The login screen described by Listing 9.5.

Recipe: Adding a EULA

As discussed in Chapter 1, "Overview of Android," it is often useful to have an End User License Agreement (EULA) display when a user first installs and runs an app. If the user does not accept it, the downloaded application does not run. After a user does accept it, the EULA is never shown again.

This EULA functionality is already implemented and available publicly under the Apache License as the `Eula` class shown in Listing 9.7. It uses `SharedPreferences` with the boolean `PREFERENCE_EULA_ACCEPTED` to determine whether the EULA was previously accepted or not accepted.

Listing 9.7 **src/com/cookbook/eula_example/Eula.java**

```
/*
 * Copyright (C) 2008 The Android Open Source Project
 *
 * Licensed under the Apache License, Version 2.0 (the "License");
 * you may not use this file except in compliance with the License.
 * You may obtain a copy of the License at
 *
 *      http://www.apache.org/licenses/LICENSE-2.0
 *
```

```
 * Unless required by applicable law or agreed to in writing, software
 * distributed under the License is distributed on an "AS IS" BASIS,
 * WITHOUT WARRANTIES OR CONDITIONS OF ANY KIND, either express or implied.
 * See the License for the specific language governing permissions and
 * limitations under the License.
 */

package com.cookbook.eula_example;

import android.app.Activity;
import android.app.AlertDialog;
import android.content.DialogInterface;
import android.content.SharedPreferences;

import java.io.IOException;
import java.io.BufferedReader;
import java.io.InputStreamReader;
import java.io.Closeable;

/**
 * Displays an EULA ("End User License Agreement") that the user has to accept
before
 * using the application.
 */
class Eula {
    private static final String ASSET_EULA = "EULA";
    private static final String PREFERENCE_EULA_ACCEPTED = "eula.accepted";
    private static final String PREFERENCES_EULA = "eula";

    /**
     * callback to let the activity know when the user accepts the EULA.
     */
    static interface OnEulaAgreedTo {
        void onEulaAgreedTo();
    }

    /**
     * Displays the EULA if necessary.
     */
    static boolean show(final Activity activity) {

        final SharedPreferences preferences =
                          activity.getSharedPreferences(
                                 PREFERENCES_EULA, Activity.MODE_PRIVATE);
        //to test:
        //  preferences.edit()
        //     .putBoolean(PREFERENCE_EULA_ACCEPTED, false).commit();
```

```
        if (!preferences.getBoolean(PREFERENCE_EULA_ACCEPTED, false)) {
            final AlertDialog.Builder builder =
                          new AlertDialog.Builder(activity);
            builder.setTitle(R.string.eula_title);
            builder.setCancelable(true);
            builder.setPositiveButton(R.string.eula_accept,
                                 new DialogInterface.OnClickListener() {
                public void onClick(DialogInterface dialog, int which) {
                    accept(preferences);
                    if (activity instanceof OnEulaAgreedTo) {
                        ((OnEulaAgreedTo) activity).onEulaAgreedTo();
                    }
                }
            });
            builder.setNegativeButton(R.string.eula_refuse,
                                 new DialogInterface.OnClickListener() {
                public void onClick(DialogInterface dialog, int which) {
                    refuse(activity);
                }
            });
            builder.setOnCancelListener(
                                 new DialogInterface.OnCancelListener() {
                public void onCancel(DialogInterface dialog) {
                    refuse(activity);
                }
            });
            builder.setMessage(readEula(activity));
            builder.create().show();
            return false;
        }
        return true;
    }

    private static void accept(SharedPreferences preferences) {
        preferences.edit().putBoolean(PREFERENCE_EULA_ACCEPTED,
                                     true).commit();
    }

    private static void refuse(Activity activity) {
        activity.finish();
    }

    private static CharSequence readEula(Activity activity) {
        BufferedReader in = null;
        try {
            in = new BufferedReader(new
                InputStreamReader(activity.getAssets().open(ASSET_EULA)));
```

```
            String line;
            StringBuilder buffer = new StringBuilder();
            while ((line = in.readLine()) != null)
                buffer.append(line).append('\n');
            return buffer;
        } catch (IOException e) {
            return "";
        } finally {
            closeStream(in);
        }
    }

    /**
     * Closes the specified stream.
     */
    private static void closeStream(Closeable stream) {
        if (stream != null) {
            try {
                stream.close();
            } catch (IOException e) {
                // Ignore
            }
        }
    }
}
```

The `Eula` class needs to be customized as follows:

1. The actual text of the EULA needs to be put in a text file called **EULA** (as specified by the `ASSET_EULA` variable in Listing 9.7) and placed in the **assets/** directory of the Android project. This is loaded by the `readEula()` method of the `Eula` class.

2. There are few strings that need to be specified for the Acceptance dialog box. These can be collected in the string's resource file. An example wording is shown in Listing 9.8.

Listing 9.8 **res/values/strings.xml**

```
<?xml version="1.0" encoding="utf-8"?>
<resources>
    <string name="hello">Welcome to MyApp</string>
    <string name="app_name">MyApp</string>
    <string name="eula_title">License Agreement</string>
    <string name="eula_accept">Accept</string>
    <string name="eula_refuse">Don\'t Accept</string>
</resources>
```

Then, any application can automatically have the EULA functionality by simply putting the following line in the `onCreate()` method of the main activity of the application:

```
Eula.show(this);
```

SQLite Database

For more complex data structures, a database provides a quicker and more flexible access method than flat files or shared preferences. Android provides a built-in database called SQLite that provides full relational database capability utilizing SQL commands. Each application that uses SQLite has its own instance of the database, which is by default accessible only from the application itself. The database is stored in the **/data/data/<package_name>/databases** folder of an Android device. A Content Provider can be used to share the database information between applications. The different steps for utilizing SQLite are

1. Create a database.
2. Open the database.
3. Create a table.
4. Create an insert interface for datasets.
5. Create a query interface for datasets.
6. Close the database.

The next recipe provides a general method to accomplish these steps.

Recipe: Creating a Separate Database Package

A good modular structure to classes is essential for more complicated Android projects. Here, the database class is put in its own package **com.cookbook.data** so it is easy to reuse. This package contains three classes: `MyDB`, `MyDBhelper`, and `Constants`.

The `MyDB` class is shown in Listing 9.9. It contains a `SQLiteDatabase` instance and a `MyDBhelper` class (described in the following) with the methods that follow:

- `MyDB()`—Initializes a `MyDBhelper` instance (the constructor).
- `open()`—Initializes a `SQLiteDatabase` instance using the `MyDBhelper`. This opens a writeable database connection. If SQLite throws any exception, it tries to get a readable database instead.
- `close()`—Closes the database connection.
- `insertdiary()`—Saves a diary entry to the database as name-value pairs in a `ContentValues` instance, and then passes the data to the `SQLitedatabase` instance to do an insert.

- `getdiaries()`—Reads the diary entries from the database, saves them in a `Cursor` class, and returns it from the method.

Listing 9.9 **src/com/cookbook/data/MyDB.java**

```
package com.cookbook.data;

import android.content.ContentValues;
import android.content.Context;
import android.database.Cursor;
import android.database.sqlite.SQLiteDatabase;
import android.database.sqlite.SQLiteException;
import android.util.Log;

public class MyDB {
    private SQLiteDatabase db;
    private final Context context;
    private final MyDBhelper dbhelper;
    public MyDB(Context c){
        context = c;
        dbhelper = new MyDBhelper(context, Constants.DATABASE_NAME, null,
                                           Constants.DATABASE_VERSION);
    }
    public void close()
    {
        db.close();
    }
    public void open() throws SQLiteException
    {
        try {
            db = dbhelper.getWritableDatabase();
        } catch(SQLiteException ex) {
            Log.v("Open database exception caught", ex.getMessage());
            db = dbhelper.getReadableDatabase();
        }
    }
    public long insertdiary(String title, String content)
    {
        try{
            ContentValues newTaskValue = new ContentValues();
            newTaskValue.put(Constants.TITLE_NAME, title);
            newTaskValue.put(Constants.CONTENT_NAME, content);
            newTaskValue.put(Constants.DATE_NAME,
                             java.lang.System.currentTimeMillis());
            return db.insert(Constants.TABLE_NAME, null, newTaskValue);
        } catch(SQLiteException ex) {
```

```
            Log.v("Insert into database exception caught",
                  ex.getMessage());
            return -1;
        }
    }
    public Cursor getdiaries()
    {
        Cursor c =  db.query(Constants.TABLE_NAME, null, null,
                             null, null, null, null);
        return c;
    }
}
```

The `MyDBhelper` class extends `SQLiteOpenHelper` and is shown in Listing 9.10. The `SQLiteOpenHelper` framework provides methods to manage database creation and upgrades. The database is initialized in the class constructor `MyDBhelper()`. This requires the context and database name to be specified for creation of the database file under **/data/data/com.cookbook.datastorage/databases** and database schema version to determine whether the `onCreate()` or `onUpgrade()` method is called.

Tables can be added in the `onCreate()` method using a custom SQL command such as:

```
create table MyTable (key_id integer primary key autoincrement,
                      title text not null, content text not null,
                      recorddate long);
```

Whenever a database needs to be upgraded (when a user downloads a new version of an application, for example), the change in database version number calls the `onUpgrade()` method. This can be used to alter or drop tables as needed to update the tables to the new schema.

Listing 9.10 **src/com/cookbook/data/MyDBhelper.java**

```
package com.cookbook.data;

import android.content.Context;
import android.database.sqlite.SQLiteDatabase;
import android.database.sqlite.SQLiteException;
import android.database.sqlite.SQLiteOpenHelper;
import android.database.sqlite.SQLiteDatabase.CursorFactory;
import android.util.Log;

public class MyDBhelper extends SQLiteOpenHelper{
    private static final String CREATE_TABLE="create table "+
    Constants.TABLE_NAME+" ("+
    Constants.KEY_ID+" integer primary key autoincrement, "+
    Constants.TITLE_NAME+" text not null, "+
    Constants.CONTENT_NAME+" text not null, "+
    Constants.DATE_NAME+" long);";
```

```
    public MyDBhelper(Context context, String name, CursorFactory factory,
                      int version) {
        super(context, name, factory, version);
    }

    @Override
    public void onCreate(SQLiteDatabase db) {
        Log.v("MyDBhelper onCreate","Creating all the tables");
        try {
            db.execSQL(CREATE_TABLE);
        } catch(SQLiteException ex) {
            Log.v("Create table exception", ex.getMessage());
        }
    }

    @Override
    public void onUpgrade(SQLiteDatabase db, int oldVersion,
                          int newVersion) {
        Log.w("TaskDBAdapter", "Upgrading from version "+oldVersion
                               +" to "+newVersion
                               +", which will destroy all old data");
        db.execSQL("drop table if exists "+Constants.TABLE_NAME);
        onCreate(db);
    }
}
```

The third file of the **com.cookbook.data** package is the `Constants` class shown in Listing 9.11. This class is used to hold all the String constants because they are utilized in both `MyDB` and `MyDBhelper`.

Listing 9.11 **src/com/cookbook/data/Constants.java**

```
package com.cookbook.data;

public class Constants {
    public static final String DATABASE_NAME="datastorage";
    public static final int DATABASE_VERSION=1;
    public static final String TABLE_NAME="diaries";
    public static final String TITLE_NAME="title";
    public static final String CONTENT_NAME="content";
    public static final String DATE_NAME="recorddate";
    public static final String KEY_ID="_id";
}
```

Recipe: Using a Separate Database Package

This recipe demonstrates SQLite data storage utilizing the previous recipe's database package. It also ties together the login screen from the "Changing the UI Based on Stored Data" recipe and enables the creation and listing of personal diary entries. First, a layout XML file for creating diary entries—**diary.xml**—is shown in Listing 9.12 with its output screen shown in Figure 9.3.

Listing 9.12 **res/layout/diary.xml**

```
<?xml version="1.0" encoding="utf-8"?>
<LinearLayout xmlns:android="http://schemas.android.com/apk/res/android"
    android:orientation="vertical"
    android:layout_width="fill_parent"
    android:layout_height="fill_parent"
    >
    <TextView
        android:layout_width="fill_parent"
        android:layout_height="wrap_content"
        android:text="Diary Title"
    />
    <EditText
        android:id="@+id/diarydescriptionText"
        android:layout_width="fill_parent"
        android:layout_height="wrap_content"
    />
    <TextView
        android:layout_width="fill_parent"
        android:layout_height="wrap_content"
        android:text="Content"
    />
    <EditText
        android:id="@+id/diarycontentText"
        android:layout_width="fill_parent"
        android:layout_height="200dp"
    />
    <Button
        android:id="@+id/submitButton"
        android:layout_width="wrap_content"
        android:layout_height="wrap_content"
        android:text="submit"
        android:textSize="20dp"
    />
</LinearLayout>
```

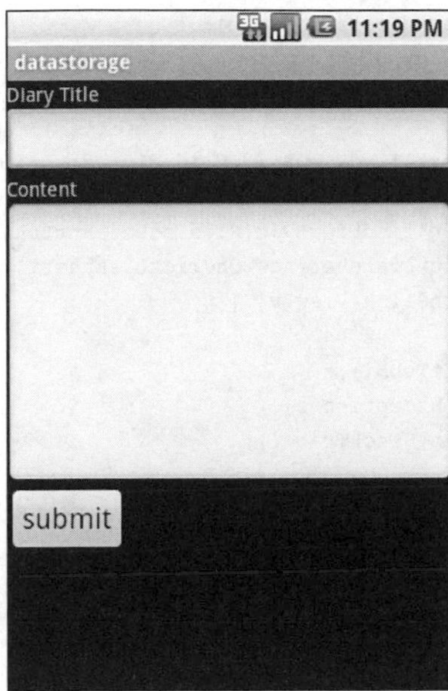

Figure 9.3 The diary entry creation screen.

The main activity is **Diary.java,** shown in Listing 9.13. The `com.cookbook.data` package needs to be imported, and the `MyDB` object is declared, initialized, and opened for use. It also displays the **diary.xml** layout and handles the submit button press to save data to the database.

Listing 9.13 **src/com/cookbook/datastorage/Diary.java**

```
package com.cookbook.datastorage;

import android.app.Activity;
import android.content.Intent;
import android.os.Bundle;
import android.view.View;
import android.view.View.OnClickListener;
import android.widget.Button;
import android.widget.EditText;

import com.cookbook.data.MyDB;
public class Diary extends Activity {
    EditText titleET, contentET;
    Button submitBT;
    MyDB dba;

    @Override
    public void onCreate(Bundle savedInstanceState) {
```

```
        super.onCreate(savedInstanceState);
        setContentView(R.layout.diary);
        dba = new MyDB(this);
        dba.open();
        titleET = (EditText)findViewById(R.id.diarydescriptionText);
        contentET = (EditText)findViewById(R.id.diarycontentText);
        submitBT = (Button)findViewById(R.id.submitButton);
        submitBT.setOnClickListener(new OnClickListener() {
            public void onClick(View v) {
                try {
                    saveItToDB();
                } catch (Exception e) {
                    e.printStackTrace();
                }
            }
        });
    }
    public void saveItToDB() {
        dba.insertdiary(titleET.getText().toString(),
                        contentET.getText().toString());
        dba.close();
        titleET.setText("");
        contentET.setText("");
        Intent i = new Intent(Diary.this, DisplayDiaries.class);
        startActivity(i);
    }
}
```

The **DataStorage.java** class is the same as in Listing 9.6 with the **MyPreferences.class** changed to launch the **Diary.class** when the login is successful:

```
Toast.makeText(DataStorage.this, "login passed!!",
               Toast.LENGTH_SHORT).show();
Intent i = new Intent(DataStorage.this, Diary.class);
startActivity(i);
```

Finally, the AndroidManifest XML file must be updated to include the new activities, as shown in Listing 9.14.

Listing 9.14 **AndroidManifest.xml**

```
<?xml version="1.0" encoding="utf-8"?>
<manifest xmlns:android="http://schemas.android.com/apk/res/android"
      package="com.cookbook.datastorage"
      android:versionCode="1" android:versionName="1.0">
    <application android:icon="@drawable/icon"
                 android:label="@string/app_name">
```

```
        <activity android:name=".DataStorage"
                  android:label="@string/app_name">
            <intent-filter>
              <action android:name="android.intent.action.MAIN" />
              <category android:name="android.intent.category.LAUNCHER" />
            </intent-filter>
        </activity>
        <activity android:name=".MyPreferences" />
        <activity android:name=".Diary"/>
    </application>
    <uses-sdk android:minSdkVersion="7" />
</manifest>
```

Now that a separate database has been integrated, the layout for the list of entries is discussed in the next recipe to complete the diary application.

Recipe: Creating a Personal Diary

This recipe leverages the `ListView` object to display multiple entries from a SQLite database table. It shows these items in a vertically scrolling list. The `ListView` needs a data adapter to tell the View whenever the underlying data changes. Two XML files need to be created: **diaries.xml,** which populates the `ListView` shown in Listing 9.15, and **diaryrow.xml,** which populates the row inside the `ListView` shown in Listing 9.16.

Listing 9.15 **res/layout/diaries.xml**

```
<?xml version="1.0" encoding="utf-8"?>
<LinearLayout xmlns:android="http://schemas.android.com/apk/res/android"
    android:orientation="vertical"
    android:layout_width="fill_parent"
    android:layout_height="fill_parent">
        <ListView
            android:layout_width="fill_parent" android:dividerHeight="1px"
            android:layout_height="fill_parent"
            android:id="list">
        </ListView>
</LinearLayout>
```

Listing 9.16 **res/layout/diaryrow.xml**

```
<?xml version="1.0" encoding="utf-8"?>
<RelativeLayout android:layout_width="wrap_content"
    android:layout_height="wrap_content" android:orientation="vertical"
    android:layout_alignLeft="@+id/name" android:layout_below="@+id/name"
    xmlns:android="http://schemas.android.com/apk/res/android"
```

```
    android:padding="12dip">
    <TextView android:layout_width="wrap_content"
        android:layout_height="wrap_content" android:id="@+id/name"
        android:layout_marginRight="4dp" android:text="Diary Title "
        android:textStyle="bold" android:textSize="16dip"  />
    <TextView android:id="@+id/datetext"
        android:layout_width="wrap_content"
        android:layout_height="wrap_content" android:text="Date Recorded"
        android:textSize="14dip" />
</RelativeLayout>
```

The activity **DisplayDiaries.java** extends `ListActivity` to display a `ListView`. Inside this class are two inner classes defined: `MyDiary` is a data class to hold the content of the diary entry (title, content, and date), and `DiaryAdapter` is a `BaseAdapter` class to handle data retrieval from the database (using `getdata()`). The following methods are derived from `BaseAdapter` and called by `ListView`:

- `getCount()`—Returns how many items on the adapter
- `getItem()`—Returns the item specified
- `getItemID()`—Returns the ID of item (for this example, there is no item ID)
- `getView()`—Returns a view for each item

Note that `ListView` calls `getView()` to draw the view for each item. To improve the UI rendering performance, the view returned by `getView()` should be recycled as much as possible. This is done by creating a `ViewHolder` class to hold the views.

When `getView()` is called, the view currently displayed to the user is also passed in, which is when it is saved in the `ViewHolder` and tagged. On subsequent calls to `getView()` with the same view, the tag identifies the view as already in the `ViewHolder`. In this case, the content can be changed on the existing view rather than create a new one.

The main activity is shown in Listing 9.17, and the resulting view of diary entries in a `ListView` is shown in Figure 9.4.

Listing 9.17 **src/com/cookbook/datastorage/DisplayDiaries.java**

```
package com.cookbook.datastorage;

import java.text.DateFormat;
import java.util.ArrayList;
import java.util.Date;

import android.app.ListActivity;
import android.content.Context;
import android.database.Cursor;
import android.os.Bundle;
import android.view.LayoutInflater;
import android.view.View;
```

```
import android.view.ViewGroup;
import android.widget.BaseAdapter;
import android.widget.TextView;

import com.cookbook.data.Constants;
import com.cookbook.data.MyDB;

public class DisplayDiaries extends ListActivity {
    MyDB dba;
    DiaryAdapter myAdapter;
    private class MyDiary{
        public MyDiary(String t, String c, String r){
            title=t;
            content=c;
            recorddate=r;
        }
        public String title;
        public String content;
        public String recorddate;
    }
    @Override
    protected void onCreate(Bundle savedInstanceState) {
        dba = new MyDB(this);
        dba.open();
        setContentView(R.layout.diaries);

        super.onCreate(savedInstanceState);
        myAdapter = new DiaryAdapter(this);
        this.setListAdapter(myAdapter);
    }

    private class DiaryAdapter extends BaseAdapter {
        private LayoutInflater mInflater;
        private ArrayList<MyDiary> diaries;
        public DiaryAdapter(Context context) {
            mInflater = LayoutInflater.from(context);
            diaries = new ArrayList<MyDiary>();
            getdata();
        }
        public void getdata(){
            Cursor c = dba.getdiaries();
            startManagingCursor(c);
            if(c.moveToFirst()){
                do{
                   String title =
                      c.getString(c.getColumnIndex(Constants.TITLE_NAME));
```

```
                String content =
                 c.getString(c.getColumnIndex(Constants.CONTENT_NAME));
                DateFormat dateFormat =
                 DateFormat.getDateTimeInstance();
                String datedata = dateFormat.format(new
                 Date(c.getLong(c.getColumnIndex(
                                    Constants.DATE_NAME))).getTime());
                 MyDiary temp = new MyDiary(title,content,datedata);
                 diaries.add(temp);
            } while(c.moveToNext());
        }
    }

    @Override
    public int getCount() {return diaries.size();}
    public MyDiary getItem(int i) {return diaries.get(i);}
    public long getItemId(int i) {return i;}
    public View getView(int arg0, View arg1, ViewGroup arg2) {
        final ViewHolder holder;
        View v = arg1;
        if ((v == null) || (v.getTag() == null)) {
            v = mInflater.inflate(R.layout.diaryrow, null);
            holder = new ViewHolder();
            holder.mTitle = (TextView)v.findViewById(R.id.name);
            holder.mDate = (TextView)v.findViewById(R.id.datetext);
            v.setTag(holder);
        } else {
            holder = (ViewHolder) v.getTag();
        }

        holder.mdiary = getItem(arg0);
        holder.mTitle.setText(holder.mdiary.title);
        holder.mDate.setText(holder.mdiary.recorddate);

        v.setTag(holder);

        return v;
    }

    public class ViewHolder {
        MyDiary mdiary;
        TextView mTitle;
        TextView mDate;
    }
  }
}
```

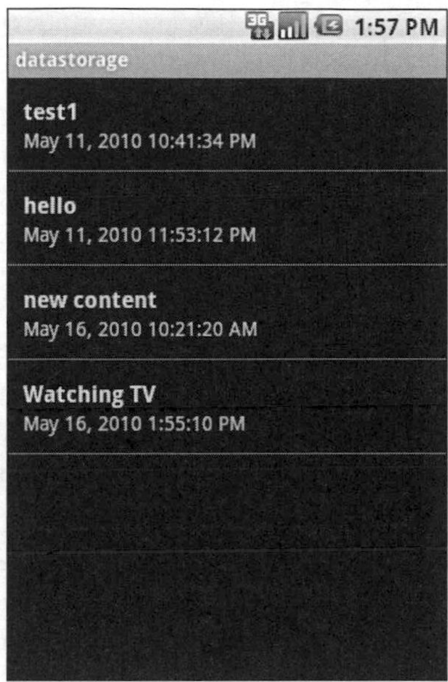

Figure 9.4 The ListView of diary entries.

Content Provider

Every application has its own sandbox and cannot access data from other applications. If access to functions not provided by its own sandbox is required, the application must explicitly declare permission upfront before installation. Android provides an interface called `ContentProvider` to act as a bridge between applications, enabling them to share and change each other's data. A content provider allows a clean separation between the application layer and data layer. It requires a permission setting in the AndroidManifest XML file and can be accessed using a simple URI model.

Some native databases Android makes available as content providers are

- Browser—Read or modify bookmarks, browser history, or web searches.
- CallLog—View or update the call history.
- Contacts—Retrieve, modify, or store the personal contacts. Contact information is stored in a three-tier data model of tables under a `ContactsContract` object:
  - `ContactsContract.Data`—Contains all kinds of personal data. There is a predefined set of common data, such as phone numbers and email addresses, but the format of this table can be application-specific.
  - `ContactsContract.RawContacts`—Contains a set of Data objects associated with a single account or person.

    - `ContactsContract.Contacts`—Contains an aggregate of one or more RawContacts, presumably describing the same person.

- LiveFolders—A special folder whose content is provided by a ContentProvider.
- MediaStore—Access audio, video, and images.
- Setting—View and retrieve Bluetooth settings, ring tones, and other device preferences.
- SearchRecentSuggestions—Can be configured to operate with a search suggestions provider.
- SyncStateContract—ContentProvider contract for associating data with a data array account. Providers that want to store this data in a standard way can use this.
- UserDictionary—Provides user-defined words used by input methods during predictive text input. Applications and input methods can add words to the dictionary. Words can have associated frequency information and locale information.

To access a content provider, the application needs to get a `contentResolver` instance to query, insert, delete, and update the data from the content provider, as shown in the following example:

```
ContentResolver crInstance = getContentResolver(); //get a content Resolver
instance
crInstance.query(People.CONTENT_URI, null, null, null, null); //query contacts
ContentValues new_Values= new ContentValues();
crInstance.insert(People.CONTENT_URI, new_Values); // insert new values
crInstance.delete(People_URI, null, null); //delete all contacts

ContentValues update_Values= new ContentValues();
crInstance.update(People_URI, update_Value, null,null); //update values
```

Each content provider needs to have a Uniform Resource Identifier (URI), which is used for registration and permission access. The URI must be unique between providers and have the generic suggested format:

```
content://<package name>.provider.<custom ContentProvider name>/<DataPath>
```

For simplicity, it can also be just `content://com.cookbook.datastorage/diaries`, which is used in the next recipe. The `Urimatcher` is utilized in the `ContentProvider` to ensure a proper URI is passed.

Recipe: Creating a Custom Content Provider

After getting a sense of how to use a content provider, it is time to integrate one into the diary project used in previous recipes. This recipe shows how to expose diary entries to other selected applications. A custom content provider just extends the Android `ContentProvider` class, which contains six methods to optionally override:

- `query()`—Allows third-party applications to retrieve content.
- `insert()`—Allows third-party applications to insert content.
- `update()`—Allows third-party applications to update content.
- `delete()`—Allows third-party applications to delete content.
- `getType()`—Allows third-party applications to read each of URI structures supported.
- `onCreate()`—Creates a database instance to help retrieve the content.

For example, if other applications are allowed to read only content from the provider, just `onCreate()` and `query()` need to be overridden.

A custom `ContentProvider` is shown in Listing 9.18; it has one URI added to `UriMatcher` based on the package `com.cookbook.datastorage` and the database table name `diaries`. The `onCreate()` method forms a `MyDB` object with code in Listing 9.9. It is responsible for the database access. The `query()` method retrieves all records from the diaries database, which is passed as the `uri` argument. In case of a more specific selection of records, the other arguments of this method would be utilized.

Listing 9.18 **src/com/cookbook/datastorage/DiaryContentProvider.java**

```
package com.cookbook.datastorage;

import android.content.ContentProvider;
import android.content.ContentValues;
import android.content.UriMatcher;
import android.database.Cursor;
import android.database.sqlite.SQLiteQueryBuilder;
import android.net.Uri;

import com.cookbook.data.Constants;
import com.cookbook.data.MyDB;

public class DiaryContentProvider extends ContentProvider {

    private MyDB dba;
    private static final  UriMatcher sUriMatcher;
    //the code returned for URI match to components
    private static final int DIARIES=1;
    public  static final  String AUTHORITY = "com.cookbook.datastorage";
    static {
                sUriMatcher = new UriMatcher(UriMatcher.NO_MATCH);
                sUriMatcher.addURI(AUTHORITY, Constants.TABLE_NAME,
                                   DIARIES);
    }
    @Override
```

```
    public int delete(Uri uri, String selection, String[] selectionArgs) {
        return 0;
    }
    public String getType(Uri uri) {return null;}
    public Uri insert(Uri uri, ContentValues values) {return null;}
    public int update(Uri uri, ContentValues values, String selection,
        String[] selectionArgs) {return 0;}

    @Override
    public boolean onCreate() {
        dba = new MyDB(this.getContext());
        dba.open();
        return false;
    }

    @Override
    public Cursor query(Uri uri, String[] projection, String selection,
            String[] selectionArgs, String sortOrder) {
        Cursor c=null;
        switch (sUriMatcher.match(uri)) {
                case DIARIES:
                    c = dba.getdiaries();
                    break;
                default:
                    throw new IllegalArgumentException(
                                                  "Unknown URI " + uri);
        }
        c.setNotificationUri(getContext().getContentResolver(), uri);
        return c;
    }
}
```

The provider needs to be specified in the AndroidManifest XML file to be accessible, as shown in Listing 9.19.

Listing 9.19 **AndroidManifest.xml**

```
<?xml version="1.0" encoding="utf-8"?>
<manifest xmlns:android="http://schemas.android.com/apk/res/android"
      package="com.cookbook.datastorage"
      android:versionCode="1"
      android:versionName="1.0">
    <application android:icon="@drawable/icon"
                 android:label="@string/app_name">
```

```
        <activity android:name=".DataStorage"
                  android:label="@string/app_name">
            <intent-filter>
              <action android:name="android.intent.action.MAIN" />
              <category android:name="android.intent.category.LAUNCHER" />
            </intent-filter>
        </activity>
        <activity android:name=".MyPreferences" />
        <activity android:name=".Diary"/>
        <activity android:name=".DisplayDiaries"/>
        <provider android:name="DiaryContentProvider"
            android:authorities="com.cookbook.datastorage" />
    </application>
    <uses-sdk android:minSdkVersion="7" />
</manifest>
```

Now the content provider is ready for other applications to use. To test this content provider, a new Android project can be created called **DataStorageTester** with main activity `DataStorageTester`. This is shown in Listing 9.20. An instance of the `ContentResult` is created to query the data from the `DataStorage` content provider. After a `Cursor` is returned, the testing function parses the second column of each data entry and concatenates into a `String` to display on the screen using a `StringBuilder` object.

Listing 9.20 **src/com/cookbook/datastorage_tester/DataStorageTester.java**

```
package com.cookbook.datastorage_tester;

import android.app.Activity;
import android.content.ContentResolver;
import android.database.Cursor;
import android.net.Uri;
import android.os.Bundle;
import android.widget.TextView;

public class DataStorageTester extends Activity {
    TextView tv;

    @Override
    public void onCreate(Bundle savedInstanceState) {
        super.onCreate(savedInstanceState);
        setContentView(R.layout.main);
        tv = (TextView) findViewById(R.id.output);
        String myUri = "content://com.cookbook.datastorage/diaries";
        Uri CONTENT_URI = Uri.parse(myUri);
```

```
        //get ContentResolver instance
        ContentResolver crInstance = getContentResolver();
        Cursor c = crInstance.query(CONTENT_URI, null, null, null, null);
        startManagingCursor(c);
        StringBuilder sb = new StringBuilder();
        if(c.moveToFirst()){
            do{
                sb.append(c.getString(1)).append("\n");

            }while(c.moveToNext());
        }
        tv.setText(sb.toString());

    }
}
```

Inside the **main.xml** layout file, an ID needs to be added for the `TextView` output, as shown in Listing 9.21.

Listing 9.21 **res/layout/main.xml**

```
<?xml version="1.0" encoding="utf-8"?>
<LinearLayout xmlns:android="http://schemas.android.com/apk/res/android"
    android:orientation="vertical"
    android:layout_width="fill_parent"
    android:layout_height="fill_parent"
    >
<TextView
    android:id="@+id/output"
    android:layout_width="fill_parent"
    android:layout_height="wrap_content"
    android:text="@string/hello"
    />
</LinearLayout>
```

Running the testing function displays the diary entry titles, as shown in Figure 9.5.

Figure 9.5 The result of a query in a Content Provider to the separate diary application.

File Saving and Loading

In addition to the Android-specific data storage methods mentioned previously, the standard **java.io.File** Java package is available, too. This provides for flat file manipulation, such as `FileInputStream`, `FileOutputStream`, `InputStream`, and `OutputStream`. An example is reading from and writing to a file:

```
FileInputStream fis = openFileInput("myfile.txt");
FileOutputStream fos = openFileOutput("myfile.txt",
                                Context.MODE_WORLD_WRITABLE);
```

Another example is saving the bitmap camera picture to a PNG file, as follows:

```
Bitmap takenPicture;
FileOutputStream out = openFileOutput("mypic.png",
                                Context.MODE_WORLD_WRITEABLE);
takenPicture.compress(CompressFormat.PNG, 100, out);
out.flush();
out.close();
```

The files in the resources directories can also be opened. For example, to open **myrawfile.txt** located in the **res/raw** folder, use the following:

```
InputStream is = this.getResource()
                        .openRawResource(R.raw.myrawfile.txt);
```

10

Location-Based Services

Location-Based Services (LBS) enable some of the most popular mobile applications. Location can be integrated with many functions, such as Internet searching, picture taking, gaming, and social networking. Developers can leverage the available location technology to make their applications more relevant and local.

This chapter introduces methods to obtain the device's location and then track, geocode, and map it. In addition, there are recipes on overlaying the map with markers and views.

Location Basics

An application requires the following to access the location services from the Android system:

- `LocationManager`—Class providing access to Android system location services
- `LocationListener`—Interface for receiving notifications from the `LocationManager` when the location has changed
- `Location`—Class representing a geographic location determined at a particular time

The `LocationManager` needs to be initialized with the Android system service called `LOCATION_SERVICE`. This provides the application with the device's current location, movement and can also alert when the device enters or leaves a defined area. An example of initialization is

```
LocationManager mLocationManager;
mLocationManager = (LocationManager)
            getSystemService(Context.LOCATION_SERVICE);
```

After the `LocationManager` instance is initiated, a location provider needs to be selected. Different location technologies might be available on the device (such as Assisted Global Positioning System (AGPS), Wi-Fi, and so on), and a general way to find a proper location provider is to define the accuracy and power requirement. This can be done using the `Criteria` class defined in `android.location.Criteria`. This enables the Android system to find the best available location technology for the specified requirements. An example of selecting a location provider based on criteria is

```
Criteria criteria = new Criteria();
criteria.setAccuracy(Criteria.ACCURACY_FINE);
criteria.setPowerRequirement(Criteria.POWER_LOW);
String locationprovider =
            mLocationManager.getBestProvider(criteria, true);
```

It is also possible to specify the location estimation technology using the location manager's `getProvider()` method. The two most common providers are the satellite-based Global Positioning System (GPS) (specified by `LocationManager.GPS_PROVIDER`) and cell-tower identification (specified by `LocationManager.NETWORK_PROVIDER`). The former is more accurate, but the latter is useful when a direct view of the sky is not available such as indoors.

Unless otherwise noted, all recipes in this will utilize the following two support files. First, the main layout needs a `TextView` as shown in Listing 10.1 for displaying the location data.

Listing 10.1 **res/layout/main.xml**

```
<?xml version="1.0" encoding="utf-8"?>
<LinearLayout xmlns:android="http://schemas.android.com/apk/res/android"
    android:orientation="vertical"
    android:layout_width="fill_parent"
    android:layout_height="fill_parent"
    >
<TextView
    android:id="@+id/tv1"
    android:layout_width="fill_parent"
    android:layout_height="wrap_content"
    android:text="@string/hello"
    />
</LinearLayout>
```

Second, permission to utilize location information needs to be granted in the **AndroidManifest.xml** file, as shown in Listing 10.2 (only the package name needs to be changed for each recipe). For a more accurate location, such as GPS, add the `ACCESS_FINE_LOCATION` permission. Otherwise, add the `ACCESS_COARSE_LOCATION` permission.

Listing 10.2 **AndroidManifest.xml**

```
<?xml version="1.0" encoding="utf-8"?>
<manifest xmlns:android="http://schemas.android.com/apk/res/android"
      package="com.cookbook.mylocationpackage"
      android:versionCode="1"
```

```
        android:versionName="1.0">
    <application android:icon="@drawable/icon"
                 android:label="@string/app_name">
        <activity android:name=".MyLocation"
                  android:label="@string/app_name">
            <intent-filter>
              <action android:name="android.intent.action.MAIN" />
              <category android:name="android.intent.category.LAUNCHER" />
            </intent-filter>
        </activity>
    </application>
    <uses-sdk android:minSdkVersion="4" />

<uses-permission android:name="android.permission.ACCESS_FINE_LOCATION"/>
</manifest>
```

Recipe: Retrieving Last Location

Because it might take time to produce a location estimation, `getLastKnownLocation()` can be called to retrieve the location last saved for a given provider. The location contains a latitude, longitude, and Coordinated Universal Time (UTC) timestamp. Depending on the provider, information on altitude, speed, and bearing might also be included (use `getAltitude()`, `getSpeed()`, and `getBearing()` on the Location object to retrieve these and `getExtras()` to retrieve satellite information). The latitude and longitude are displayed to the screen in this recipe. The main activity is shown in Listing 10.3.

Listing 10.3 **src/com/cookbook/lastlocation/MyLocation.java**

```
package com.cookbook.lastlocation;

import android.app.Activity;
import android.content.Context;
import android.location.Criteria;
import android.location.Location;
import android.location.LocationManager;
import android.os.Bundle;
import android.widget.TextView;

public class MyLocation extends Activity {
    LocationManager mLocationManager;
    TextView tv;

    @Override
    public void onCreate(Bundle savedInstanceState) {
        super.onCreate(savedInstanceState);
        setContentView(R.layout.main);
        tv = (TextView) findViewById(R.id.tv1);
```

```
        mLocationManager = (LocationManager)
                getSystemService(Context.LOCATION_SERVICE);

        Criteria criteria = new Criteria();
        criteria.setAccuracy(Criteria.ACCURACY_FINE);
        criteria.setPowerRequirement(Criteria.POWER_LOW);
        String locationprovider =
                mLocationManager.getBestProvider(criteria,true);
        Location mLocation =
                mLocationManager.getLastKnownLocation(locationprovider);

        tv.setText("Last location lat:" + mLocation.getLatitude()
                 + " long:" + mLocation.getLongitude());
    }
}
```

Recipe: Updating Location Upon Change

The `LocationListener` interface is used to receive notifications when the location has changed. The location manager's `requestLocationUpdates()` method needs to be called after a location provider is initialized to specify when the current activity is to be notified of changes. It depends on the following parameters:

- `provider`—The location provider the application uses.
- `minTime`—The minimum time between updates in milliseconds (although the system might increase this time to conserve power).
- `minDistance`—The minimum distance change before updates in meters.
- `listener`—The location listener should receive the updates.

The location listener's `onLocationChanged()` method can be overridden to specify an action to be done with the new location. Listing 10.4 shows how this is put together for 5 seconds of time and changes of more than 2 meters between updates. An actual implementation should use larger values between updates to save battery life. Also note that no heavy processing should be done in the `onLocationChanged()` method. Rather, copy the data and pass it off to a thread.

Listing 10.4 **src/com/cookbook/update_location/MyLocation.java**

```
package com.cookbook.update_location;

import android.app.Activity;
import android.content.Context;
import android.location.Criteria;
import android.location.Location;
import android.location.LocationListener;
```

```
import android.location.LocationManager;
import android.os.Bundle;
import android.widget.TextView;

public class MyLocation extends Activity implements LocationListener {
    LocationManager mLocationManager;
    TextView tv;
    Location mLocation;

    @Override
    public void onCreate(Bundle savedInstanceState) {
        super.onCreate(savedInstanceState);
        setContentView(R.layout.main);
        tv = (TextView) findViewById(R.id.tv1);

        mLocationManager = (LocationManager)
                getSystemService(Context.LOCATION_SERVICE);

        Criteria criteria = new Criteria();
        criteria.setAccuracy(Criteria.ACCURACY_FINE);
        criteria.setPowerRequirement(Criteria.POWER_LOW);
        String locationprovider =
                mLocationManager.getBestProvider(criteria,true);

        mLocation =
                mLocationManager.getLastKnownLocation(locationprovider);
        mLocationManager.requestLocationUpdates(
                    locationprovider, 5000, 2.0, this);
    }

    @Override
    public void onLocationChanged(Location location) {
        mLocation = location;
        showupdate();
    }
    // these methods are required
    public void onProviderDisabled(String arg0) {}
    public void onProviderEnabled(String provider) {}
    public void onStatusChanged(String a, int b, Bundle c) {}

    public void showupdate(){
        tv.setText("Last location lat:"+mLocation.getLatitude()
                  + " long:" + mLocation.getLongitude());
    }
}
```

Note that rather than implementing the `LocationListener` at the activity level, it can also be declared as a separate inner class as follows. This can easily be added to any of the following recipes to provide an update mechanism to the location:

```
    mLocationManager.requestLocationUpdates(
                    locationprovider, 5000, 2.0, myLocL);
}

private final LocationListener myLocL = new LocationListener(){
    @Override
    public void onLocationChanged(Location location){
        mLocation = location;
        showupdate();
    }

    // these methods are required
    public void onProviderDisabled(String arg0) {}
    public void onProviderEnabled(String provider) {}
    public void onStatusChanged(String a, int b, Bundle c) {}
};
```

Recipe: Listing All Enabled Providers

This recipe lists the different location providers available on a given Android device. One example output is shown in Figure 10.1, but may be different depending on the device. The main activity is shown in Listing 10.5. To see a list of possible providers, the `getProviders(true)` method is used. To contrast with the previous recipe, the `LocationListener` is declared as an anonymous inner class without loss of functionality.

Listing 10.5 **src/com/cookbook/show_providers/MyLocation.java**

```
package com.cookbook.show_providers;

import java.util.List;

import android.app.Activity;
import android.content.Context;
import android.location.Criteria;
import android.location.Location;
import android.location.LocationListener;
import android.location.LocationManager;
import android.os.Bundle;
import android.widget.TextView;

public class MyLocation extends Activity {
    LocationManager mLocationManager;
    TextView tv;
```

```
    Location mLocation;

    @Override
    public void onCreate(Bundle savedInstanceState) {
        super.onCreate(savedInstanceState);
        setContentView(R.layout.main);
        tv = (TextView) findViewById(R.id.tv1);
        mLocationManager = (LocationManager)
                            getSystemService(Context.LOCATION_SERVICE);
        Criteria criteria = new Criteria();
        criteria.setAccuracy(Criteria.ACCURACY_FINE);
        criteria.setPowerRequirement(Criteria.POWER_LOW);
        String locationprovider =
                       mLocationManager.getBestProvider(criteria,true);

        List<String> providers = mLocationManager.getProviders(true);
        StringBuilder mSB = new StringBuilder("Providers:\n");
        for(int i = 0; i<providers.size(); i++) {
          mLocationManager.requestLocationUpdates(
            providers.get(i), 5000, 2.0f, new LocationListener(){

            // these methods are required
            public void onLocationChanged(Location location) {}
            public void onProviderDisabled(String arg0) {}
            public void onProviderEnabled(String provider) {}
            public void onStatusChanged(String a, int b, Bundle c) {}
          });
          mSB.append(providers.get(i)).append(": \n");
          mLocation =
              mLocationManager.getLastKnownLocation(providers.get(i));
          if(mLocation != null) {
              mSB.append(mLocation.getLatitude()).append(" , ");
              mSB.append(mLocation.getLongitude()).append("\n");
          } else {
              mSB.append("Location can not be found");
          }
        }
        tv.setText(mSB.toString());
    }
}
```

Figure 10.1 Example output of all enabled location providers at their lastKnownLocation using an actual Android device.

Recipe: Translating a Location to Address (Reverse Geocoding)

The Geocoder class provides a method to translate from an address into a latitude-longitude coordinate (geocoding) and from a latitude-longitude coordinate into an address (reverse geocoding). Reverse geocoding might produce only a partial address, such as city and postal code, depending on the level of detail available to the location provider.

This recipe uses reverse geocoding to get an address from the device's location and display to the screen, as shown in Figure 10.2. The Geocoder instance needs to be initiated with a context and optionally with a locale if different from the system locale. Here, it is explicitly set to `Locale.ENGLISH`. Then the `getFromLocation()` method provides a list of addresses associated with the area around the provided location. Here the maximum number of returned results is set to one (for instance, the most likely address).

The Geocoder returns a `List` of `android.location.Address` objects. This translation to an address depends on a backend service that is not included in the core Android framework. The Google Maps API provides a client Geocoder service, for example. However, the translation returns an empty list if no such service exists on the target device. The address as a list of strings is dumped line by line into a `String` for display on the screen. The main activity is shown in Listing 10.6.

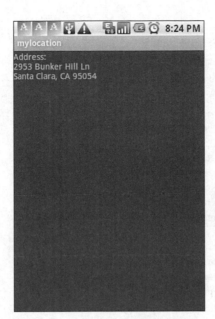

Figure 10.2 Reverse geocoding example, which converts a latitude-longitude coordinate into an address.

Listing 10.6 **src/com/cookbook/rev_geocoding/MyLocation.java**

```
package com.cookbook.rev_geocoding;

import java.io.IOException;
import java.util.List;
import java.util.Locale;

import android.app.Activity;
import android.content.Context;
import android.location.Address;
import android.location.Criteria;
import android.location.Geocoder;
import android.location.Location;
import android.location.LocationListener;
import android.location.LocationManager;
import android.os.Bundle;
import android.util.Log;
import android.widget.TextView;
```

```
public class MyLocation extends Activity {
    LocationManager mLocationManager;
    Location mLocation;
    TextView tv;

    @Override
    public void onCreate(Bundle savedInstanceState) {
        super.onCreate(savedInstanceState);

        setContentView(R.layout.main);
        tv = (TextView) findViewById(R.id.tv1);

        mLocationManager = (LocationManager)
                  getSystemService(Context.LOCATION_SERVICE);

        Criteria criteria = new Criteria();
        criteria.setAccuracy(Criteria.ACCURACY_FINE);
        criteria.setPowerRequirement(Criteria.POWER_LOW);
        String locationprovider =
                  mLocationManager.getBestProvider(criteria,true);

        mLocation =
                  mLocationManager.getLastKnownLocation(locationprovider);

        List<Address> addresses;
        try {
          Geocoder mGC = new Geocoder(this, Locale.ENGLISH);
          addresses = mGC.getFromLocation(mLocation.getLatitude(),
                                          mLocation.getLongitude(), 1);
          if(addresses != null) {
            Address currentAddr = addresses.get(0);
            StringBuilder mSB = new StringBuilder("Address:\n");
            for(int i=0; i<currentAddr.getMaxAddressLineIndex(); i++) {
              mSB.append(currentAddr.getAddressLine(i)).append("\n");
            }

            tv.setText(mSB.toString());
          }
        } catch(IOException e) {
            tv.setText(e.getMessage());
        }
      }
}
```

Recipe: Translating an Address to Location (Geocoding)

This recipe shows how to translate an address to a longitude-latitude coordinate called geocoding. It is almost the same as the previous recipe, except the `getFromLocationName()` method is used instead of `getFromLocation()`. Listing 10.7 shows the recipe, which takes a specific address in the `String myAddress`, converts it to a location, and then displays it to the screen, as shown in Figure 10.3.

Listing 10.7 **src/com/cookbook/geocoding/MyLocation.java**

```
package com.cookbook.geocoding;

import java.io.IOException;
import java.util.List;
import java.util.Locale;

import android.app.Activity;
import android.content.Context;
import android.location.Address;
import android.location.Criteria;
import android.location.Geocoder;
import android.location.Location;
import android.location.LocationListener;
import android.location.LocationManager;
import android.os.Bundle;
import android.widget.TextView;

public class MyLocation extends Activity {
    LocationManager mLocationManager;
    Location mLocation;
    TextView tv;

    @Override
    public void onCreate(Bundle savedInstanceState) {
        super.onCreate(savedInstanceState);

        setContentView(R.layout.main);
        tv = (TextView) findViewById(R.id.tv1);

        mLocationManager = (LocationManager)
                getSystemService(Context.LOCATION_SERVICE);

        Criteria criteria = new Criteria();
        criteria.setAccuracy(Criteria.ACCURACY_FINE);
        criteria.setPowerRequirement(Criteria.POWER_LOW);
        String locationprovider =
                mLocationManager.getBestProvider(criteria,true);
```

```
        mLocation =
                mLocationManager.getLastKnownLocation(locationprovider);

        List<Address> addresses;

        String myAddress="Seattle,WA";
        Geocoder gc = new Geocoder(this);
        try {
            addresses = gc.getFromLocationName(myAddress, 1);
            if(addresses != null) {
                Address x = addresses.get(0);
                StringBuilder mSB = new StringBuilder("Address:\n");

                mSB.append("latitude: ").append(x.getLatitude());
                mSB.append("\nlongitude: ").append(x.getLongitude());
                tv.setText(mSB.toString());
            }
        } catch(IOException e) {
            tv.setText(e.getMessage());
        }
    }
}
```

Figure 10.3 Geocoding example, which converts an address string into a latitude-longitude coordinate.

Using Google Maps

Google maps can be used on the Android system in two ways: user access through a browser and application access through the Google Maps Application Programming Interface (API). The MapView class is a wrapper around the Google Maps API. To use MapView, the following setup is needed:

1. Download and install the Google API's Software Development Kit (SDK):
    1. Use the Android SDK and Android Virtual Device (AVD) manager in Eclipse to download the Google API.
    2. Right-click the project that uses the API, and then select **Properties**.
    3. Select **Android,** and then select **Google API** to enable it for this project.
2. Obtain a valid Maps API key to use the Google Maps service (see http://code.google.com/android/add-ons/google-apis/mapkey.html):
    1. Use the **keytool** command to generate an MD5 certificate fingerprint for the key **alias_name**:
    ```
    > keytool -list -alias alias_name -keystore my.keystore
    > result:(Certificate fingerprint (MD5):
            94:1E:43:49:87:73:BB:E6:A6:88:D7:20:F1:8E:B5)
    ```
    2. Use the MD5 keystore to sign up for the Google Maps service at **http://code.google.com/android/maps-api-signup.html.**
    3. A Maps API key is provided upon signup. Use this key with `MapView`.
3. Include `<uses-library android:name="com.google.android.maps" />` in the **AndroidManifest.xml** file to inform the Android system that the application uses the `com.google.android.maps` library from the Google API's SDK.
4. Add the `android.permission.INTERNET` permission to the **AndroidManifest.xml** file so the application is allowed to use the Internet to receive data from the Google Maps service.
5. Include a `MapView` in the layout XML file.

More specifically, the two supporting files needed for a Google Maps activity are as follows. First, the AndroidManifest XML file needs the proper maps library and permissions, as shown in Listing 10.8.

Listing 10.8 **AndroidManifest.xml**

```
<?xml version="1.0" encoding="utf-8"?>
<manifest xmlns:android="http://schemas.android.com/apk/res/android"
      package="com.cookbook.using_gmaps"
      android:versionCode="1"
      android:versionName="1.0">
    <application android:icon="@drawable/icon"
                 android:label="@string/app_name">
        <activity android:name=".MyLocation"
                  android:label="@string/app_name">
            <intent-filter>
              <action android:name="android.intent.action.MAIN" />
              <category android:name="android.intent.category.LAUNCHER" />
            </intent-filter>
        </activity>
    <uses-library android:name="com.google.android.maps" />
    </application>
    <uses-sdk android:minSdkVersion="4" />
<uses-permission android:name="android.permission.INTERNET" />
<uses-permission android:name="android.permission.ACCESS_FINE_LOCATION"/>
</manifest>
```

Second, the layout XML file needs the proper MapView declared to show the Google Map, as shown in Listing 10.9. It can also declare whether the user can interact with the map by declaring the `clickable` element, which is `false` by default.

Listing 10.9 **res/layout/main.xml**

```
<?xml version="1.0" encoding="utf-8"?>
<LinearLayout xmlns:android="http://schemas.android.com/apk/res/android"
    android:orientation="vertical"
    android:layout_width="fill_parent"
    android:layout_height="fill_parent"
    >
<TextView
    android:id="@+id/tv1"
    android:layout_width="fill_parent"
    android:layout_height="wrap_content"
    android:text="@string/hello"
    />
<com.google.android.maps.MapView
    android:id="@+id/map1"
    android:layout_width="fill_parent"
    android:layout_height="fill_parent"
    android:clickable="true"
```

```
    android:apiKey="0ZDUMMY13442HjX491CODE44MSsJzfDVlIQ"
    />
</LinearLayout>
```

This is utilized in the following recipes.

Recipe: Adding Google Maps to an Application

To display a Google Map, the main activity should extend `MapActivity`, as shown in Listing 10.10. It also must point to the layout ID for the map in the main layout XML file, called `map1` here. Note that the `isRouteDisplayed()` method needs to be implemented, too. The resulting display looks like Figure 10.4.

Listing 10.10 **src/com/cookbook/using_gmaps/MyLocation.java**

```
package com.cookbook.using_gmaps;

import android.content.Context;
import android.location.Criteria;
import android.location.Location;
import android.location.LocationManager;
import android.os.Bundle;
import android.widget.TextView;

import com.google.android.maps.MapActivity;
import com.google.android.maps.MapView;

public class MyLocation extends MapActivity {
    LocationManager mLocationManager;
    Location mLocation;
    TextView tv;

    @Override
    public void onCreate(Bundle savedInstanceState) {
        super.onCreate(savedInstanceState);

        setContentView(R.layout.main);
        MapView mapView = (MapView) findViewById(R.id.map1);
        tv = (TextView) findViewById(R.id.tv1);

        mLocationManager = (LocationManager)
                getSystemService(Context.LOCATION_SERVICE);

        Criteria criteria = new Criteria();
        criteria.setAccuracy(Criteria.ACCURACY_FINE);
        criteria.setPowerRequirement(Criteria.POWER_LOW);
        String locationprovider =
                mLocationManager.getBestProvider(criteria,true);
```

```
        mLocation =
                    mLocationManager.getLastKnownLocation(locationprovider);

        tv.setText("Last location lat:" + mLocation.getLatitude()
                     + " long:" + mLocation.getLongitude());
    }

    @Override
    protected boolean isRouteDisplayed() {
        // this method is required
        return false;
    }
}
```

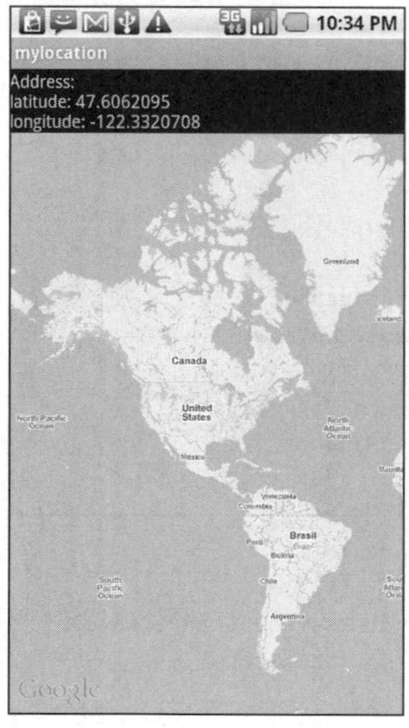

Figure 10.4 Example of Google Maps used from inside an application.

Recipe: Adding Markers on a Map

The `ItemizedOverlay` class provides a way to draw markers and layovers on top of a MapView. It manages a set of `OverlayItem` elements, such as an image, in a list and handles the drawing, placement, click handling, focus control, and layout optimization for each element. Create a class that extends `ItemizedOverlay` and override the following:

- `addOverlay()`—Adds an `OverlayItem` to the `ArrayList`. This calls `populate()`, which reads the item and prepares it to be drawn.
- `createItem()`—Called by `populate()` to retrieve the given `OverlayItem`.
- `size()`—Returns the number of `OverlayItem` elements in the `ArrayList`.
- `onTap()`—Callback method when a marker is clicked.

The newly created class is given in Listing 10.11 and provides the result in Figure 10.5.

Listing 10.11 **src/com/cookbook/adding_markers/MyMarkerLayer.java**

```
package com.cookbook.adding_markers;

import java.util.ArrayList;

import android.app.AlertDialog;
import android.content.DialogInterface;
import android.graphics.drawable.Drawable;

import com.google.android.maps.ItemizedOverlay;
import com.google.android.maps.OverlayItem;

public class MyMarkerLayer extends ItemizedOverlay {

    private ArrayList<OverlayItem> mOverlays =
              new ArrayList<OverlayItem>();

    public MyMarkerLayer(Drawable defaultMarker) {
        super(boundCenterBottom(defaultMarker));
        populate();
    }
    public void addOverlayItem(OverlayItem overlay) {
        mOverlays.add(overlay);
        populate();
    }
    @Override
    protected OverlayItem createItem(int i) {
        return mOverlays.get(i);
    }
    @Override
    public int size() {
        return mOverlays.size();
    }
```

```
    @Override
    protected boolean onTap(int index) {
        AlertDialog.Builder dialog =
              new AlertDialog.Builder(MyLocation.mContext);
        dialog.setTitle(mOverlays.get(index).getTitle());
        dialog.setMessage(mOverlays.get(index).getSnippet());
        dialog.setPositiveButton("Ok",
          new DialogInterface.OnClickListener() {
            public void onClick(DialogInterface dialog, int whichButton) {
                dialog.cancel();
          }
        });
        dialog.setNegativeButton("Cancel",
          new DialogInterface.OnClickListener() {
            public void onClick(DialogInterface dialog, int whichButton) {
                dialog.cancel();
          }
        });
        dialog.show();
        return super.onTap(index);
    }
}
```

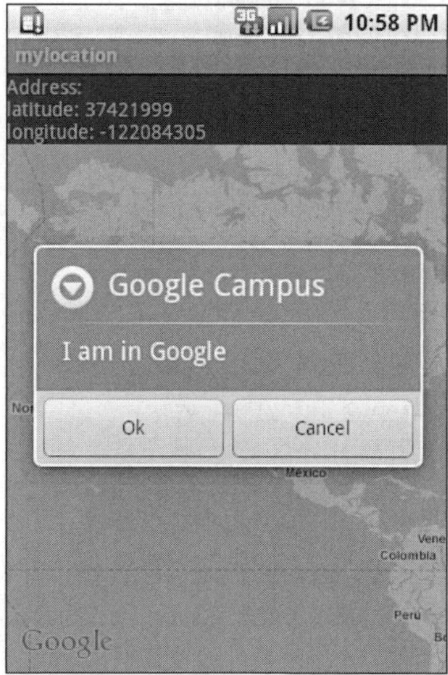

Figure 10.5 Adding a clickable marker to a map.

A few comments on the MyMarkerLayer class that are highlighted in Listing 10.11:

- An `OverlayItem` container `mOverlays` is declared to save all the items passed to the Overlay.
- A binding point for where all overlaid items are attached to the map needs to be defined before any overlay item is drawn. To specify the bottom center of the map as that point, `boundCenterBottom` is added to the class constructor.
- The required methods are overridden: `addOverlay()`, `createItem()`, `size()`, and `onTap()`. Here, the `onTap()` method provides a dialog box when the item is clicked.
- The `populate()` method is added to the end of the constructor and `addOverlay()`. This tells the `MyMarkerLayer` class to prepare all `OverlayItem` elements and draw each one on the map.

Now, this `ItemizedOverlay` can be added to the `MapActivity` created in the previous recipe. As highlighted in Listing 10.12, the activity:

1. Retrieves the existing map overlay items using the `getOverlays()` method from MapView. The marker layer is added to this container at the end of the function.
2. Defines an instance of the `MyMarkerLayer` to handle the overlay items.
3. Retrieves the latitude and longitude (in degrees) of the address. This defines the point of interest using a `GeoPoint` class. `GeoPoint` takes input in microdegrees, so the latitude and longitude each needs to be multiplied by one million (`1E6`).
4. Uses a map controller to animate to the `GeoPoint` and zoom the view. Also, it enables user-controlled zoom using `setBuiltInZoomControls()`.
5. Defines an `OverlayItem` as a message at the `GeoPoint` of interest.
6. Adds the item to the `MyMarkerLayer` using the `addOverlayItem()` method. It then puts the now defined `MyMarkerLayer` into the existing overlay list retrieved in step 1.

Listing 10.12 **src/com/cookbook/adding_markers/MyLocation.java**

```
package com.cookbook.adding_markers;

import java.io.IOException;
import java.util.List;

import android.content.Context;
import android.graphics.drawable.Drawable;
import android.location.Address;
import android.location.Geocoder;
import android.os.Bundle;
import android.widget.TextView;
```

```
import com.google.android.maps.GeoPoint;
import com.google.android.maps.MapActivity;
import com.google.android.maps.MapController;
import com.google.android.maps.MapView;
import com.google.android.maps.Overlay;

public class MyLocation extends MapActivity {
    TextView tv;
    List<Overlay> mapOverlays;
    MyMarkerLayer markerlayer;
    private MapController mc;
    public static Context mContext;

    @Override
    public void onCreate(Bundle savedInstanceState) {
        super.onCreate(savedInstanceState);
        mContext = this;
        setContentView(R.layout.main);
        MapView mapView = (MapView) findViewById(R.id.map1);
        tv = (TextView) findViewById(R.id.tv1);

        mapOverlays = mapView.getOverlays();
        Drawable drawable =
                 this.getResources().getDrawable(R.drawable.icon);
        markerlayer = new MyMarkerLayer(drawable);

        List<Address> addresses;
        String myAddress="1600 Amphitheatre Parkway, Mountain View, CA";

        int geolat = 0;
        int geolon = 0;

        Geocoder gc = new Geocoder(this);
        try {
            addresses = gc.getFromLocationName(myAddress, 1);
            if(addresses != null) {
              Address x = addresses.get(0);

              geolat = (int)(x.getLatitude()*1E6);
              geolon = (int)(x.getLongitude()*1E6);
            }
        } catch(IOException e) {
            tv.setText(e.getMessage());
        }

        mapView.setBuiltInZoomControls(true);
        GeoPoint point = new GeoPoint(geolat,geolon);
        mc = mapView.getController();
```

```
            mc.animateTo(point);
            mc.setZoom(3);

            OverlayItem overlayitem =
                    new OverlayItem(point, "Google Campus", "I am at Google");
            markerlayer.addOverlayItem(overlayitem);
            mapOverlays.add(markerlayer);
        }

    @Override
    protected boolean isRouteDisplayed() { return false; }
}
```

Recipe: Adding Views to a Map

The developer can add any `View` or `ViewGroup` to the `MapView`. This recipe shows the addition of two simple elements to a map: `TextView` and `Button`. When the button is clicked, the text in the `TextView` changes. These two views are added to `MapView` by calling the `addView()` method with `LayoutParams`. Here, the location of the elements are specified in (x,y) screen coordinates, but developers can also provide a `GeoPoint` to the `LayoutParams` instead. Listing 10.13 shows the main activity, which also requires the `MyMarkerLayer` class defined in the previous recipe (Listing 10.11 with the first line changed to reflect the proper package). This results in the map view shown in Figure 10.6.

Listing 10.13 **src/com/cookbook/mylocation/MyLocation.java**

```
package com.cookbook.mylocation;

import java.io.IOException;
import java.util.List;

import android.content.Context;
import android.content.Intent;
import android.graphics.Color;
import android.graphics.drawable.Drawable;
import android.location.Address;
import android.location.Geocoder;
import android.os.Bundle;
import android.view.View;
import android.view.View.OnClickListener;
import android.widget.Button;
import android.widget.TextView;
import com.google.android.maps.GeoPoint;
import com.google.android.maps.MapActivity;
import com.google.android.maps.MapController;
```

```
import com.google.android.maps.MapView;
import com.google.android.maps.Overlay;

public class MyLocation extends MapActivity {
    TextView tv;
    List<Overlay> mapOverlays;
    MyMarkerLayer markerlayer;
    private MapController mc;
    MapView.LayoutParams mScreenLayoutParams;
    public static Context mContext;

    @Override
    public void onCreate(Bundle savedInstanceState) {
        super.onCreate(savedInstanceState);
        mContext = this;
        setContentView(R.layout.main);

        MapView mapView = (MapView) findViewById(R.id.map1);
        mc = mapView.getController();
        tv = (TextView) findViewById(R.id.tv1);
        mapOverlays = mapView.getOverlays();
        Drawable drawable =
                   this.getResources().getDrawable(R.drawable.icon);
        markerlayer = new MyMarkerLayer(drawable);

        List<Address> addresses;
        String myAddress="1600 Amphitheatre Parkway, Mountain View, CA";

        int geolat = 0;
        int geolon = 0;

        Geocoder gc = new Geocoder(this);
        try {
          addresses = gc.getFromLocationName(myAddress, 1);
          if(addresses != null) {
              Address x = addresses.get(0);

              StringBuilder mSB = new StringBuilder("Address:\n");
              geolat =(int)(x.getLatitude()*1E6);
              geolon = (int)(x.getLongitude()*1E6);
              mSB.append("latitude: ").append(geolat).append("\n");
              mSB.append("longitude: ").append(geolon);
              tv.setText(mSB.toString());
          }
```

```
        } catch(IOException e) {
          tv.setText(e.getMessage());
        }

        int x = 50;
        int y = 50;
        mScreenLayoutParams =
             new MapView.LayoutParams(MapView.LayoutParams.WRAP_CONTENT,
                                      MapView.LayoutParams.WRAP_CONTENT,
                                      x,y,MapView.LayoutParams.LEFT);

        final TextView tv = new TextView(this);
        tv.setText("Adding View to Google Map");
        tv.setTextColor(Color.BLUE);
        tv.setTextSize(20);
        mapView.addView(tv, mScreenLayoutParams);

        x = 250;
        y = 250;
        mScreenLayoutParams =
             new MapView.LayoutParams(MapView.LayoutParams.WRAP_CONTENT,
                                      MapView.LayoutParams.WRAP_CONTENT,
                                      x,y,
                                      MapView.LayoutParams.BOTTOM_CENTER);

        Button clickMe = new Button(this);
        clickMe.setText("Click Me");
        clickMe.setOnClickListener(new OnClickListener() {
            public void onClick(View v) {
                tv.setTextColor(Color.RED);
                tv.setText("Let's play");
            }
        });

        mapView.addView(clickMe, mScreenLayoutParams);
    }

    @Override
    protected boolean isRouteDisplayed() { return false; }
}
```

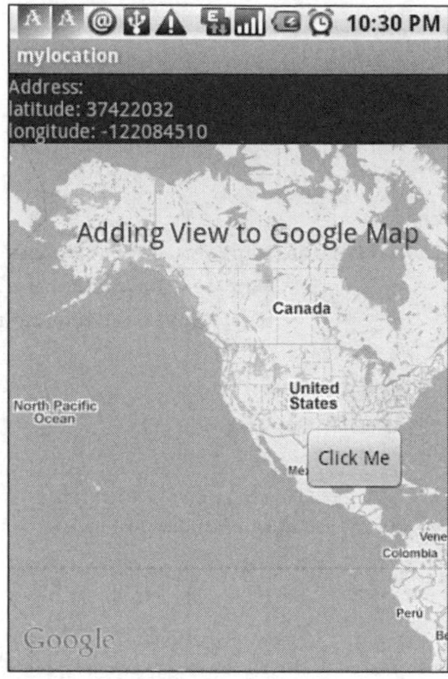

Figure 10.6 Adding views to a map.

Recipe: Marking the Device's Current Location on a Map

A convenient built-in overlay is `MyLocationOverlay`, which automatically draws the user's current location on a map as a blue dot. It can also show accuracy and which direction the user is pointing (bearing). There are four significant methods that are often used:

- `enableCompass()`—Allows the user to see the compass indicator on the map
- `enableMyLocation()`—Registers the location for most accurate location fix updates and draws a blinking blue dot surrounded by an outlining blue disk to represent accuracy
- `getMyLocation()`—Returns a GeoPoint with the current location data
- `getOrientation()`—Returns the most recently set compass bearing

These methods provide an easy way for developers to utilize the compass in maps.

Recipe: Setting up a Proximity Alert

The `LocationManager` provides a method to set a proximity alert. This triggers an alert when a user enters or leaves a defined area. The area is specified by a latitude-longitude coordinate and a radius in meters. The alert is specified with a `PendingIntent` to be launched whenever a user enters or leaves the specified area. An expiration time for the alert can also be defined. An example of how to implement this is shown in Listing 10.14.

Listing 10.14 **Example of Setting Up a Proximity Alert**

```
double mlatitude=35.41;
double mlongitude=139.46;

float mRadius=500f; // in meters

long expiration=-1; //-1 never expires or use milliseconds

Intent mIntent = new Intent("You entered the defined area");
PendingIntent mFireIntent
              = PendingIntent.getBroadCast(this, -1, mIntent, 0);

mLocationManager.addProximityAlert(mlatitude, mlongitude,
                                   mRadius, expiration, mFireIntent);
```

11

Advanced Android Development

This chapter is a collection of advanced techniques that are useful to make an application more robust, faster, and in some cases, to improve the user interface. First, an example of customizing an Android standard view is shown. Then, the Native Development Kit (NDK) is introduced as a method for reducing overhead and improving time on complex computations. Android security is then discussed. Next, a way to do inter-process communication between two different processes is presented. This is followed by data backup to the cloud, which is a feature introduced in Android 2.2. Finally, some techniques for user interface animation are shown.

Android Custom View

As discussed in Chapter 4, "User Interface Layout," Android has two types of views: `View` objects and `ViewGroup` objects. A custom view can be created by either starting from scratch or inheriting an existing view structure. Some standard widgets are defined by the Android Framework under the `View` and `ViewGroup` class, and if possible, the customization should start with one of these:

- Views—`Button`, `EditText`, `TextView`, `ImageView`, and so on
- ViewGroups—`LinearLayout`, `ListView`, `RelativeLayout`, `RadioGroup`, and so on

Recipe: Customizing a Button

This recipe customizes a button using a class called `myButton`. It extends the `Button` widget so that the component inherits most of the `Button` features. To customize a widget, the most important methods are `onMeasure()` and `onDraw()`.

The `onMeasure()` method determines the size requirements for a widget. It takes two parameters: the width and height measure specification. Customized widgets should calculate the width and height based on the contents inside the widget, and then call `setMeasuredDimension()` with these values. If this is not done, an `illegalStateException` is thrown by `measure()`.

The `onDraw()` method allows customized drawing on the widget. Drawing is handled by walking down the tree and rendering view by view. All parents are drawn before the children get drawn. If a background drawable is set for a view, then the view draws that before calling back to its `onDraw()` method.

Inside the `myButton` class, eight member methods and two constructors are implemented. The member functions are

- `setText()`—Set the text that is drawn on the button.
- `setTextSize()`—Set the text size.
- `setTextColor()`—Set the text color.
- `measureWidth()`—Measure the width of the button widget.
- `measureHeight()`—Measure the height of the button widget.
- `drawArcs()`—Draw arcs.
- `onDraw()`—Draw the graphics on the button widget.
- `onMeasure()`—Measure and set the boundary of the button widget.

The methods `setText()`, `setTextSize()`, and `setTextColor()` change the text attributes. Every time the text is changed, the `invalidate()` method needs to be called to force the view to redraw the button widget and reflect the change. The method `requestLayout()` is called in the `setText()` and `setTextSize()` methods but not in the `setTextColor()` method. This is because the layout is only needed when the boundary of the widget changes, which is not the case with text color change.

Inside `onMeasure()`, the `setMeasuredDimension()` method is called with `measureWidth()` and `measureHeight()`. It is an important step for customizing the `View`.

The methods `measureWidth()` and `measureHeight()` are called with the size of the parent view and need to return the proper width and height values of the custom view based on the requested mode of measurement. If the `EXACTLY` mode of measurement is specified, then the method needs to return the value given from parent `View`. If the `AT_MOST` mode is specified, then the method can return the smaller of the two values—content size and parent view size—to ensure the content is sized properly. Otherwise, the method calculates the width and height based on the content inside the widget. In this recipe, the content size is based on the text size.

The method `drawArcs()` is a straightforward function that draws arcs on the button. This is called by `onDraw()` as the text is drawn. Animation of the arcs also takes place here. Every time the arc is drawn, its length is incremented a little and the gradient is rotated making a nice animation.

The class for the custom button is shown in Listing 11.1. A constructor method is required, and here, two `MyButton()` methods are shown depending on arguments. Each initializes the label view with the custom attributes. The `android.graphics.*` libraries are similar in format to Java for graphics manipulations, such as `Matrix` and `Paint`.

Listing 11.1 **src/com/cookbook/advance/MyButton.java**

```
package com.cookbook.advance.customComponent;

import android.content.Context;
import android.graphics.Canvas;
import android.graphics.Color;
import android.graphics.Matrix;
import android.graphics.Paint;
import android.graphics.RectF;
import android.graphics.Shader;
import android.graphics.SweepGradient;
import android.util.AttributeSet;
import android.util.Log;
import android.widget.Button;

public class MyButton extends Button {
    private Paint mTextPaint, mPaint;
    private String mText;
    private int mAscent;
    private Shader mShader;
    private Matrix  mMatrix = new Matrix();
    private float mStart;
    private float mSweep;
    private float mRotate;
    private static final float SWEEP_INC = 2;
    private static final float START_INC = 15;

    public MyButton(Context context) {
        super(context);
        initLabelView();
    }

    public MyButton(Context context, AttributeSet attrs) {
        super(context, attrs);
        initLabelView();
    }

    private final void initLabelView() {
        mTextPaint = new Paint();
        mTextPaint.setAntiAlias(true);
        mTextPaint.setTextSize(16);
        mTextPaint.setColor(0xFF000000);
        setPadding(15, 15, 15, 15);
        mPaint = new Paint();
        mPaint.setAntiAlias(true);
        mPaint.setStrokeWidth(4);
```

```
        mPaint.setAntiAlias(true);
        mPaint.setStyle(Paint.Style.STROKE);
        mShader = new SweepGradient(this.getMeasuredWidth()/2,
                                    this.getMeasuredHeight()/2,
                                new int[] { Color.GREEN,
                                            Color.RED,
                                            Color.CYAN,Color.DKGRAY },
                                null);
        mPaint.setShader(mShader);
    }

    public void setText(String text) {
        mText = text;
        requestLayout();
        invalidate();
    }

    public void setTextSize(int size) {
        mTextPaint.setTextSize(size);
        requestLayout();
        invalidate();
    }

    public void setTextColor(int color) {
        mTextPaint.setColor(color);
        invalidate();
    }

    @Override
    protected void onMeasure(int widthMeasureSpec, int heightMeasureSpec){
        setMeasuredDimension(measureWidth(widthMeasureSpec),
                measureHeight(heightMeasureSpec));
    }

    private int measureWidth(int measureSpec) {
        int result = 0;
        int specMode = MeasureSpec.getMode(measureSpec);
        int specSize = MeasureSpec.getSize(measureSpec);

        if (specMode == MeasureSpec.EXACTLY) {
            // We were told how big to be
            result = specSize;
        } else {
            // Measure the text
            result = (int) mTextPaint.measureText(mText)
                    + getPaddingLeft()
```

```
                + getPaddingRight();
        if (specMode == MeasureSpec.AT_MOST) {
            result = Math.min(result, specSize);
        }
    }

    return result;
}

private int measureHeight(int measureSpec) {
    int result = 0;
    int specMode = MeasureSpec.getMode(measureSpec);
    int specSize = MeasureSpec.getSize(measureSpec);

    mAscent = (int) mTextPaint.ascent();
    if (specMode == MeasureSpec.EXACTLY) {
        // We were told how big to be
        result = specSize;
    } else {
        // Measure the text (beware: ascent is a negative number)
        result = (int) (-mAscent + mTextPaint.descent())
                        + getPaddingTop() + getPaddingBottom();
        if (specMode == MeasureSpec.AT_MOST) {
            Log.v("Messure Height", "At most Height:"+specSize);
            result = Math.min(result, specSize);
        }
    }
    return result;
}

private void drawArcs(Canvas canvas, RectF oval, boolean useCenter,
        Paint paint) {
    canvas.drawArc(oval, mStart, mSweep, useCenter, paint);
}

@Override protected void onDraw(Canvas canvas) {
    mMatrix.setRotate(mRotate, this.getMeasuredWidth()/2,
                    this.getMeasuredHeight()/2);
    mShader.setLocalMatrix(mMatrix);
    mRotate += 3;
    if (mRotate >= 360) {
        mRotate = 0;
    }
    RectF drawRect = new RectF();
    drawRect.set(this.getWidth()-mTextPaint.measureText(mText),
              (this.getHeight()-mTextPaint.getTextSize())/2,
```

```
                    mTextPaint.measureText(mText),
            this.getHeight()-(this.getHeight()-mTextPaint.getTextSize())/2);
            drawArcs(canvas, drawRect, false, mPaint);
            mSweep += SWEEP_INC;
            if (mSweep > 360) {
                mSweep -= 360;
                mStart += START_INC;
                if (mStart >= 360) {
                    mStart -= 360;
                }
            }
            if(mSweep >180){
                canvas.drawText(mText, getPaddingLeft(),
                                getPaddingTop() -mAscent, mTextPaint);
            }
            invalidate();
        }
}
```

This custom `Button` widget can then be used in a layout as shown in Listing 11.2.

Listing 11.2 **res/layout/main.xml**

```
<?xml version="1.0" encoding="utf-8"?>
<LinearLayout xmlns:android="http://schemas.android.com/apk/res/android"
    android:orientation="vertical"
    android:layout_width="fill_parent"
    android:layout_height="fill_parent"
    android:gravity="center_vertical"
    >
<com.cookbook.advance.customComponent.MyButton
    android:layout_width="wrap_content"
    android:layout_height="wrap_content"
    android:id="@+id/mybutton1"
    />
</LinearLayout>
```

The layout XML has only one `ViewGroup`, `LinearLayout`, and one `View`, called by its definition location `com.cookbook.advance.customComponent.myButton`. This can be used in an activity, as shown in Listing 11.3.

Listing 11.3 **src/com/cookbook/advance/ShowMyButton.java**

```
package com.cookbook.advance.customComponent;

import android.app.Activity;
import android.os.Bundle;
```

```
public class ShowMyButton extends Activity{

    @Override
    protected void onCreate(Bundle savedInstanceState) {
        super.onCreate(savedInstanceState);

        setContentView(R.layout.main);
        MyButton myb = (MyButton)findViewById(R.id.mybutton1);
        myb.setText("Hello Students");
        myb.setTextSize(40);

    }
}
```

This shows the custom button is used the same as a normal `Button` widget. The resulting custom button is shown in Figure 11.1.

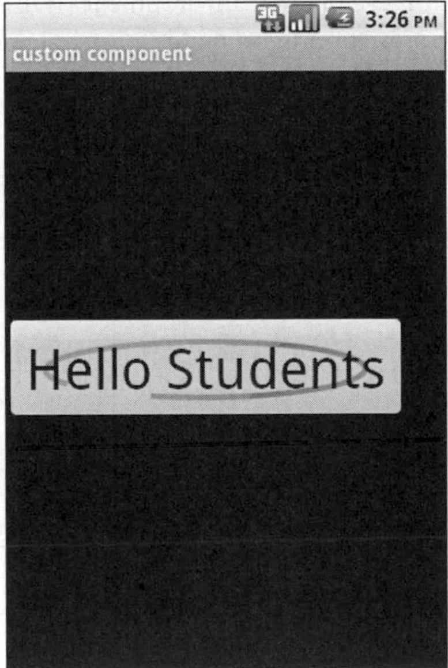

Figure 11.1 An example of a custom button.

Android Native Components

When a computationally intensive function is critical to an Android application, it might be worthwhile to move the intensive computation to native C or C++ for efficiency. The Android NDK exists to help in the development of a native component. The NDK is a companion to the Android Software Development Kit (SDK) and includes a bundle of libraries that can be used to build C/C++ libraries. Steps to set up and build an Android native component are

1. Download the Android NDK from http://developer.android.com/sdk/ndk/, which includes detailed documents on usage.
2. Create an Android project through the normal means under the NDK directory.
3. Create a **jni/** folder under the project created in step 2.
4. Create the necessary C/C++ program files under the **jni/** folder.
5. Create an **Android.mk** make file.
6. Run the build script (**ndk-build** for NDK-r4) from the project directory.
7. Inside the Android Java project, import the library and call the native functions.

Using the Eclipse Integrated Development Environment (IDE), the native libraries are properly bundled with the application upon build.

Recipe: Developing a Native Component

In this recipe, a C program is used to create a numerical factorial function. Then, an activity in Java calls the C library function and shows the result on the screen. First of all, the C program is shown in Listing 11.4.

Listing 11.4 **jni/cookbook.c**

```
#include <string.h>
#include <jni.h>

jint factorial(jint n){
    if(n == 1){
      return 1;
    }
    return factorial(n-1)*n;
}

jint Java_com_cookbook_advance_ndk_ndk_factorial( JNIEnv* env,
                                                  jobject thiz, jint n ) {
    return factorial(n);
}
```

Inside this C program, there is a special type `jint`, which is the Java type defined in C/C++. This provides a way to pass native types to Java. If return values from Java to C are necessary, a casting can be done. Table 11.1 summarizes the type mapping between Java and native description.

Table 11.1 **Type Mapping Between Java and Native**

Java Type in C/C++	Native Type	Description
`jboolean`	`unsigned char`	unsigned 8 bits
`jbyte`	`signed char`	signed 8 bits
`jchar`	`unsigned short`	unsigned 16 bits
`jshort`	`short`	signed 16 bits
`jint`	`long`	signed 32 bits
`jfloat`	`float`	32 bits
`jlong`	`long long _int64`	signed 64 bits
`jdouble`	`double`	64 bits

There are two functions inside the C program. The first `factorial` function is used to do actual calculations. Java calls the second function. The name of the function should always be defined as the `JAVA_CLASSNAME_METHOD` format for interface.

There are three parameters in the second function: a `JNIEnv` pointer, a `jobject` pointer, and a Java argument the Java method declares. `JNIEnv` is a Java Native Interface (JNI) pointer passed as an argument for each native function. These functions are mapped to a Java method that is the structure that contains the interface to the Java Virtual Machine (JVM). It includes the functions necessary to interact with the JVM and to work with Java objects. In this example, it does not use any Java functions. The only argument needed for this program is the Java argument `jint n`.

The makefile for the builder is shown in Listing 11.5. It should be placed at the same location as the C program. It contains a definition of the `LOCAL_PATH` for the builder and a call to `CLEAR_VARS` to clean up all `LOCAL_*` variables before each build. Then, the `LOCAL_MODULE` is identified as the name of the custom library `ndkcookbook` and identifies the source code files to build. After all these declarations, it includes the `BUILD_SHARED_LIBRARY`. This is a generic makefile for building a simple program. More detailed information on the makefile format is provided in the **ANDROID-MK.TXT** file under the **docs/** directory of the NDK.

Listing 11.5 **jni/Android.mk**

```
LOCAL_PATH := $(call my-dir)

include $(CLEAR_VARS)

LOCAL_MODULE    := ndkcookbook
LOCAL_SRC_FILES := cookbook.c

include $(BUILD_SHARED_LIBRARY)
```

The next step is to build the native library. With NDK-r4, calling the provided build script **ndk-build** at the NDK root directory of the project builds the libraries with an associated makefile. For older versions, the command **make APP=NAME_OF_APPLICATION** is needed. After the libraries are built, a **lib/** folder is created containing the native library **libndkcookbook.so**. In NDK-r4, it also contains two gdb files that help with debugging.

The Android activity that utilizes this library calls the `System.loadLibrary()` to load the **ndkcookbook** library. Then, the native function needs to be declared. This is shown in Listing 11.6. The output is shown in Figure 11.2.

Listing 11.6 **src/com/cookbook/advance/ndk/ndk.java**

```
package com.cookbook.advance.ndk;

import android.app.Activity;
import android.widget.TextView;
import android.os.Bundle;
public class ndk extends Activity {
    @Override
    public void onCreate(Bundle savedInstanceState) {
        super.onCreate(savedInstanceState);
        TextView tv = new TextView(this);
        tv.setText(" native calculation on factorial :"+factorial(30));
        setContentView(tv);
    }
    public static native int factorial(int n);
    static {
        System.loadLibrary("ndkcookbook");
    }
}
```

Figure 11.2 Output of the NDK application.

Android Security

Android is a multiprocess system. Each application runs on top of the Android Dalvik machine. Each Dalvik machine runs on top of a Linux process. Each process runs in its own sandbox, which means it can access only the resources it creates.

By default, each application is assigned a unique Linux user ID. It is possible to configure multiple applications to share the same user ID. This allows those applications to have the same permission to access the resources.

To access resources outside of the application sandbox, the application needs to request permission from the Android system. Most of the native components in Android have permission restrictions. The permissions requested in the application manifest are exposed to the user during installation. If a user allows installation of the application, then the permissions are granted. Permissions cannot be added after the application is installed. The permissions are defined under `android.Manifest.permission`.

As discussed in Chapter 1, "Overview of Android," each application needs a self-signed private keystore that contains a certificate. This keystore is used to identify the author of the application, but does not manage permissions of the applications. An application can grant permission to a given group using the `permission` tag in the AndroidManifest file.

Recipe: Declaring and Enforcing Permissions

Permissions can be assigned to activities, broadcast receivers, content providers, and services. To assign a permission, the `permission` element needs to be declared in the desired Android component in the AndroidManifest XML file. For example:

```
<permission android:name="com.myapp"
    android:label="my app"
    android:description="using my app"
    android:permissionGroup="android.permission-group.COST_MONEY"
    android:protectionLevel="dangerous" />
```

This provides a method not only to specify the permission needed, but also the level of access with the `protectionLevel` attribute. There are four levels of access: `normal`, `dangerous`, `signature`, and `signatureOrSystem`. The `permissionGroup` attribute is used only to help the system display permissions to the user, which is optional. The possible permission groups are

```
permission group:android.permission-group.DEVELOPMENT_TOOLS
permission group:android.permission-group.PERSONAL_INFO
permission group:android.permission-group.COST_MONEY
permission group:android.permission-group.LOCATION
permission group:android.permission-group.MESSAGES
permission group:android.permission-group.NETWORK
permission group:android.permission-group.ACCOUNTS
permission group:android.permission-group.STORAGE
permission group:android.permission-group.PHONE_CALLS
permission group:android.permission-group.HARDWARE_CONTROLS
permission group:android.permission-group.SYSTEM_TOOLS
```

The label, description, and name attributes are ways to make the permission more descriptive.

Android Inter-Process Communication

If two applications need to share resources but cannot get granted permissions, it is possible to define an inter-process communication (IPC) message. To support IPC, an interface is needed to serve as a bridge between applications. This is provided by the Android Interface Definition Language (AIDL).

Defining AIDL is similar to a Java interface. In fact, it can be easily done in Eclipse by creating a new Java interface, and after the definitions are complete, changing the suffix of the file from **.java** to **.aidl.**

The data types that AIDL currently supports are

- Java primitives that include `int`, `boolean`, `float`
- `String`
- `CharSequence`

- `List`
- `Map`
- Other AIDL-generated interfaces
- Custom classes that implement the `Parcelable` protocol and are passed by value

Recipe: Implementing a Remote Procedure Call

This recipe implements a remote procedure call (RPC) between two activities. First, an AIDL interface can be defined, as shown in Listing 11.7.

Listing 11.7 **IAdditionalService.aidl under the com.cookbook.advance.rpc.**

```
package com.cookbook.advance.rpc;

// Declare the interface.
interface IAdditionService {
    int factorial(in int value);
}
```

After the AIDL file is created, Eclipse generates an **IAdditionalService.java** file under the **gen/** folder when the project is built. The contents of this file should not be modified. It contains a stub class that is needed to implement the remote service.

Inside the first activity, **rpcService,** an `mBinder` member is declared as the stub from the `IAdditionalService`. It can also be interpreted as an `IBinder`. In the `onCreate()` method, the `mBinder` is initiated and defined to call the `factorial()` function. During the `onBind()`, it returns `mBinder` to the caller. After the `onBind()` is ready, the other process activities are able to connect to the service. This is shown in Listing 11.8.

Listing 11.8 **src/com/cookbook/advance/rpc/rpcService.java**

```
package com.cookbook.advance.rpc;

import android.app.Service;
import android.content.Intent;
import android.os.IBinder;
import android.os.RemoteException;

public class RPCService extends Service {

  IAdditionService.Stub mBinder;
  @Override
  public void onCreate() {
    super.onCreate();
    mBinder = new IAdditionService.Stub() {
        public int factorial(int value1) throws RemoteException {
            int result=1;
```

```
            for(int i=1; i<=value1; i++){
                result*=i;
            }
            return result;
        }
    };
  }

  @Override
  public IBinder onBind(Intent intent) {
    return mBinder;
  }

  @Override
  public void onDestroy() {
    super.onDestroy();
  }
}
```

Now the second activity that runs in a different process must be specified. The associated layout file is shown in Listing 11.9. Inside the layout, it has three views that actually serve the main roles. `EditText` takes the input from the user, the `Button` triggers the `factorial()` function call, and the `TextView` with ID `result` is used for displaying the result from factorial.

Listing 11.9 **res/layout/main.xml**

```
<?xml version="1.0" encoding="utf-8"?>
<LinearLayout xmlns:android="http://schemas.android.com/apk/res/android"
  android:orientation="vertical" android:layout_width="fill_parent"
  android:layout_height="fill_parent">
  <TextView android:layout_width="fill_parent"
    android:layout_height="wrap_content"
    android:text="Android CookBook RPC Demo"
    android:textSize="22dp" />
  <LinearLayout
  android:orientation="horizontal" android:layout_width="fill_parent"
  android:layout_height="wrap_content">
  <EditText android:layout_width="wrap_content"
    android:layout_height="wrap_content" android:id="@+id/value1"
    android:hint="0-30"></EditText>
  <Button android:layout_width="wrap_content"
    android:layout_height="wrap_content" android:id="@+id/buttonCalc"
    android:text="GET"></Button>
    </LinearLayout>
  <TextView android:layout_width="wrap_content"
```

```
    android:layout_height="wrap_content" android:text="result"
    android:textSize="36dp" android:id="@+id/result"></TextView>
</LinearLayout>
```

The AndroidManifest is shown in Listing 11.10. Inside the service tag, there is an extra attribute `android:process=".remoteService"`. This asks the system to create a new process named `remoteService` to run the second activity.

Listing 11.10 **AndroidManifest.xml**

```
<?xml version="1.0" encoding="utf-8"?>
<manifest xmlns:android="http://schemas.android.com/apk/res/android"
  package="com.cookbook.advance.rpc"
  android:versionCode="1" android:versionName="1.0">
  <application android:icon="@drawable/icon"
               android:label="@string/app_name" >
    <activity android:name=".rpc" android:label="@string/app_name">
      <intent-filter>
        <action android:name="android.intent.action.MAIN" />
        <category android:name="android.intent.category.LAUNCHER" />
      </intent-filter>
    </activity>

    <service android:name=".rpcService" android:process=".remoteService"/>
  </application>
  <uses-sdk android:minSdkVersion="7" />
</manifest>
```

The second activity is shown in Listing 11.11. It needs to call `bindService()` to retrieve the `factorial()` method provided in the `rpcService`. The `bindService()` requires a service connection instance as the interface for monitoring the state of an application service. Therefore, this activity has an inner class `myServiceConnection` that implements the service connection.

The `myServiceConnection` and `IAdditionService` classes are instantiated in the `rpc` activity. The `myServiceConnection` listens to the `onServiceConnected` and `onServiceDisconnected` callback functions. The `onServiceConnected` passes the `IBinder` instance to the `IAdditionService` instance. The `onServiceDisconnected` callback function puts the `IAdditionService` instance to `null`.

There are also two methods defined inside the `rpc` activity that are `initService()` and `releaseService()`. The `initService()` tries to initiate a new `myServiceConnetion`. Then, it creates a new intent for a specific package name and class name and passes it to the `bindService` along with the `myServiceConnection` instance and a flag `BIND_AUTO_CREATE`. After the service is bound, the `onServiceConnected` callback function is triggered and it passes the `IBinder` to the `IAdditionService` instance so the `rpc` activity can start to call the factorial method. The output is shown in Figure 11.3.

Listing 11.11 **src/com/cookbook/advance/rpc/rpc.java**

```
package com.cookbook.advance.rpc;

import android.app.Activity;
import android.content.ComponentName;
import android.content.Context;
import android.content.Intent;
import android.content.ServiceConnection;
import android.os.Bundle;
import android.os.IBinder;
import android.os.RemoteException;
import android.view.View;
import android.view.View.OnClickListener;
import android.widget.Button;
import android.widget.EditText;
import android.widget.TextView;
import android.widget.Toast;

public class rpc extends Activity {
  IAdditionService service;
  myServiceConnection connection;

  class myServiceConnection implements ServiceConnection {

    public void onServiceConnected(ComponentName name,
                                   IBinder boundService) {
      service = IAdditionService.Stub.asInterface((IBinder) boundService);
      Toast.makeText(rpc.this, "Service connected", Toast.LENGTH_SHORT)
          .show();
    }

    public void onServiceDisconnected(ComponentName name) {
      service = null;
      Toast.makeText(rpc.this, "Service disconnected", Toast.LENGTH_SHORT)
          .show();
    }
  }
```

```
private void initService() {
  connection = new myServiceConnection();
  Intent i = new Intent();
  i.setClassName("com.cookbook.advance.rpc",
                com.cookbook.advance.rpc.rpcService.class.getName());
  if(!bindService(i, connection, Context.BIND_AUTO_CREATE)) {
      Toast.makeText(rpc.this, "Bind Service Failed", Toast.LENGTH_LONG)
      .show();
  }
}

private void releaseService() {
  unbindService(connection);
  connection = null;
}

@Override
public void onCreate(Bundle savedInstanceState) {
  super.onCreate(savedInstanceState);
  setContentView(R.layout.main);

  initService();

  Button buttonCalc = (Button) findViewById(R.id.buttonCalc);

  buttonCalc.setOnClickListener(new OnClickListener() {
    TextView result = (TextView) findViewById(R.id.result);
    EditText value1 = (EditText) findViewById(R.id.value1);

    public void onClick(View v) {
      int v1, res = -1;
      try {
          v1 = Integer.parseInt(value1.getText().toString());
          res = service.factorial(v1);
      } catch (RemoteException e) {
        e.printStackTrace();
      }
      result.setText(new Integer(res).toString());
    }
  });
}
```

```
    @Override
    protected void onDestroy() {
      releaseService();
    }
  }
```

Figure 11.3 Output of the AIDL application.

Android Backup Manager

In Android devices, end users store a lot of data on different applications like notes, game data, application settings, address book entries, and so on. All these data cannot be recovered after they are gone. In the past, developers needed to find alternative ways to back up application data to a remote server. With the introduction of Android 2.2, the support for an Android backup service hosted by Google was introduced. All the application data can use the backup service to store any data to the cloud.

Recipe: Creating a Backup of Runtime Data

Android provides the `BackupManager` class for developers to notify the `Backup` service to do backup and restore operations. After the notification is received, the backup manager requests backup data from the application and delivers it to a cloud storage server during backup. It also retrieves backup data from the backup transport and returns it to applications during a restore process.

A backup agent is the interface where the `BackupManager` communicates with the applications. To create a backup agent for applications, developers can extend the `BackupAgent` in their class. Inside any class that extends `BackupAgent`, two methods need to be overridden: `onBackup()` and `onRestore()`. The `onBackup()` method is triggered whenever there is a `dataChanged()` method call. The `onRestore()` method is triggered whenever there is a `requestRestore()` method call:

```
public class MyBackupAgent extends BackupAgent {

        @Override
        public void onCreate() {
            ...
        }

        @Override
        public void onBackup(ParcelFileDescriptor oldState,
                              BackupDataOutput data,
                           ParcelFileDescriptor newState){

            ...
        }
        @Override
        public void onRestore(BackupDataInput data, int appVersionCode,
                                ParcelFileDescriptor newState){
        ...
        }
}
```

The `onBackup()` method has three parameters that are passed and used by the backup manager:

- `oldState`—Return the state from the last backup
- `data`—The data that is backed up
- `newState`—Write the current state of the backup, which becomes the `oldState` for the next backup

In implementing the `onBackup()` method, the `oldState` that the `BackupManager` passes in should be checked against the current data state. If it is the same, there is no need to do the backup. If it is not the same, the `data` passed to the method should be written, and the `newState` should be updated for the backup.

The `onRestore()` method has three parameters passed and used by the backup manager as well:

- `data`—The data from the last backup.
- `appVersionCode`—The application's version code during the backup operation. The version code is defined as the attribute `android:versionCode` in the Android-Manifest XML file.
- `newState`—Write the current state as the restore point.

Any data conversions required in changes from version to version should be done in the `onRestore()` method. That is the reason the `BackupManager` passes the `appVersionCode`. After the data is restored to the application, the state of the application changes. At this point, a `newState` needs to be written.

Recipe: Backing Up Files to the Cloud

The `BackupAgent` is intended to save application run-time data. To save files, there is another agent named `BackupAgentHelper`. This is the wrapper class for the backup agent class. It supports two different kinds of backup helpers:

- `SharedPreferencesBackupHelper` to backup `SharedPreferences` files
- `FileBackupHelper` to backup files

This is shown in Listing 11.12.

Listing 11.12 **Example of Extending the BackupAgentHelper**

```
public class MyFileBackupAgentHelper extends BackupAgentHelper {
        @Override
        public void onCreate() {
           FileBackupHelper filehelper = new FileBackupHelper(this,
                                                           DATA_FILE_NAME);
           addHelper(FILE_HELPER_KEY, helper);
           SharedPreferencesBackupHelper xmlhelper
                         = new SharedPreferencesBackupHelper(this, PREFS);
           addHelper(PREFS_BACKUP_KEY, helper);
         }
}
```

All backup agent helpers need an `onCreate()` method. The `BackupAgent` can have more than one backup helper. In the class extended with `BackupAgentHelper`, it does not need to override `onBackup` and `onRestore` because it is handled well by the `BackupAgent`.

Recipe: Triggering Backup and Restore

To trigger a backup or restore, the backup agent for the application needs to be defined. This can be done by adding an `android:backupAgent` attribute inside the application tag. This is shown in Listing 11.13.

Listing 11.13 **AndroidManifest.xml**

```
<manifest xmlns:android="http://schemas.android.com/apk/res/android"
        package="com.cookbook.databackuprestore"
        android:versionCode="1"
        android:versionName="1.0">
        <uses-sdk android:minSdkVersion="8"/>
        <application android:label="Backup/Restore"
```

```
        android:backupAgent="myBackupAgent">
        <activity android:name="MyBandRActivity">
        <intent-filter>
        <action android:name="android.intent.action.MAIN" />
            <category android:name="android.intent.category.LAUNCHER" />
          </intent-filter>
        </activity>
        </application>
</manifest>
```

Anytime the application triggers a backup or restore to the `BackupManager`, it initiates with the identified backup agent. For example, with the main activity excerpt as follows:

```
public class MyBandRActivity extends Activity {

       BackupManager mBackupManager;

       @Override
       public void onCreate(Bundle savedInstanceState) {
           super.onCreate(savedInstanceState);
           ...
           mBackupManager = new BackupManager(this);
       }

       void dataUpdate() {
           ...
           // We also need to perform an initial backup; ask for one
           mBackupManager.dataChanged();
       }
}
```

Inside the `MyBandRActivity` activity, the `BackupManager` instance is created in the `onCreate()` function. To ask for a backup, the `dataChanged()` function is called from the `BackupManager`. Then the `BackupManager` finds the `BackupAgent` defined in the AndroidManifest file and calls its `onBackup()` method.

Android provides two ways to trigger the restore. The first method is to use `requestRestore()` from the `BackupManager`. This method triggers a call to the backup agent's `onRestore()` method. Another way to trigger a restore is whenever the user does a factory data reset or when the application is reinstalled. The Android system then automatically triggers the restore for the application.

Besides triggering the backup and restore in an Android application, Android also provides a command-line script **bmgr** that can do the same thing. To trigger the backup, type

```
> adb shell bmgr backup <package>
```

To trigger the restore, type

```
> adb shell bmgr restore <package>
```

Whenever there is a backup request to the backup manager, it might not start the backup until a time it determines is appropriate. To force the `BackupManager` to do the backup right away, type

```
> adb shell bmgr run
```

Android Animation

Android provides two types of animation: frame-by-frame and Tween animation. Frame-by-frame animation shows a sequence of pictures in order. It enables developers to define the pictures to display, and then show them like a slideshow.

Frame-by-frame animation first needs an `animation-list` element in the layout file containing a list of `item` elements specifying an ordered list of the different pictures to display. The `oneshot` attribute specifies whether the animation is played only once or repeatedly. The animation list XML file is shown in Listing 11.14.

Listing 11.14 **res/anim/animated.xml**

```
<?xml version="1.0" encoding="utf-8"?>
<animation-list xmlns:android="http://schemas.android.com/apk/res/android"
     android:oneshot="false">
    <item android:drawable="@drawable/anddev1" android:duration="200" />
    <item android:drawable="@drawable/anddev2" android:duration="200" />
    <item android:drawable="@drawable/anddev3" android:duration="200" />
</animation-list>
```

To display the frame-by-frame animation, set the animation to a view's background:

```
ImageView im = (ImageView) this.findViewById(R.id.myanimated);
im.setBackgroundResource(R.anim.animated);
AnimationDrawable ad = (AnimationDrawable)im.getBackground();
ad.start();
```

After the view background is set, a drawable can be retrieved by calling `getBackground()` and casting it to `AnimationDrawable`. Then, calling the `start()` method starts the animation.

Tween animation uses a different approach that creates an animation by performing a series of transformations on a single image. In Android, it provides access to the following classes that are the basis for all the animations:

- AlphaAnimation—Controls transparency changes
- RotateAnimation—Controls rotations
- ScaleAnimation—Controls growing or shrinking
- TranslateAnimation—Controls position changes

These four Animation classes can be used for transitions between activities, layouts, views and so on. All these can be defined in the layout XML file as `<alpha>`, `<rotate>`, `<scale>`, and `<translate>`. They all have to be contained within an AnimationSet `<set>`:

- `<alpha>` attributes:

  `android:fromAlpha, android:toAlpha`

  The alpha value translates the opacity from 0.0 (transparent) to 1.0 (opaque).
- `<rotate>` attributes:

  `android:fromDegrees, android:toDegrees,`

  `android:pivotX, android:pivotY`

  The rotate specifies the angle to rotate an animation around a center of rotation defined as the pivot.
- `<scale>` attributes:

  `android:fromXScale, android:toXScale,`

  `android:fromYScale, android:toYScale,`

  `android:pivotX, android:pivotY`

  The scale specifies how to change the size of a view in the x-axis or y-axis. The pivot location that stays fixed under the scaling can also be specified.
- `<translate>` attributes:

  `android:fromXDelta, android:toXDelta,`

  `android:fromYDelta, android:toYDelta`

  The translate specifies the amount of translation to perform on a View.

Recipe: Creating an Animation

This recipe creates a new mail animation that can be used when mail is received. The main layout file is shown in Listing 11.15 and is shown in Figure 11.4.

Listing 11.15 **res/layout/main.xml**

```
<?xml version="1.0" encoding="utf-8"?>
<LinearLayout xmlns:android="http://schemas.android.com/apk/res/android"
    android:orientation="vertical"
    android:layout_width="fill_parent"
    android:layout_height="fill_parent"
    android:gravity="center"
    >

    <ImageView
    android:id="@+id/myanimated"
    android:layout_width="wrap_content"
    android:layout_height="wrap_content"
```

```
        android:src="@drawable/mail"
    />
    <Button
    android:id="@+id/startAnimated"
    android:layout_width="wrap_content"
    android:layout_height="wrap_content"
    android:text="you've got mail"
    />
</LinearLayout>
```

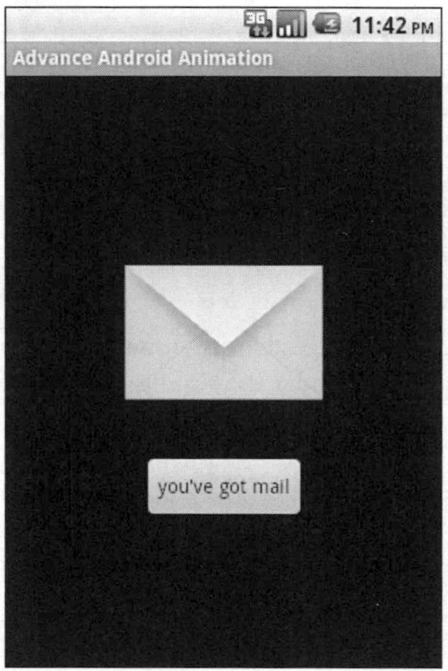

Figure 11.4 Based layout for the animation.

To animate this view, an animation set needs to be defined. In Eclipse, right-click the **res/** folder and select **New → Android XML File**. Then, fill the filename as **animated.xml** and select the file-type as **Animation.** Then, the file can be edited to create the content shown in Listing 11.16.

Listing 11.16 **res/anim/animated.xml**

```
<?xml version="1.0" encoding="utf-8"?>

<set xmlns:android="http://schemas.android.com/apk/res/and-
roid" android:interpolator="@android:anim/accelerate_interpolator">
```

```
    <translate android:fromXDelta="100%p" android:toXDelta="0"
android:duration="5000" />
    <alpha android:fromAlpha="0.0" android:toAlpha="1.0" android:duration="3000" />
            <rotate
            android:fromDegrees="0"
            android:toDegrees="-45"
            android:toYScale="0.0"
            android:pivotX="50%"
            android:pivotY="50%"
            android:startOffset="700"
            android:duration="3000" />

          <scale
            android:fromXScale="0.0"
            android:toXScale="1.4"
            android:fromYScale="0.0"
            android:toYScale="1.0"
            android:pivotX="50%"
            android:pivotY="50%"
            android:startOffset="700"
            android:duration="3000"
            android:fillBefore="false" />
</set>
```

The main activity is shown in Listing 11.17. It is a simple activity that creates an `Animation` object by using the `AnimationUtils` to load the `animationSet` defined in the animation. Then, every time the user clicks on the button, it uses the image view object to run animation by calling the `startAnimation()` method using the `Animation` object already loaded.

Listing 11.17 **src/com/cookbook/advance/myanimation.java**

```
package com.cookbook.advance;

import android.app.Activity;
import android.os.Bundle;
import android.view.View;
import android.view.View.OnClickListener;
import android.view.animation.Animation;
import android.view.animation.AnimationUtils;
import android.widget.Button;
import android.widget.ImageView;

public class myanimation extends Activity {
    /** Called when the activity is first created. */
    @Override
```

```
    public void onCreate(Bundle savedInstanceState) {
        super.onCreate(savedInstanceState);
        setContentView(R.layout.main);

        final ImageView im
                = (ImageView) this.findViewById(R.id.myanimated);
        final Animation an
                = AnimationUtils.loadAnimation(this, R.anim.animated);

        im.setVisibility(View.INVISIBLE);
        Button bt = (Button) this.findViewById(R.id.startAnimated);
        bt.setOnClickListener(new OnClickListener(){
            public void onClick(View view){
                im.setVisibility(View.VISIBLE);
                im.startAnimation(an);
            }

        });
    }
}
```

12

Debugging

Debugging software can easily take as long as or longer than the development itself. Understanding the different ways to debug common problems can save a lot of time and effort. This chapter introduces the basic approach of debugging Android applications, and it examines the many tools available. First, the common Eclipse Integrated Development Environment (IDE) debugging tools are discussed. Then, the Android tools provided from the Android Software Development Kit (SDK) are discussed. Finally, the tools available on the Android system are discussed. Each application is different, so the appropriate debugging methodology depends on the characteristics of the application itself.

Eclipse Built-in Debug Tools

The Eclipse IDE with the Android Developer Tools (ADT) plugin is a user-friendly development environment. It includes a What-You-See-Is-What-You-Get (WYSIWYG) user interface and the tools needed to convert resource layout files into the necessary ingredients to build an Android executable. A step-by-step guide to setting up the configuration follows. Eclipse 3.4 (Ganymede) is assumed, although most steps are the same between Eclipse versions.

Recipe: Specifying a Run Configuration

The run configuration is a separate profile for each application. It tells Eclipse how to run the project, start the Activity, and whether to install the application on the emulator or a connected device. The ADT automatically creates a run configuration for each application when it is first created, but it can be customized as described here.

To create a new run configuration or edit an existing one, select **Run → Run Configurations...** (or **Debug Configurations...**) in Eclipse to launch the Run Configurations menu shown in Figure 12.1. Inside the run configuration, there are three tabs related to application testing:

- Android—Specify the project and activity to launch.
- Target—Select the virtual device upon which the application will run. For the emulator environment, the launch parameters are specified here, such as the network speed and latency. This allows for a more realistic simulation of the wireless link conditions to test how the application behaves. Developers can also choose to wipe out the persistent storage of the emulator with every launch.
- Common—Specify where the run configuration settings are saved and also whether the configuration is displayed in the Favorite menu.

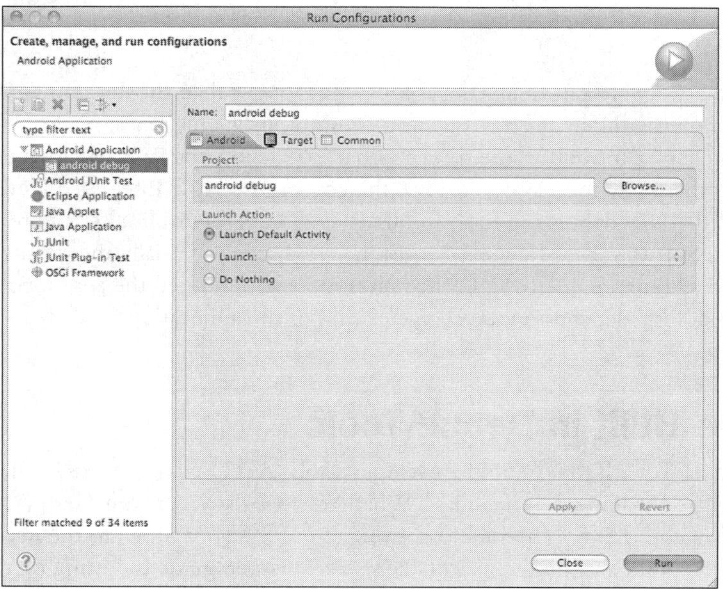

Figure 12.1 The Run Configurations menu in Eclipse.

After these settings are properly set, the application can be run on the target device with a single click of the Run button. If an actual Android device is not connected to the host computer or the target chosen is a virtual device, the emulator is launched to run the application.

Recipe: Using the DDMS

After the application is run on a target, the Dalvik Debug Monitoring Service (DDMS) can be opened to examine the status of the devices, as shown in Figure 12.2. DDMS can be run from the command line or by selecting **Window → Open Perspective → DDMS** in Eclipse.

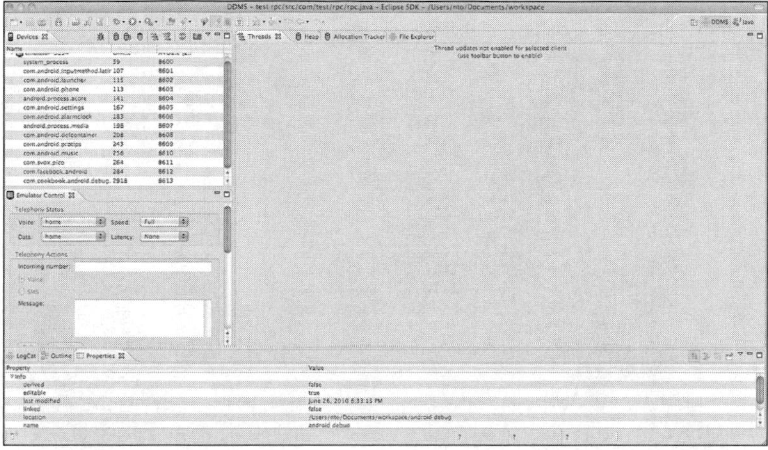

Figure 12.2 The DDMS Control Panel.

Inside the DDMS are four panels that provide different kinds of debugging data:

- Devices—Displays the connected Android devices including emulators and actual Android devices.
- Emulator Control—Provides multiple controls for injecting events and data into the emulator such as Telephony Status, Telephony Action, and Location Control:
  - The Telephony Status specifies the voice and data format, network speed, and latency.
  - The Telephony Actions provides a way to make a fake voice phone call or Short Message Service (SMS) message to the emulator. If an SMS is specified, the message content can be defined.
  - The Location Control provides a way to send a fake Global Positioning System (GPS) signal to the GPS provider in the emulator.
- Bottom Panel—Contains three tabs: LogCat, Outline, and Properties. The LogCat tab shows all the logging data from the device in real-time. It includes system log messages and user-generated log messages accessed using the `Log` class in applications.
- The Device Status Panel—The top, right panel contains four tabs: Thread, Heap, Allocation Tracker, and File Explorer. These are mostly used to analyze the process. Clicking the device in the Devices tab can cause these four tabs to reflect the currently selected device/emulator's running values, as shown in Figure 12.3.

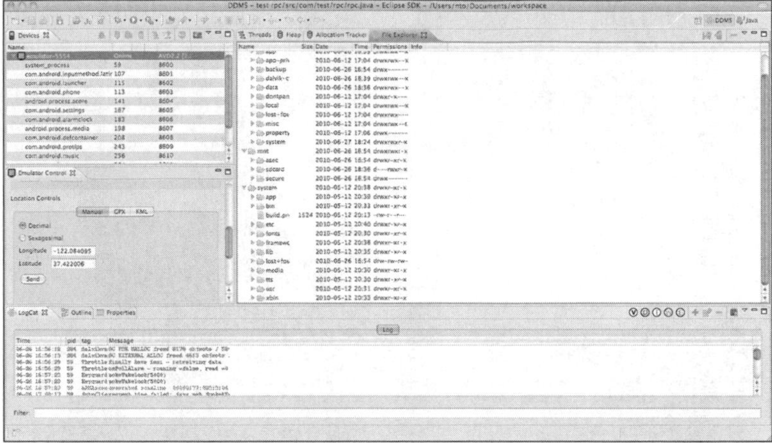

Figure 12.3 The DDMS Control Panel with the Device Status Panel open.

Recipe: Debugging Through Breakpoints

Developers can also run applications in debug mode and insert breakpoints to freeze an application in run-time. First, the application needs to be launched in debug mode, which displays the dialog shown in Figure 12.4. If Yes is selected, it switches to the Debug perspective shown in Figure 12.5.

The Debug perspective displays the source file in a window along with some other windows including variables, breakpoints, outline, and others. Developers can toggle a breakpoint by double-clicking in the left-hand margin next to the line where the code execution should freeze. A breakpoint is set when a small blue circle is present on that line.

Using breakpoints is a standard debug method for embedded programmers. The ability to stop at an instruction, step through functions, see variable values in memory, and modify values in run-time provides a powerful method to chase down complicated bugs and unexpected behavior.

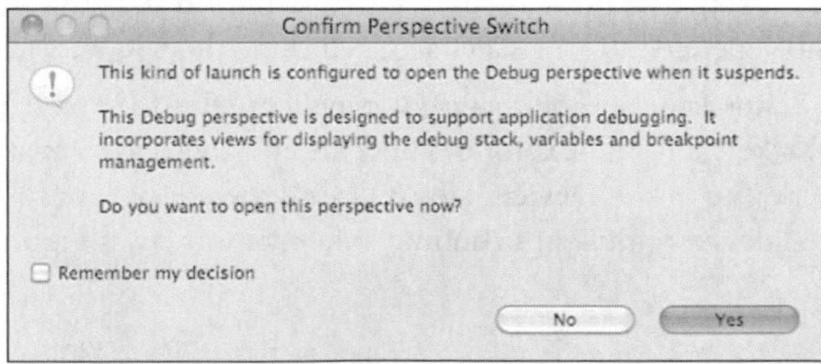

Figure 12.4 The Confirm Perspective Switch dialog box.

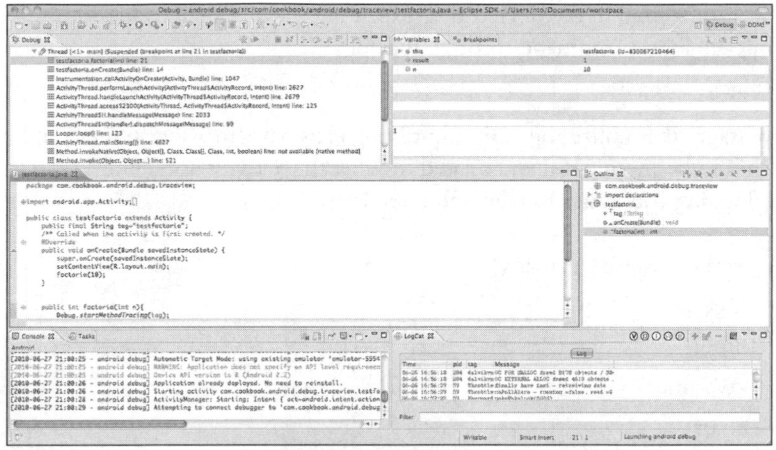

Figure 12.5 The Debug perspective in Eclipse.

Android SDK Debug Tools

The Android SDK provides multiple standalone tools for use in debugging. The Android Debug Bridge, LogCat, Hierarchy Viewer, and TraceView tools are discussed here. They can be found in the **tools/** directory of the Android SDK installation.

Recipe: Using the Android Debug Bridge

The Android Debug Bridge (ADB) provides a way to manage the state of an emulator instance or USB-connected Android device. The ADB is built of three components: a client, a server, and a daemon. The client component is initiated by the ADB shell script on the development machine. The server component runs as a background process on the development machine. This server can be started or stopped using one of the following commands:

```
> adb start-server
> adb kill-server
```

The daemon component is a background process that runs on the emulator or Android device.

Recipe: Using LogCat

Logcat is the real-time logging tool Android provides. It collects all system and application log data in circular buffers, which can then be viewed and filtered. It can be accessed as a standalone tool or as part of the DDMS tool.

LogCat can be used in the device after executing the adb shell to log into the device or by using the logcat command through the adb:

```
> [adb] logcat [<option>] ... [<filter-spec>] ...
```

All the messages that utilize the android.util.Log class have an associated tag and priority. The tag should be meaningful and related to what the activity does. The tag and priority make the logging data easier to read and filter. Possible tags are

- V—Verbose (lowest priority)
- D—Debug
- I—Info
- W—Warning
- E—Error
- F—Fatal
- S—Silent (highest priority, on which nothing is ever printed)

The LogCat data has a multitude of information, and filters should be used to avoid overload by specifying the **tag:priority** argument to the **logcat** command. For example:

```
> adb logcat ActivityManager:V *:S
```

This shows verbose (V) data on the ActivityManager while silencing (S) all other log commands.

A circular buffer system is used inside Android logging. By default, all information is logged to the main log buffer. With the Android 2.2 SDK, there are two other buffers: one that contains radio/telephony-related messages and one that contains event-related messages. Different buffers can be enabled using the **-b** switch. For example:

```
> adb logcat -b events
```

This buffer also shows event-related messages:

```
I/menu_opened(  135): 0
I/notification_cancel(   74): [com.android.phone,1,0]
I/am_finish_activity(   74):
[1128378040,38,com.android.contacts/.DialtactsActivity,app-request]
I/am_pause_activity(   74):
[1128378040,com.android.contacts/.DialtactsActivity]
I/am_on_paused_called(  135): com.android.contacts.RecentCallsListActivity
I/am_on_paused_called(  135): com.android.contacts.DialtactsActivity
I/am_resume_activity(   74): [1127710848,2,com.android.launcher/.Launcher]
I/am_on_resume_called(  135): com.android.launcher.Launcher
I/am_destroy_activity(   74):
[1128378040,38,com.android.contacts/.DialtactsActivity]
I/power_sleep_requested(   74): 0
I/power_screen_state(   74): [0,1,468,1]
```

```
I/power_screen_broadcast_send(   74): 1
I/screen_toggled(   74): 0
I/am_pause_activity(   74): [1127710848,com.android.launcher/.Launcher]
```

Another example follows

```
> adb logcat -b radio
```

This shows radio/telephony-related messages:

```
D/RILJ (  132): [2981]< GPRS_REGISTRATION_STATE {1, null, null, 2}
D/RILJ (  132): [2982]< REGISTRATION_STATE {1, null, null, 2, null, null,
null, null, null, null, null, null, null, null}
D/RILJ (  132): [2983]< QUERY_NETWORK_SELECTION_MODE {0}
D/GSM  (  132): Poll ServiceState done:  oldSS=[0 home T - Mobile T - Mo-
bile 31026  Unknown CSS not supported -1 -1RoamInd: -1DefRoamInd: -1]
newSS=[0 home T - Mobile T - Mobile 31026  Unknown CSS not supported -1 -
1RoamInd: -1DefRoamInd: -1] oldGprs=0 newGprs=0 oldType=EDGE newType=EDGE
D/RILJ (  132): [UNSL]< UNSOL_NITZ_TIME_RECEIVED 10/06/26,21:49:56-28,1
I/GSM  (  132): NITZ: 10/06/26,21:49:56-28,1,237945599 start=237945602
delay=3
D/RILJ (  132): [UNSL]< UNSOL_RESPONSE_NETWORK_STATE_CHANGED
D/RILJ (  132): [2984]> OPERATOR
D/RILJ (  132): [2985]> GPRS_REGISTRATION_STATE
D/RILJ (  132): [2984]< OPERATOR {T - Mobile, T - Mobile, 31026}
D/RILJ (  132): [2986]> REGISTRATION_STATE
D/RILJ (  132): [2987]> QUERY_NETWORK_SELECTION_MODE
D/RILJ (  132): [2985]< GPRS_REGISTRATION_STATE {1, null, null, 2}
D/RILJ (  132): [2986]< REGISTRATION_STATE {1, null, null, 2, null, null,
null, null, null, null, null, null, null, null}
D/RILJ (  132): [2987]< QUERY_NETWORK_SELECTION_MODE {0}
```

Logcat is useful when using Java-based Android applications. However, when applications involve native components, it is harder to trace. In this case, the native components should log to system.out or system.err. By default, the Android system sends stdout and stderr (system.out and system.err) output to **/dev/null.** These can be routed to a log file with the following ADB commands:

```
> adb shell stop
> adb shell setprop log.redirect-stdio true
> adb shell start
```

This stops a running emulator/device instance; use the shell command `setprop` to enable the redirection of output and restart the instance.

Recipe: Using the Hierarchy Viewer

A useful way to debug and understand the user interface is by using the Hierarchy Viewer. It provides a visual representation of the layout's View hierarchy (the Layout View) and a magnified inspector of the display (the Pixel Perfect View).

The Hierarchy Viewer is accessed using the tool **hierarchyviewer.** Executing this program launches the interface shown in Figure 12.6. It displays a list of Android devices that are currently connected to the development machine. When a device is selected, a list of running programs on the device is shown. It is then possible to select the program intended for debug or user interface optimization.

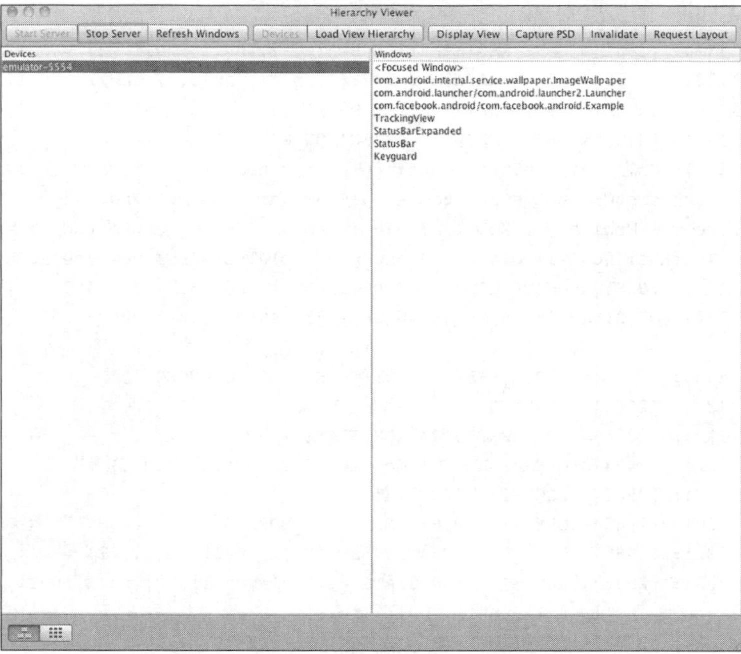

Figure 12.6 The Hierarchy Viewer tool.

After the program is selected, the Load View Hierarchy can be selected to see the View Tree constructed by the Hierarchy /Viewer. This is also called the Layout View. It contains three views:

- Tree View—A hierarchy diagram of the views on the left.
- Properties View—A list of the selected view's properties on the top, right.
- Wire-frame View—A wire-frame drawing of the layout on the bottom, right.

This is shown in Figure 12.7.

These three views are related. When one node of the view is selected, the properties view and wire-frame view are updated. In an Android system, there is a limitation on the View Tree that each application can generate. The depth of the tree cannot be deeper than 10 and the width of the tree cannot be broader than 50. In Android 1.5 or earlier, there is stack overflow exception thrown when the view tree passes that limit. Although it is good to know the limitations, a shallow layout tree always makes the application run faster and smoother. This can be accomplished using merge or RelativeLayout instead of LinearLayout to optimize the View tree.

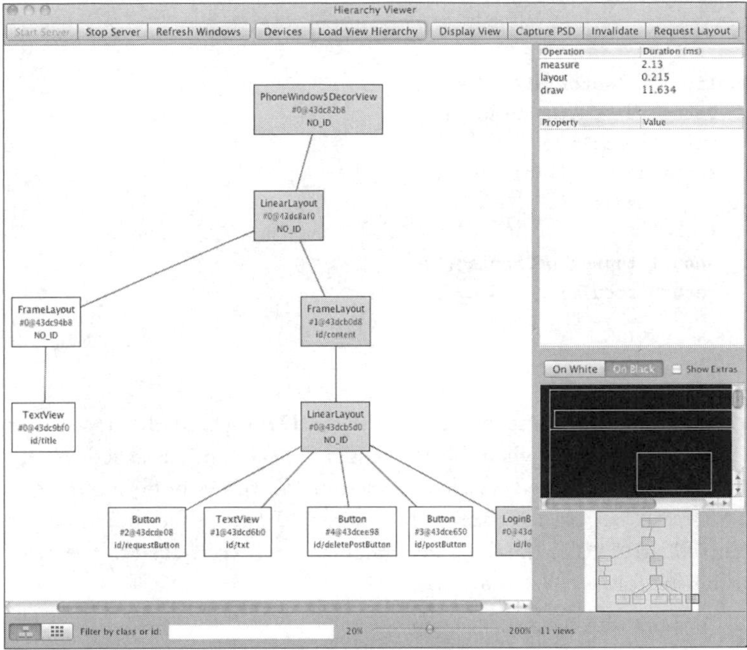

Figure 12.7 The Layout View in the Hierarchy View tool.

Recipe: Using TraceView

TraceView is a tool to optimize performance. To leverage this tool, the Debug class needs to be implemented in the application. It creates log files containing the trace information for analysis. A recipe is provided here to demonstrate how to use TraceView. This recipe specifies a factorial method and another method that calls the factorial method. Listing 12.1 shows the main activity.

Listing 12.1 **src/com/cookbook/android/debug/traceview/testfactorial.java**

```
package com.cookbook.android.debug.traceview;

import android.app.Activity;
import android.os.Bundle;
import android.os.Debug;

public class testfactorial extends Activity {
    public final String tag="testfactorial";
```

```
        @Override
        public void onCreate(Bundle savedInstanceState) {
            super.onCreate(savedInstanceState);
            setContentView(R.layout.main);
            factorial(10);
        }

        public int factorial(int n) {
           Debug.startMethodTracing(tag);
           int result=1;
           for(int i=1; i<=n; i++) {
                result*=i;
           }
           Debug.stopMethodTracing();
           return result;
        }
}
```

The `factorial()` method contains two calls to the Debug class; the trace is started in a file called **testfactorial.trace** when the `startMethodTracing()` is called. When the `stopMethodTracing()` method is called, the system continues buffering the generated trace data. After the method `factorial(10)` returns, the trace file should be generated and saved in **/sdcard/**. After the file is generated, it can be retrieved to the development machine using the following command:

```
> adb pull /sdcard/testfactorial.trace
```

The traceview tool in the Android SDK tools folder can then be used to analyze the trace file:

```
> traceview testfactorial.trace
```

After the script command is run, it produces an analysis screen, as shown in Figure 12.8.

The screen shows a Timeline Panel and a Profile Panel. The Timeline Panel on the top half of the screen describes when each thread and method started and stopped. The Profile Panel on the bottom half of the screen provides the summary of what happened inside the factorial method. By moving the cursor around in the Timeline Panel, it displays the time when the tracing started, when the method was called, and when the tracing ended.

The Profile Panel shows a summary of all the time spent in the factorial method. The panel also shows both the inclusive and exclusive times (in addition to the percentage of the total time). Exclusive time is the time spent in the method. Inclusive time is the time spent in the method plus the time spent in any called functions.

The ***.trace** file is constructed by a data file and a key file. The data file is used to hold the trace data. The key file provides a mapping from binary identifiers to thread and method names. If an older version of traceview is used, the key file and data file need to be combined into a trace file manually.

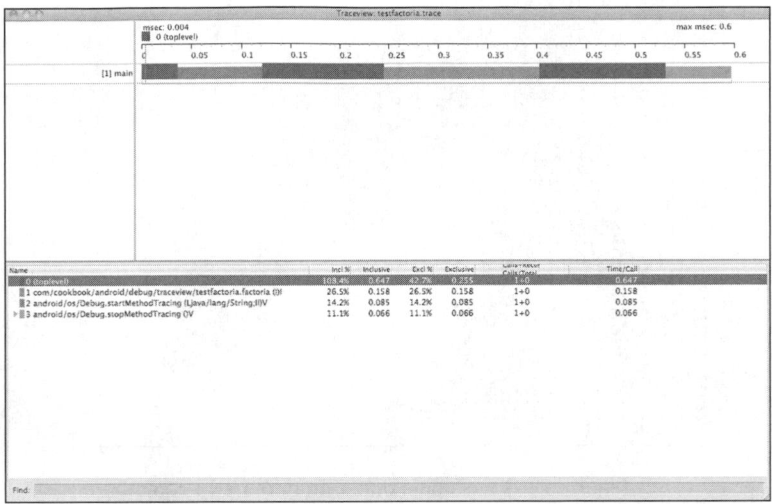

Figure 12.8 The TraceView analysis screen.

There is another way to generate a graphical call-stack diagram from trace log files in Android: dmtracedump. This tool requires the installation of the third-party Graphviz Dot utility to create the graphical output.

Android System Debug Tools

Android is built on top of Linux, so many Linux tools can be leveraged. For example, to show the applications currently running and the resources they are using, the **top** command can be used. The following command can be issued at the command line when a device is connected to a host computer through USB cable or the emulator is running:

```
> adb shell top
```

An example output from this command is shown in Figure 12.9.

The top command also shows the percentage of CPU and memory used in the overall system.

Another important tool is **ps,** which lists all the processes currently running on the Android system:

```
> adb shell ps
```

An example output from this command is shown in Figure 12.10.

Figure 12.9 Sample output from the **top** command.

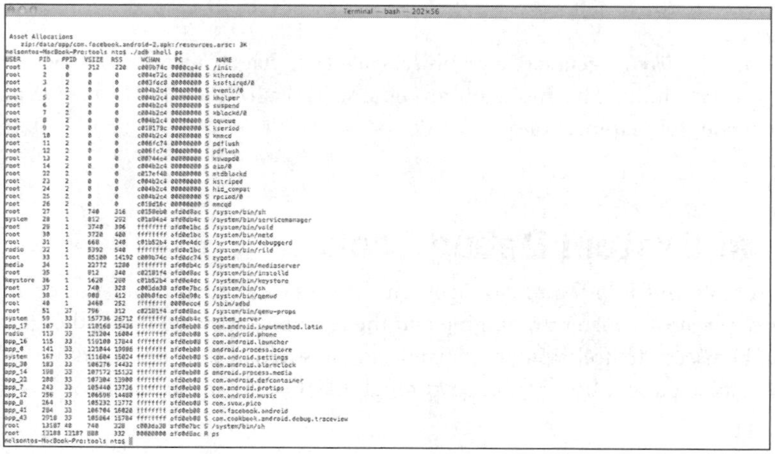

Figure 12.10 Sample output from the **ps** command.

This provides the process ID (PID) and user ID of each running process. Memory allocation can be seen using **dumpsys:**

```
> adb shell dumpsys meminfo <package name>
```

An example output from this command is shown in Figure 12.11.

```
nelsontos-MacBook-Pro:tools nto$ ./adb shell dumpsys 284
Can't find service: 284
nelsontos-MacBook-Pro:tools nto$ ./adb shell dumpsys meminfo com.facebook.android
Applications Memory Usage (kB):
Uptime: 63486347 Realtime: 63486347

** MEMINFO in pid 284 [com.facebook.android] **
                    native   dalvik    other    total
            size:     3952     3719      N/A     7671
       allocated:     3325     2621      N/A     5946
            free:       42     1098      N/A     1140
           (Pss):      790     1978     1038     3806
  (shared dirty):     1532     4160     1060     6752
    (priv dirty):      684     1184      708     2576

 Objects
           Views:        0        ViewRoots:        0
     AppContexts:        0       Activities:        0
          Assets:        2    AssetManagers:        2
   Local Binders:        5    Proxy Binders:        9
Death Recipients:        0
 OpenSSL Sockets:        0

 SQL
            heap:        0       memoryUsed:        0
pageCacheOverflo:        0  largestMemAlloc:        0


 Asset Allocations
    zip:/data/app/com.facebook.android-2.apk:/resources.arsc: 3K
nelsontos-MacBook-Pro:tools nto$ 
```

Figure 12.11 Sample output from the **dumpsys** command.

These commands provide information on Java and native components. This information is therefore useful for optimizing and analyzing Native Development Kit (NDK) applications. In addition to memory information, it includes how many views are used in the process, how many activities are used, how many application contexts are used, and so on.

Recipe: Setting up GDB Debugging

The GNU project DeBugger (GDB) is a common way to debug programs on Linux. In Android, a gdb tool is available to debug native libraries. In NDK r4, every native library is generated; it also generates a **gdbserver** and **gdb.setup**. The following commands can be used to install gdb:

```
> adb shell
> adb /data/
> mkdir myfolder
> exit
> adb push gdbserver /data/myfolder
```

To run gdb, the following command can be used:

```
> adb shell /data/myfolder/gdbserver host:port <native program>
```

For example, with a program named myprogram running on Android device with IP address 10.0.0.1 and port number 1234, the following command starts the server:

```
> adb shell /data/myfolder/gdbserver 10.0.0.1:1234 myprogram
```

Then, open another terminal and run gdb on the program:

```
> gdb myprogram
 (gdb) set sysroot ../
 (gdb) set solib-search-path ../system/lib
 (gdb) target remote localhost:1234
```

At the gdb prompt, the first command sets the root directory of the target image, the second command sets the search path of shared libraries, and the last command sets the target. After the target remote localhost:1234 is running, debugging in the gdb environment can begin.

Index

Numbers

A

B

C

D

E

H

I

M

N

P

Q-R

S

T

U

V

W

X-Y-Z

Addison-Wesley | Cisco Press | EXAM/CRAM | IBM Press | QUE | PRENTICE HALL | SAMS | Safari Books Online

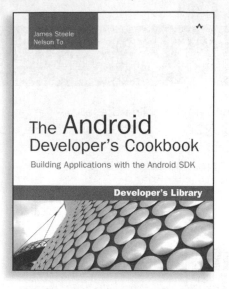